PISSARRO'S PLACES

By Ann Saul

Art Book Annex
Philadelphia
2013

Art Book Annex
225 S. 18th Street, Unit 510
Philadelphia, PA 19103
Artbookannex@yahoo.com

Designed by: Bokyoung Kim, Roger Vitkansas, Dual Corporation, New York.
Editors: Nelly Edmonson Gupta, Tracy Johnson, Danna Levy

First published 2013
Printed by Lightning Source, La Vergne, TN USA

Library of Congress Control Number: 2013903949
ISBN – 978-0-9885685-0-1 (softcover)

Publisher's Cataloging-in-Publication data

Saul, Ann.
Pissarro's places / by Ann Saul.
p. cm.
ISBN 978-0-9885685-0-1 (pbk.)
Includes bibliographical references and index.

1. Pissarro, Camille, 1830-1903. 2. Painters --France --Biography. 3. Impressionism (Art) --France. 4. Caribbean Area in art. 5. Virgin Islands of the United States in art. 6. Venezuela --In art. I. Title.

ND553.P55 .S28 2013
759.4 --dc23 2013903949

Front cover: Camille Pissarro, *Place du Théâtre-Français and the Avenue de l'Opéra, Sunlight, Winter Morning*, 1898
Back cover : Photograph of Camille Pissarro, Lionel and Sandrine Pissarro Archives

All current photographs were taken by the author during research for this book. All historic postcards are in the collection of the author. The three historic photographs of Paris (pp 110-111) are also in the author's collection.

In association with the
Normandie Impressionniste Festival

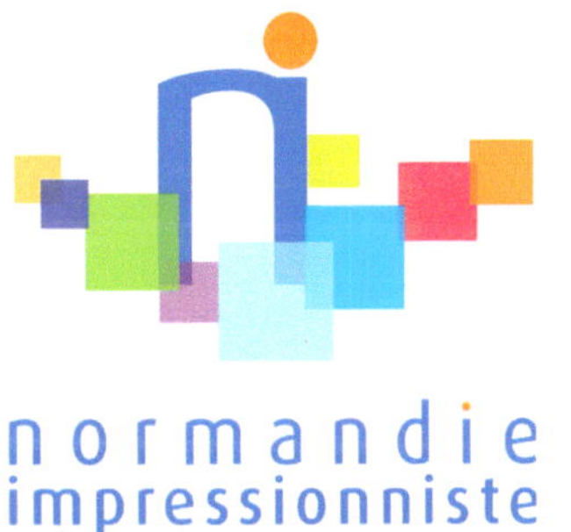

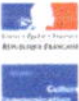
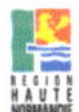

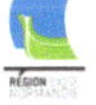

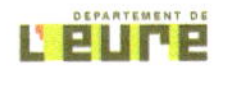

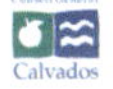

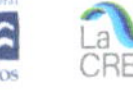

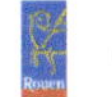
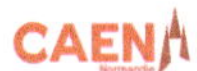

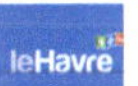

Acknowledgements

Heartfelt thanks to everyone who encouraged me to write and publish PISSARRO'S PLACES. Among the many who supported my efforts and lent assistance are: Patty Lurie, Anne Gillian, Jennifer Merdinger, Catherine Muyl, Alain Mothe, Christopher Duvivier, Lelia Pissarro, David Stern, Janice Witzel, Paul and Eileen Climance, Tamara Faulkner, Sylvain de Sutter, Jean-Marie Douillet, Claude and Sylvie Bonin-Pissarro, Jean Taquet, Bokyoung Kim, Roger Vitkansas, Katherine Donner, Tracy Johnson, Alice Rose, Danna Levy, Jane Whitehill, Nelly Edmondson Gupta, and Sandrine and Lionel Pissarro.

It has been my good fortune to have encouragement and guidance from two preeminent Pissarro scholars. Richard Brettell unknowingly set me on this path with his 1984 exhibition, "*A Day in the Country*." In recent years, he has provided invaluable information and support. Joachim Pissarro has encouraged my research and patiently answered hundreds of questions for more than fifteen years. His exhibitions and books are my inspiration. I am so grateful for their generosity.

My wonderful family has listened to my adventures, believed in me, and supported me in every possible way. My heartfelt thanks and love to them.

Everything is beautiful,
the whole secret lies in knowing how to interpret.

Camille Pissarro, 1893

Contents

Pissarro's Places

List of Paintings

Foreword

By Joachim Pissarro

The Bershad Professor of Art History and Director of the Hunter College Galleries, CUNY/City University of New York; formerly Curator at MoMA's Department of Painting and Sculpture; great-grandson of Camille Pissarro

Joachim Pissarro interviews the author of PISSARRO'S PLACES, Ann Saul:

JP: Ann Saul, this publication is very exciting, very fresh. You've done amazing research here and it's going to surprise a lot of people, myself included. I thought I knew every nook and cranny of Pissarro's varied relations throughout the world, but you've just taught us that there are many places we had missed, so many details we had not seen. So how did you come across this concept and how did you decide to launch into this?

AS: Pissarro brought me to it--studying his work and seeing these different kinds of places through his eyes. I believe that we are different people in different places; we take on the aura of that place. We respond to that place and do things differently.

Monet, Sisley and Cézanne each painted the bulk of their work in one place. Pissarro continuously sought new and different places. It was courageous because he was challenging himself with unknown artistic circumstances. This seems more difficult than continuously mining one motif or one site.

JP: Although he did that too. At Éragny, he made some 350 paintings and works of art, more than Cezanne did of Mont Sainte-Victoire. Monet also traveled to Norway, Holland, Italy, the south of France, and Algeria during his army years. Pissarro seems to have concentrated his radius of traveling within a much more concentrated area. He is a man of the North, which is paradoxical when you come from the Caribbean. Have you thought about that, why isn't he attracted to the beautiful South?

AS: He indicated at one point, I believe to Cézanne, that the light in the South was very strong. Perhaps it reminded him of St. Thomas, and the deep contrasts between bright sunlight and dark shadows did not suit him. There is one Pontoise painting of a railroad crossing, where the sunlight is very bright and there are very deep shadows. [*The Railway Crossing at Les* Pâtis *near Pontoise*, 1873-74, PDR 306
JP: Yes, that's the painting that Cezanne actually mentions

AS: It's interesting that Cezanne would point out that one because this is what he would see in his part of France. The other reason had to do with his eye infection. He talked about going other places (Amsterdam, among others), but he had to stay close to his doctor in Paris in case his eye became infected again.

JP: You've done a pretty exhaustive and exemplary job at tracking down every place that Pissarro has been, including the Carribean, so how long did this venture take you?

AS: I've been working on it nearly twenty years. I discovered Pissarro at the Art Institute of Chicago in Richard Brettell's exhibition, "*Day in the Country*" (1984). I was totally captivated by one of Pissarro's paintings, and I had to study this artist, his paintings and his world. On my second trip to France, I drove around Normandy for a month, finding the places he painted. It was quite an adventure, especially since I don't speak French.

JP: So did you manage to find a place like Montfoucault on that trip?

AS: Yes, actually I used directions from your Pissarro monograph and found Melleray-la Vallée [a nearby village]. But I didn't know where to go from there, and I saw a tour bus parked by an old stone building down the road. I discovered that this was an old cider mill, now a museum. Since I could not speak French, I wrote down my questions in advance. They understood my questions and gave me perfect instructions. Montfoucault was just down the road.

JP: When I went to Montfoucault, I tried to find it on the map and it's not there. It's a tiny, tiny little hamlet.

AS: Montfoucault is the most intensely rural place that Pissarro could have ever found himself. It reminds me of an old song from 1919 that describes a peaceful place where you can let the world go by.*

JP: You spoke very beautifully about Montfoucault, but I'm struck when I look at the spectrum of places Pissarro goes--from this extreme isolation to the bustling, buzzing city centers. He doesn't go to the outskirts of Paris; he goes to the very center, to the biggest, most busy boulevards, to the Gare St. Lazare. How do you explain this almost quasi-schizophrenic pendulum going back and forth?

AS: As you well know, Pissarro had an unusual combination of influences in his life and it made him a very complex person. He said he didn't want to leave Pontoise--the cliffs and hills and valleys, nooks and crannies, hidden spots, and woods. He would never have run out of motifs to paint. What if finances had not forced him to move to Éragny?

Once there, he created this enormous body of work, but he got bored and said so many times. This is why I think he went to the cities. He was a cosmopolitan person, an international person. As a twelve-year-old, he had traveled alone from St. Thomas to Paris for school.

JP: You're right. He could have chosen one or the other, but he chooses both. It is really interesting that at the end of his life at the age of seventy, all the Impressionists are doing very well. But Pissarro doesn't buy himself a car, and Monet did. In the 1900s having a private car was like having a private jet today. At that time, his wife is very well-dressed and his children are immaculate. They could have said goodbye to peasant life and lived in rue Rivoli. Why did he do that for the last ten years of his life? Go back and forth; that's what I find so interesting.

AS: I think Éragny was more Julie's place than Pissarro's. He obviously went where his family was, and it is beautiful in the summer. But Éragny is what it is, plain and simple, no hills, no big rivers, no woods, all out in the open. How he managed to paint so many different views of Éragny is amazing and demonstrates his inventiveness and his curiosity. Thank goodness for that one crooked apple tree!

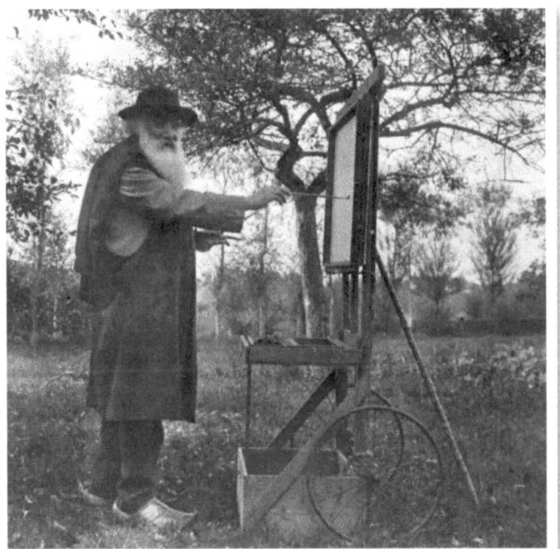

Camille Pissarro with his portable easel in his orchard by the crooked apple tree Musée Pissarro Archives, Pontoise.

* *Song "Let the Rest of the World Go By" sung by Willie Nelson on YouTube: http://www.youtube.com/watch?v=kbz0KGKV3Po*

Camille Pissarro & His Family

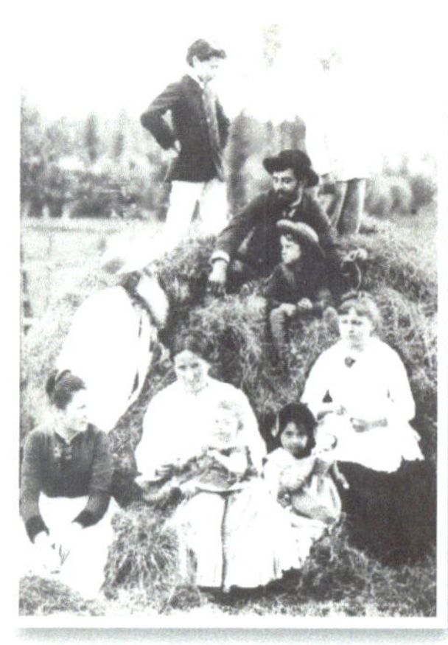

George and Félix standing, Lucien with black beard sitting beside Ludovic-Rodo, Camille Pissarro, (front row from the left) the maid, Julie, with Paulémile on her lap, Jeanne (Cocotte) and Eugenie Estruc, c. 1886, Musée Pissarro Archives, Pontoise.

Camille Pissarro

Born: July 10, 1830, St. Thomas, Virgin Islands
Died: November 13, 1903, Paris

Julie Vellay Pissarro

Born: October 2, 1838, Grancy-sur-Ource, Burgundy
Died: May 16, 1926, Éragny-sur-Epte

Their Children

Lucien Pissarro	Born: February 20, 1863, Paris Died: July 10, 1944, Hewood, Dorset, U.K.
Jeanne-Rachel Pissarro	Born: May 18, 1865, La Varenne-Saint-Hilaire Died: April 6, 1874, Pontoise
Adèle Emma Pissarro	Born: October 21, 1870, Montfoucault Died: November 5, 1870, Montfoucault
Georges-Henri Pissarro (Manzana)	Born: November 22, 1871, Louveciennes Died: January, 1961, Yvelines region west of Paris
Félix Camille Pissarro (Titi)	Born: July 24, 1874, Pontoise Died: November 25, 1897, Kew, London, U.K.
Ludovic-Rodo Pissarro (Rodo)	Born: November 21, 1878, Paris Died: October 18, 1952, Paris
Jeanne-Marguerite Pissarro (Cocotte)	Born: August 27, 1881, Pontoise Died: July 3, 1948. Paris
Paulémile Pissarro	Born: August 22, 1884, Éragny-sur-Epte Died: January 20, 1972, Clécy, Normandie

A Word with Readers

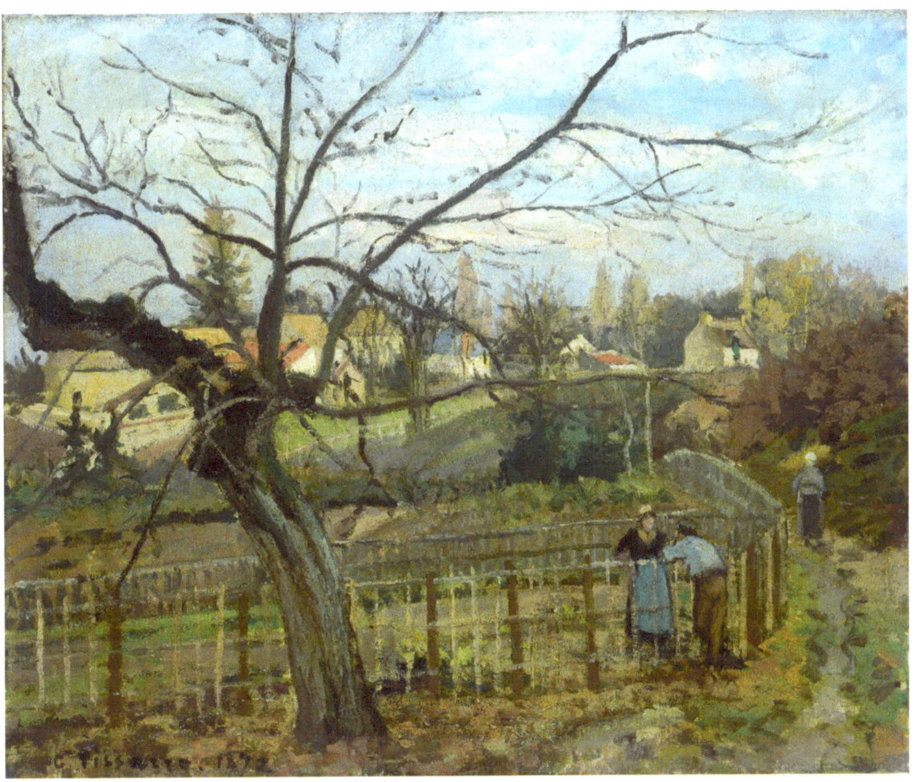

Landscape at Louveciennes, the Fence
1872
National Gallery of Art, Washington, DC
PDR 231

In Pissarro's landscapes, you virtually feel the sun and the breeze from the river—the same "sensations" he felt as he painted the canvas. This was his genius. His paintings invite us to join him in that place.

When I began to study Pissarro, I wanted to see for myself the places he painted. Thanks to many scholars who gave good directions in previous books, I found and visited most of the sites. (The one exception is Venezuela.) I was fascinated by what I found in Pissarro's places. This book looks at Pissarro's paintings in the context of the geography, history, and culture of each of the locations. To understand and enjoy Pissarro's paintings, it certainly is not necessary to visit the sites where they were painted. However, my visits to these places have produced information and insights that I never would have had otherwise. Surprisingly, some of them are much the same now as when Pissarro painted them. Others are very different, and I've seen changes in some over the 20 years I've spent traveling to them.

Being in each place gave me a sense of what Pissarro must have experienced. I stayed in Rouen for more than a week, and I could feel the pulse of the city. Just as Pissarro described, there would be clouds or rain one minute and sunny blue skies the next. The dramatic sunsets over the Seine are just as radiant as in his paintings. This is when I began to really comprehend how he painted what he saw reflected through his own "sensations."

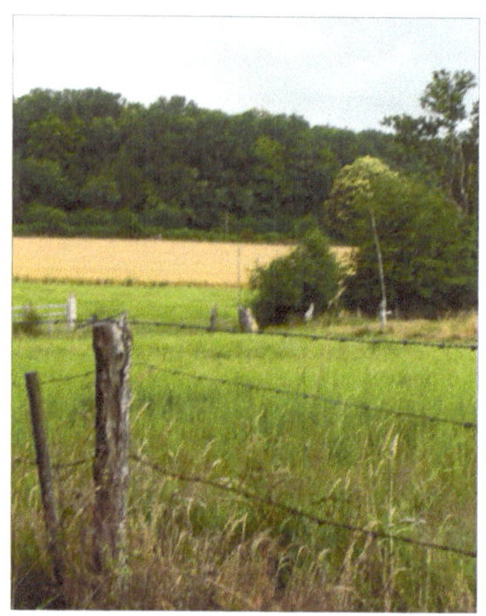

Fields at Montfoucault, near Melleray-la-Vallée

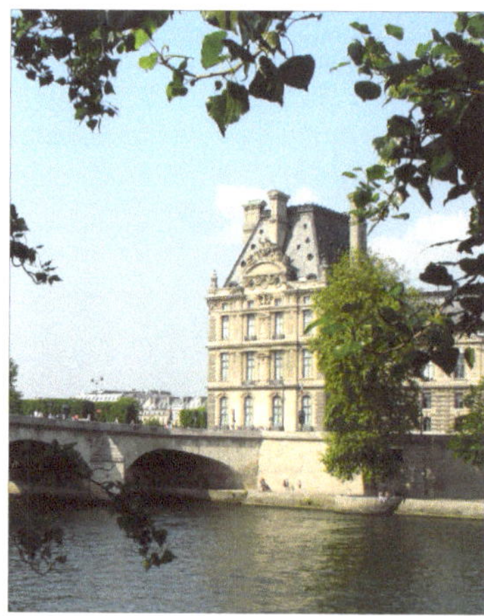

View of the Pont-Royal and the Pavillon de Flore painted by Pissarro in 1903.

Organization

This book is written for everyone who enjoys art. Each chapter stands alone, so you may choose chapters at random or read the book straight through. A short chronology of Pissarro's life is included, as well as a family tree.

Within the chapters, there are references to reproductions of Pissarro's paintings, marked by the designation: [See PDR 000]. Other pages, also marked with the PDR number, have brief comments about that specific painting. PDR 000 refers to the number in **Pissarro: Critical Catalogue**, compiled by Joachim Pissarro and Claire Durand-Ruel Snollaerts in 2005, which is the authoritative resource on Pissarro's life and paintings. (JP is the great-grandson of Camille Pissarro, and CD-RS is the great-great-granddaughter of Pissarro's art dealer, Paul Durand-Ruel.)

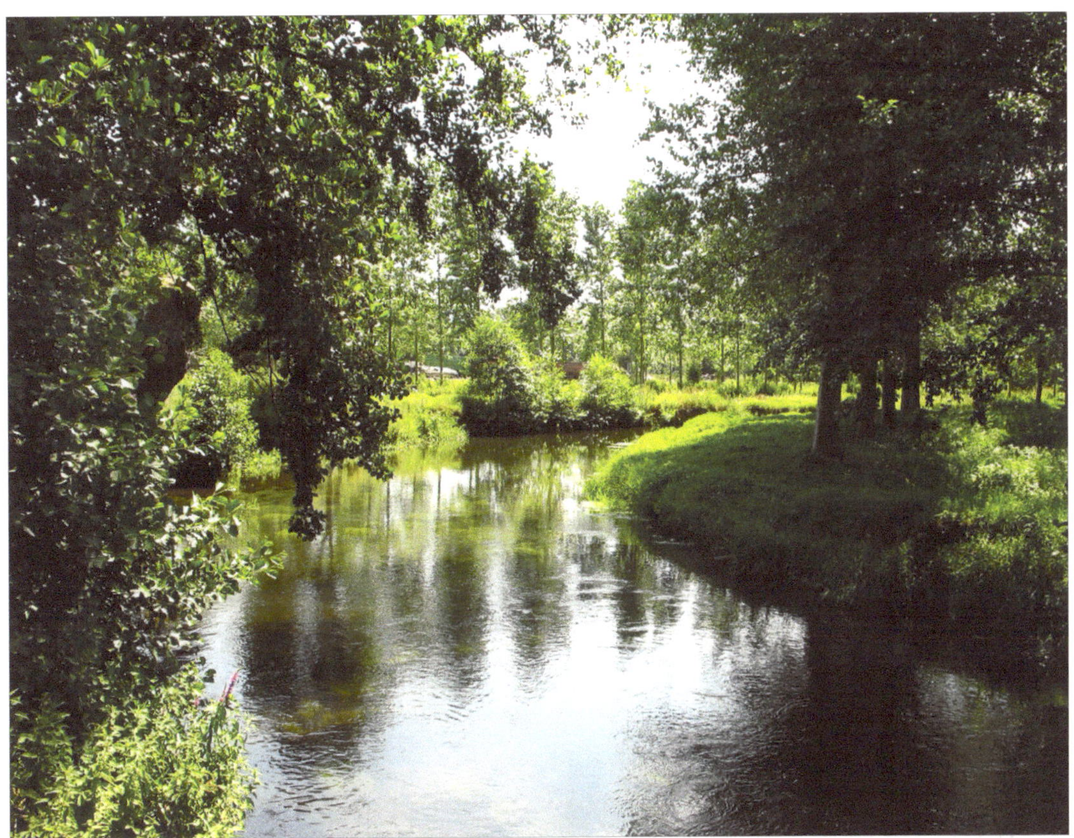

The beautiful Epte River flows behind the Pissarro home in Éragny. About 25 miles downstream, the river was dammed up by Claude Monet to create his water lily pond.

All of the paintings featured on those pages are located in public museums and are believed to be accessible to museum viewers. Of course, no photograph or online image can do proper justice to a painting, and I encourage you to see these masterpieces for yourself. If you visit a museum to see a specific Pissarro painting, email or call the museum in advance to make sure it is on view.

Although research stands behind the facts stated in this book, the narrative is written in an informal style. Issues and controversies about Pissarro's work and comparison with other artists are not dealt with here, but are left to the many fine scholarly books and references currently available, many of which are listed in the bibliography.

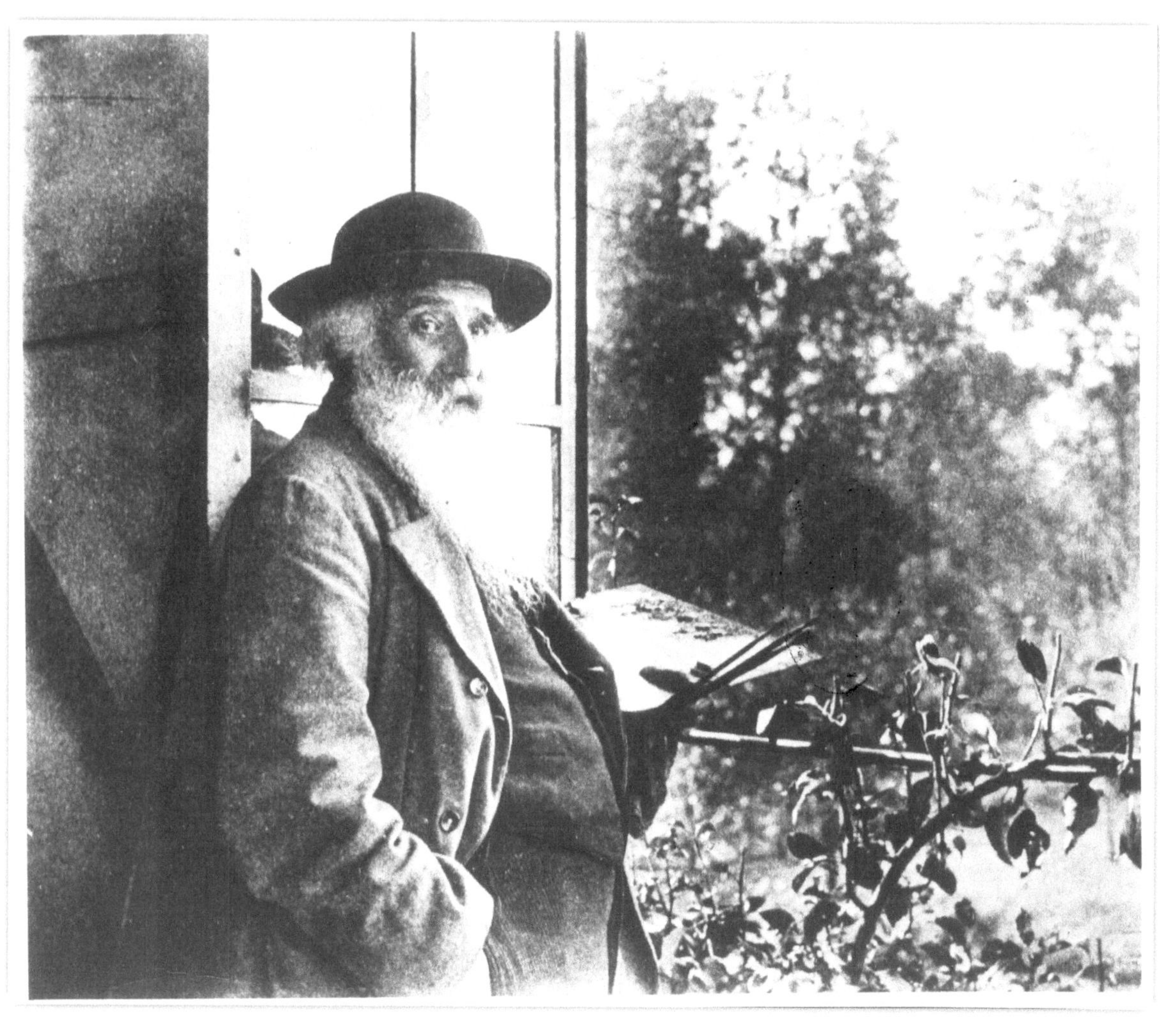

Camille Pissarro in his studio at Éragny-sur-Epte
Musée Camille Pissarro, Pontoise

Through Pissarro's Eyes

Camille Pissarro lets us see places as he saw them, through the prism of his "sensations." Describing the similarities between his work and Cézanne's, Pissarro said, "*My goodness, we were always together! But what is certain is that each of us kept the only thing that matters, 'one's own sensation....'*"

Because Pissarro places such importance on the word "sensation," we need to understand what he meant. In the English language, the word "sensation" may be used to explain emotional feelings, such as a sensation of happiness or gloom. It is also used to describe something that causes public excitement, such as a movie or a performer that is "the sensation of the year."

The French language definition is more specific. Joachim Pissarro, distinguished art historian and author of many books about his great-grandfather, describes it best:

> The French Impressionist concept of *sensation* is almost impossible to translate into English. It corresponds perhaps best to the notion of physical, sensorial experience—although it carries none of the psychological connotations of the term 'emotion.' It could be translated as 'feeling,' although 'feeling' carries none of the idiosyncratic and singular connotations of sensation. *Sensation* is always related to oneself as a subject: the only thing that matters, says [Camille] Pissarro, is not so much the *sensation* as one's *own* sensation: '*sa sensation*.'

Pissarro's "sensations," what he experienced when he stood in front of a landscape, were practically visceral. He literally absorbed it into his body, and it came out through his touch. By capturing his own "sensations" so honestly on canvas, Pissarro wakens our own senses.

Giving advice to his son Lucien, Pissarro said, "*But persistence, will and free sensations are necessary, one must be undetermined by anything but one's own sensation.*"

Pissarro's Influences

Pissarro's complex vision was shaped by the variegated influences of many different places and cultures. He was born in 1830 to French-Jewish parents on St. Thomas in the Virgin Islands, which was at that time a province of Denmark. As a result, he was influenced by four distinctly different cultures from the start. His mother, Rachel, was from a French-Jewish family who lived in what is now the Dominican Republic. His father, Frédéric, came from the Bordeaux region of France. It is hardly surprising that throughout his life he was drawn to new and different places to paint.

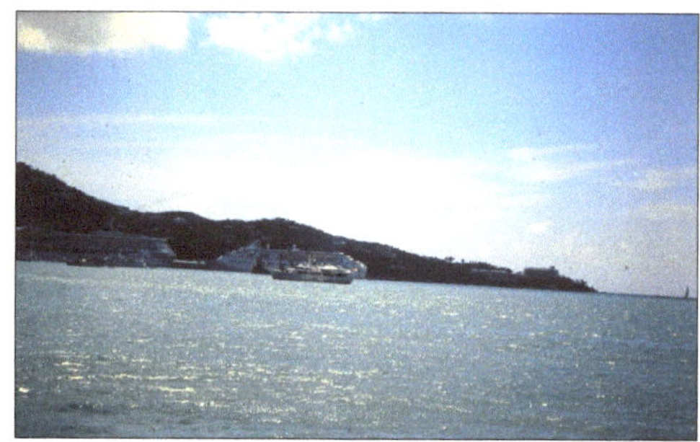

Long Bay at St. Thomas, Virgin Islands, now a popular stop for cruise ships

In the same way, we ourselves are defined by the places in which we live and visit. Places help shape our beginnings and, to some extent, who we become. Our education, cultural experiences, and attitudes are reflections of the different places where we live. The places we visit cast their unique spell on us. In each new place, we absorb the aura, adjust to local customs, and see life from a different point of view, thereby enlarging our world.

The Kinds of Places Pissarro Painted

"...The places where he lived—Caracas, Paris, Pontoise, London, Louveciennes, and Pontoise again—put their mark upon his work," observed Joachim Pissarro.

Many of Pissarro's motifs were dictated by his circumstances. His early paintings and sketches are of St. Thomas and Venezuela. In France, he painted *en plein air* in the forests and fields around Paris. He painted motifs where he lived, first at Louveciennes and later at Pontoise, where it was less expensive to raise his growing family. He painted the fields and forests at Montfoucault, the home of his close friend Ludovic Piette in northwestern France. When Pissarro and his family fled the Franco-Prussian war in 1870, he painted the southern suburbs of London. During a later period of unrest in France, Pissarro painted in Belgium. Likewise, he also painted the cities of northern

France. And he painted several hundred canvases at Éragny, a tiny village north of Paris where he and his wife Julie finally settled in 1884.

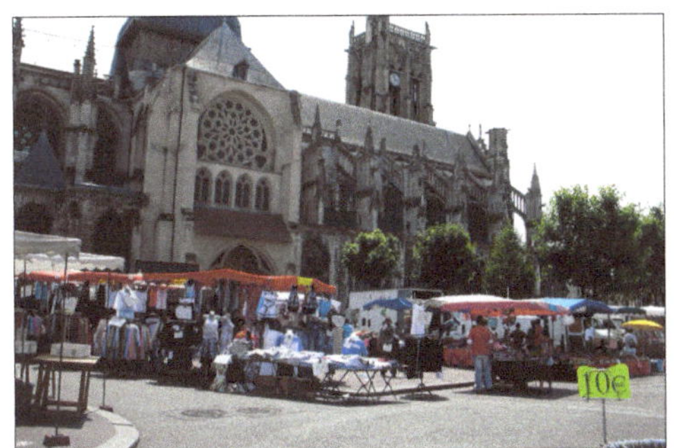

The Saturday market at Dieppe

Although Pissarro lived much of his life in rural settings, he craved the stimulation of cities bustling with industrialization and commerce. He traveled frequently to Paris, not only to sell his paintings, but also to engage in lively dialogue with other artists, writers, and philosophers. He painted what he saw in the cities—the geometric shapes of buildings, circuitous movement of traffic, and lively pedestrians. These cityscapes, which captured the spirit of Rouen, Dieppe, Le Havre, and Paris, have become some of his most beloved paintings.

Pissarro most often chose ordinary places—the orchard behind his Éragny home, the entrance to the village of Louveciennes, a busy boulevard in Paris. In a letter to his son Lucien, he wrote, *"Happy are those who see beauty in the modest spots where others see nothing. Everything is beautiful; the whole secret lies in knowing how to interpret."*

When Pissarro did paint a monument or a well-known place, such as the cathedral at Rouen, the Louvre, or l'Opéra de Paris, he often depicted it as one element among others, not as the focal point of the work.

However, making generalizations about Pissarro is dangerous because he often shatters expectations. In London, he painted Kew Gardens, already a favorite London tourist destination in 1892. For the most part, however, Pissarro bypassed fashionable locations for the commonplace (or the *common* place).

Unlike some artists, Pissarro did not take liberties with nature to the extent of adding ancient ruins or mythical creatures. Neither did he make a photographic image of the scene. He did not "prettify" or romanticize his motifs. Doing this, he felt, created a sentimentality that was false, less than the truth. One of Pissarro's early paintings prompted Émile Zola to write, "A beautiful picture by this artist is the act of an honest man."

The People in Pissarro's Places

When people appear in Pissarro's landscapes, they are elements of equal value with the rest of nature. Even landscapes without people generally show evidence of the human hand with planted fields, homes, and domestic animals.

In a painting of a south London landscape, *View of Alleyn Park, West Dulwich,* we see open fields framed on either side by trees [See PDR 190]. In the middle ground, a small valley conceals a train detectable only by the long plume of smoke trailing from its engine. With the route of the train leading the eye to the right, it is easy to miss the small man standing in the middle of the field.

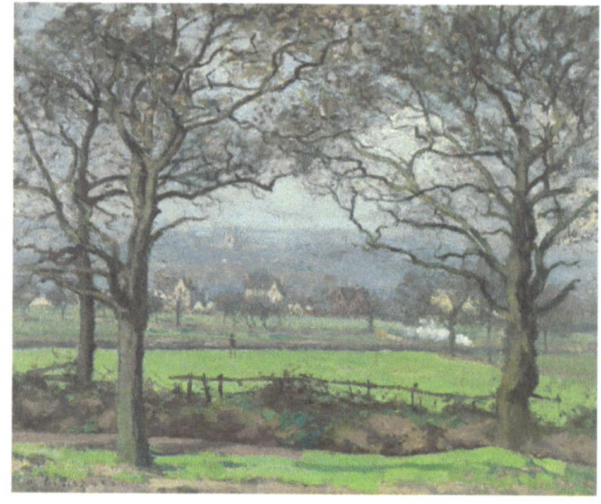

View of Alleyn Park, West Dulwich
1871
Kimbell Art Museum, Fort Worth, TX
PDR 190

In some of Pissarro's landscapes, the people are almost hidden. In the painting, *Côte des Bœufs, Pontoise*, for example, our eyes are focused on the entangled underbrush and houses that appear to be close but are difficult to reach [See PDR 488]. When we discover a woman and child hidden in the thicket by the stream, we feel startled like an interloper wandering onto private property.

Describing the artist's process, Joachim Pissarro said, "Essentially complex, his work made use of a phenomenal imagination, an unusually rich, innovative visual mind, a vast curiosity about techniques of all sorts, a profound poetic sensitivity, and an unquenchable passion for painting, as well as a strongly defined set of intellectual positions."

Pissarro's Viewpoint

For many years, Pissarro painted as other Impressionists did, *en plein air.* In all kinds of weather—snow, rain, or sun—he planted his easel in his chosen spot and painted what was in front of him. This freedom of movement changed when Pissarro

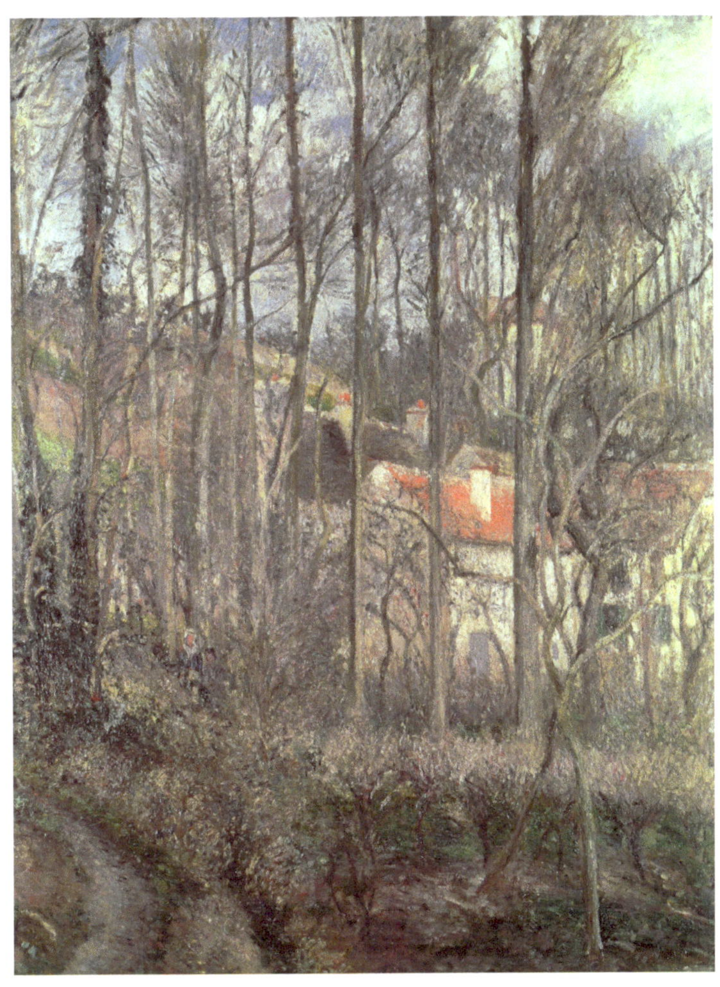

Côte des Bœufs, Pontoise
1877
The National Gallery, London, UK
PDR 488

was in his fifties. He developed an inflamed tear gland in 1887 that required a physician's care. Occasionally, Pissarro had to completely stop his work, which was very distressing to him. In January 1891, he wrote his son Lucien, "*My eyes have been so bad that I had to interrupt all that I had in view.... I have kept to my room since Friday and I probably won't be able to go out before several days.*"

Although he never completely stopped working outside, gradually he began doing more work in his studio or from windows of well-situated buildings, protected from wind and dust. In this sense, Pissarro's point of view became literal as well as intellectual. When he visited new places, he carefully chose hotels that would give him interesting views to paint. Just as he had done when he painted outside, he used his position in the window as a pivot point, finding new motifs by turning left and right or looking straight ahead.

Pissarro's virtuosity was such that from that one room on the third or fourth floor of a building, he was able to create the image as he saw it. He also was able to paint the same image as if he were closer to it. Perhaps he was using binoculars to check the details, although there's no way to verify that. At home in Éragny, his studio was situated on the top level of what had been a barn. He had large windows installed on two sides, which gave him a protected place to paint the garden, orchard, and meadows if the wind and dust were too strong outside.

This unique perspective, imposed on Pissarro by the problem with his eye, brought about some of his most memorable paintings. Published books and articles about Paris are frequently illustrated with Pissarro's artistry. And his paintings of Paris, made from above the street, are those that come to mind when most people think of the "City of Lights."

Pissarro's Places Now

Some of Pissarro's places still look nearly the same as when he painted them. This is easy to document because he frequently provided the exact location – for example, "Rue de Gisors," "Route de Versailles, Louveciennes," "Place du Havre." [See PDR 284, 224, and 986]

But how important is the place after all? Some scholars contend that the place depicted in a landscape is of little or no importance to the artistic value of a painting and has no bearing on creativity, composition, or originality. From a purely aesthetic point of view, this is a strong argument. However, this line of reasoning discounts the subliminal impact—the sensations it creates—on the artist and the viewer.

Part of the mystique of a place is that it can provide a meaningful connection. Like the face of a friend, its contours and aspects often recall something familiar. The precise location of the painting's site may be less important than the painting itself, but its impressions on the painter are at the heart of the artistic creation.

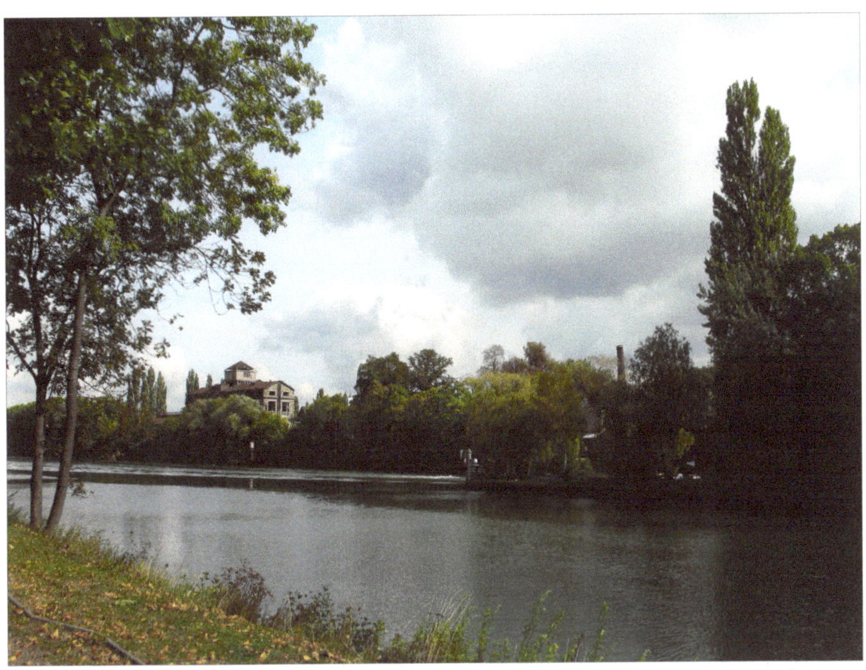

Reflections on the Oise River at Pontoise, a view Pissarro painted many times

Why visit the site painted by an artist? Seeing the exact spot is certainly not essential to the enjoyment and appreciation of a landscape painting. But standing in the artist's footprints does enhance understanding. In Pontoise, the banks of the Oise River offer the essence of Pissarro's paintings—the soft summer air, clouds scudding across the blue sky, reflections lying gently on the river's surface, the dusty towpath and barges tied along the shore, just as they were more than a century ago.

In Paris, pedestrians and traffic still crowd the Place du Havre, and the Gare Saint-Lazare is still busy with commuters hurrying to catch trains. This bustle of the city is what Pissarro must have seen, heard, and felt as he put brush to canvas.

Not everyone can visit the actual sites of famous paintings. This book is intended to transport all of us to the places Pissarro painted and offer a sense of the places themselves—the combination of history and culture that made them what they were in Pissarro's experience. And then, most importantly, to see those places through Pissarro's eyes.

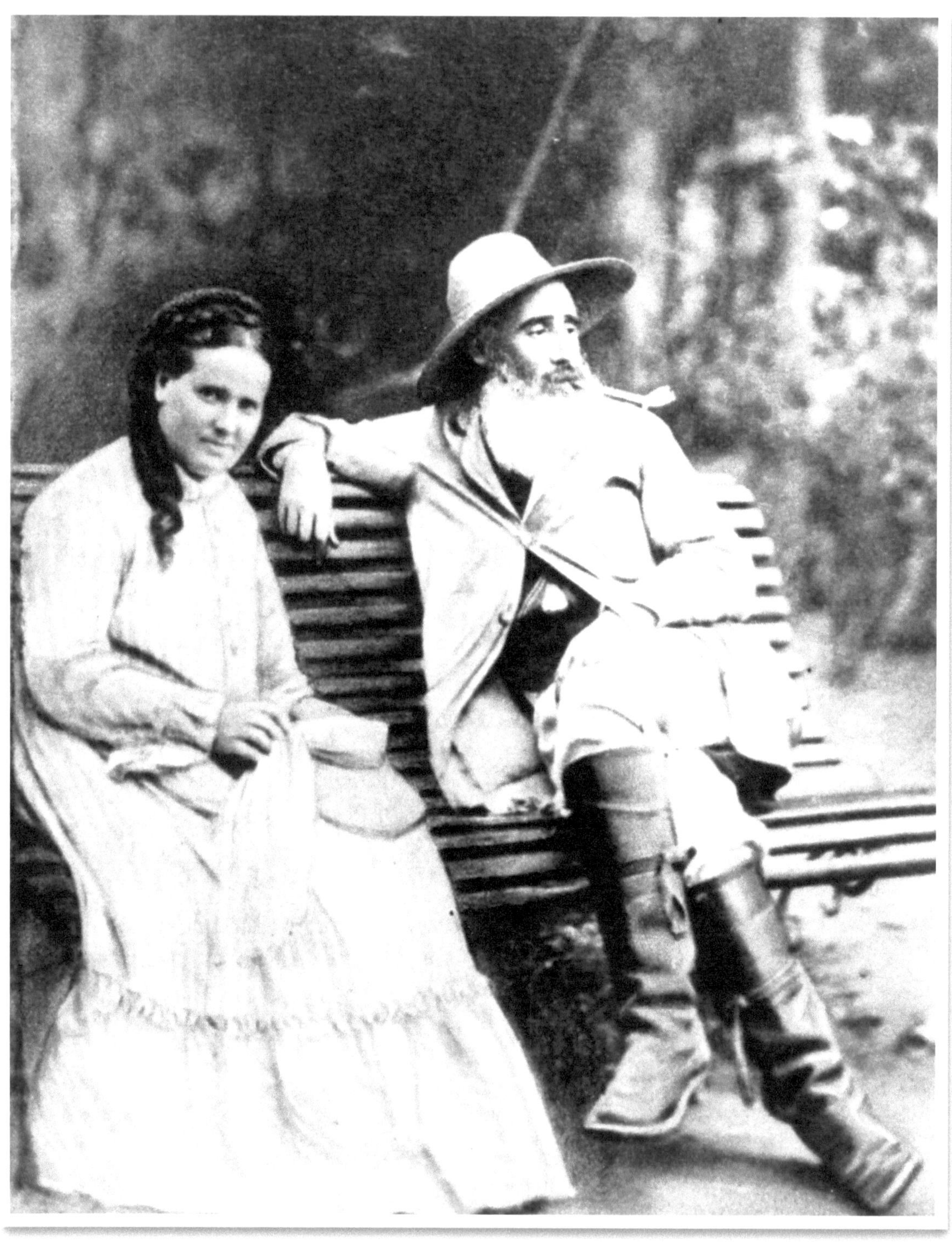

Julie and Camille Pissarro, montage of two photographs
Lionel and Sandrine Pissarro Archives

LOUVECIENNES

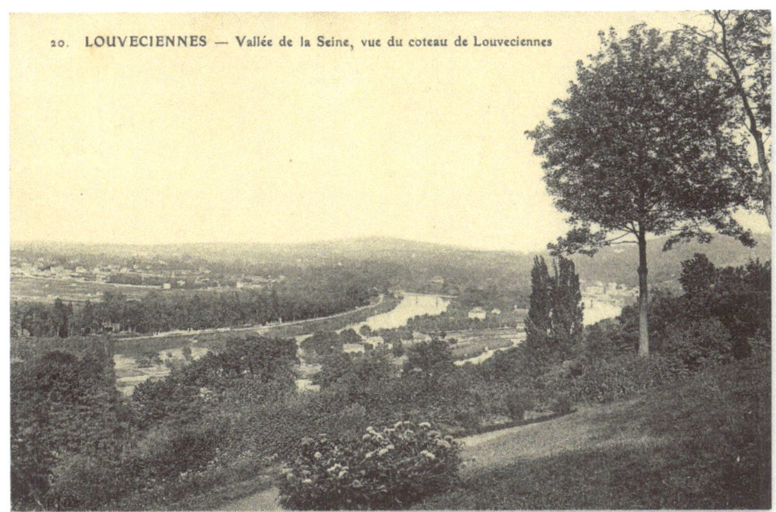

The village of Louveciennes in the curve of the River Seine

An Impressionist Place

A radical young artist named Camille Pissarro moved to Louveciennes in the spring of 1869. Soon after, three other young artists—Auguste Renoir, Alfred Sisley, and Claude Monet—converged on the scene. As they shared their revolutionary ideas and brought their ingenious notions into being, the Impressionist movement was born. Much later, Camille Pissarro would recall that "*...although I was full of ardor, I didn't conceive, even at forty, the deeper side of the movement we followed instinctively. It was in the air!*"

The four artists were friends before they moved to the area. Pissarro met Monet in 1860 at the Académie Suisse, and in 1863, he met both Renoir and Sisley at the Atelier Gleyre in Paris. But it was happenstance that brought them within walking distance of one another. A few months after Pissarro came to Louveciennes, Renoir's parents moved to the nearby hamlet Voisins, and Renoir frequently stayed with them. That same year Sisley moved to a house just a few blocks from Pissarro's home. Claude Monet lived barely a mile and a half away in Bougival, another village on the Seine.

They invented new artistic concepts and worked *en plein air*. Renoir and Monet worked together in Bougival in 1869, painting the swimming and boating activities at the "Grenouillère," a popular weekend getaway. Monet and Pissarro painted snow scenes together in January 1870 on the Route de Versailles near Pissarro's home.

The four artists also painted the same scenes, but at different times. Pissarro and Sisley both painted the Route de Saint-Germaine and the Machine de Marly. Pissarro and Monet painted similar views of the Route de Marly and the River Seine at Bougival. Pissarro, Sisley, and Renoir all painted views of the aqueduct that ran through Louveciennes. Surely, they looked at each other's work. Together, the group was inventing what they would later call "the new art," although each artist would always have his own style and character.

On the Edge of History

Because Louveciennes is only fourteen miles northwest of Paris, it was a convenient location for Pissarro. Today it is still a small town of about 8000 people. Although it has no major historical sites of its own, Louveciennes is situated near places where history was made. During the Middle Ages, it was home to farms and vineyards. When the French government made its headquarters in the neighboring town of Versailles, the forest at Louveciennes became the royal hunting grounds. In 1679, Louis XIV built the Château de Marly nearby as a retreat from his royal duties at Versailles and launched a massive landscaping project to decorate the surrounding grounds.

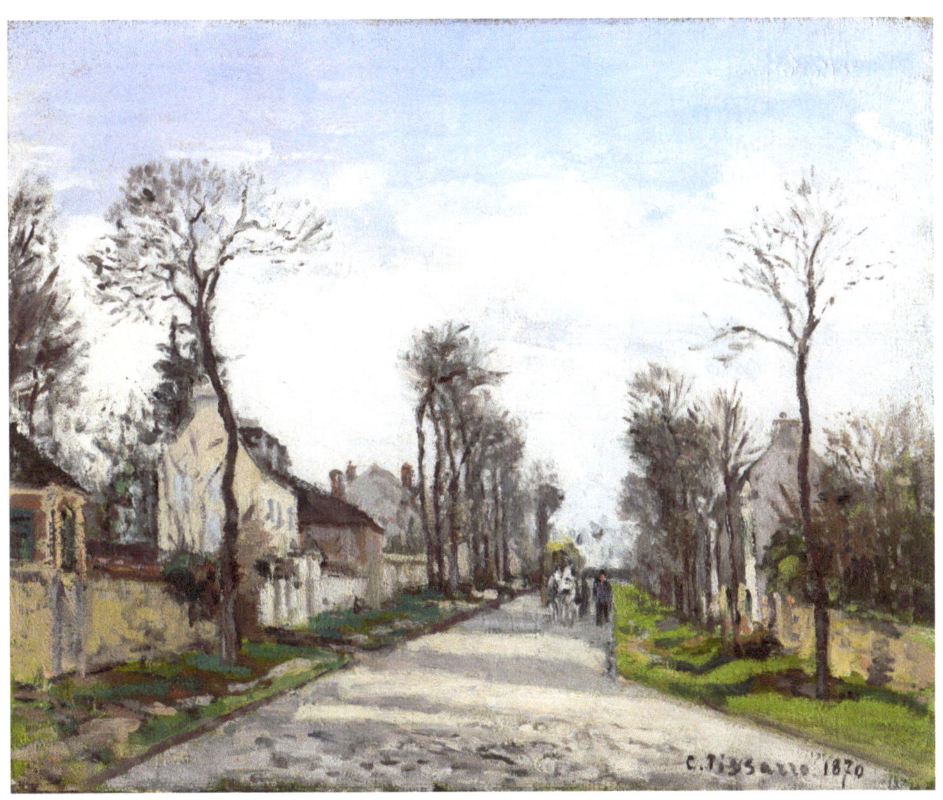

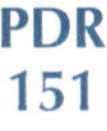

PDR 151

Route de Versailles, Louveciennes

1870

Sterling and Francine Clark Art Institute, Williamstown, MA

PDR 151

This painting is a superb example of Impressionism. The color palette is light and soft. Through the haziness of the blue sky, the pale morning sunlight bathes the façades of the houses and casts transparent shadows on the road. The brushstrokes are loose and visible. The large shadow at the lower edge was cast by something out of the picture, an objectionable practice in French academic art.

We almost hear the distant clip-clop of the horse's hooves and birds twittering in the bushes. We feel a soft breeze and the sun's warmth. Pissarro's "sensations," captured so honestly on this canvas, awaken our own senses.

Pissarro was able to capture the sense of this place because he knew it intimately. He and his family lived in the house on the left—the pink one with blue shutters.

To feed the ponds and fountains at his Marly and Versailles estates, the Sun King ordered engineers to bring water uphill from the River Seine. They constructed the Machine of Marly, considered in the seventeenth century to be one of the wonders of the world. Using fourteen paddle wheels and 250 pumps, the Machine moved water through three different reservoirs up 500 feet to an aqueduct that was 643 meters long and had 36 arches. Although the château was demolished, a later version of the Machine was still in use when Pissarro lived there. The aqueduct, which transported the water from the Seine to the reservoirs at Marly, was directly behind Pissarro's house. Its huge arches are still visible from the train station in Louveciennes [See PDR 158].

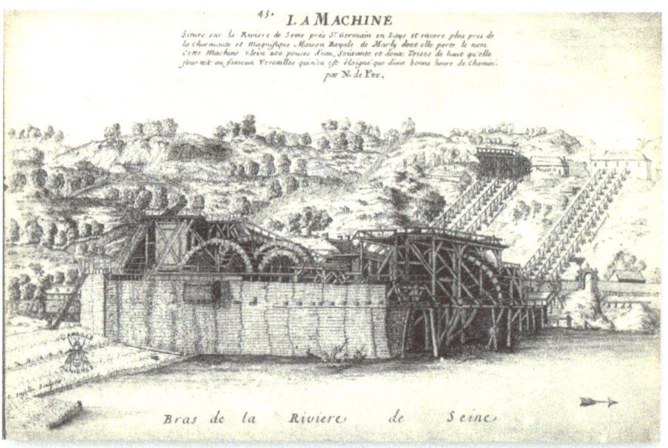

A reproduction of the original design of the Machine of Marly

The aqueduct appears as an element in two of Pissarro's paintings, but he did not focus on it or other historical spaces near Louveciennes. Instead, he set his easel near his home on the Route de Versailles, where he lived with his companion Julie Vellay and their two small children, six-year-old Lucien and four-year-old Jeanne-Rachel (called Minette). He painted the street in all kinds of weather—heavy winter snow, spring's pale sunlight, and summer rains [See PDR 151].

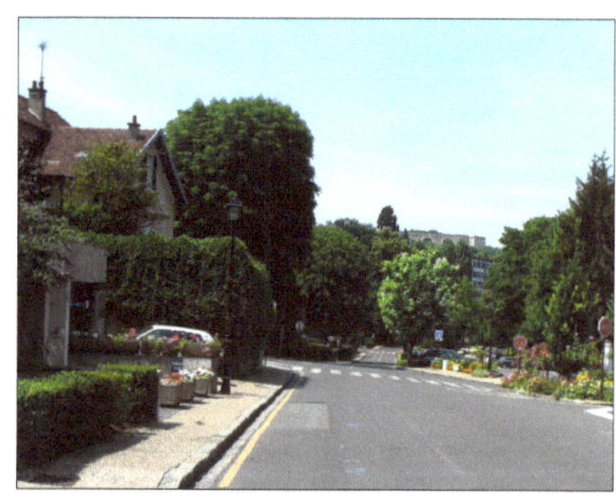
This current photograph, taken from the train station, shows the site of the aqueduct. Pissarro must have stood here to make his painting in 1870.

During this time, Pissarro's painting techniques were shifting. Christopher Lloyd, the distinguished art historian, described it like this: "The palette becomes brighter, the light sharper, and the artist's eye becomes more investigative, examining moving surfaces, such as water and foliage, or luminous surfaces, such as snow and blossom."

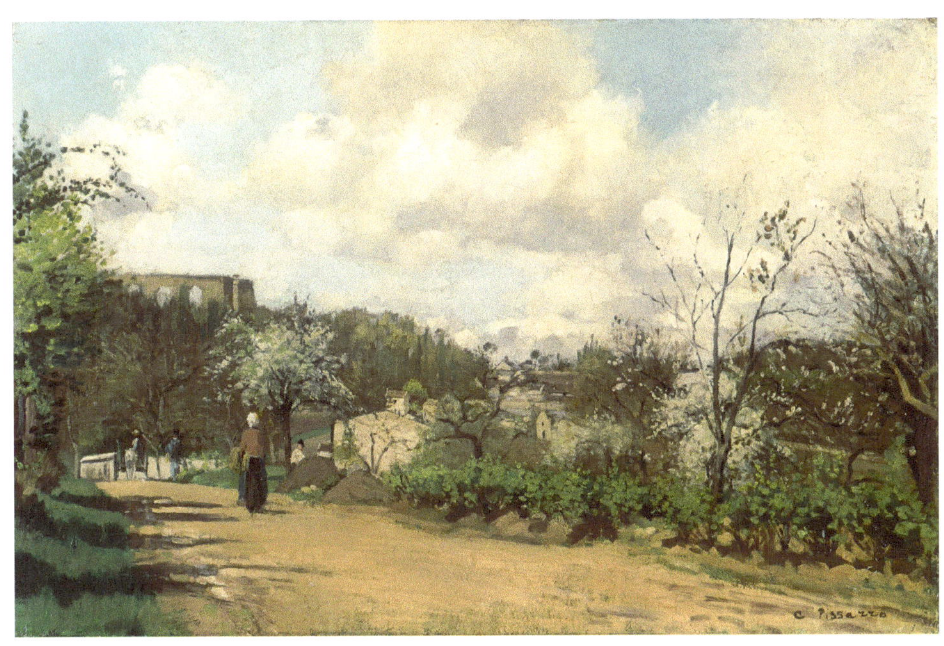

View of the Aqueduct at Louveciennes, Spring

1870

The National Gallery, London, UK

PDR 158

PDR 158

This view of the aqueduct is easily visible from the front of the Louveciennes train station, just as it was in Pissarro's time.

Despite its landmark status, the aqueduct is not the major focal point of this painting. It is placed on the far left side in the middle ground, and its earthy colors blend perfectly with the distant vegetation. In the center of the painting is a cluster of white houses below street level, bookended by white flowering fruit trees, suggesting early springtime.

As he does in many paintings, Pissarro includes a few people, all of whom are ignoring our view as they walk away from us or continue their daily chores. Pissarro's irrepressible sense of humor surfaces in the unassuming man working by the pile of dirt under the flowering trees. A close look reveals that Pissarro has provided him with a handsome pair of suspenders!

About the same time, Renoir painted a view almost identical to this, and a few years later, in 1874, Sisley also painted the aqueduct, although his viewpoint was much closer to the massive structure.

Painting for the Salon

During the period from 1859 to 1870, eleven paintings by Pissarro were accepted for the Salon, the annual juried art exhibition. In 1869, one of Pissarro's paintings was placed, in his own words, *"impossibly high up over a door."* Needless to say, it did not attract the attention of art critics. However in 1870, the Salon accepted two of his paintings, and those were noticed. One of the art critics, Zacharie Astruc, said, "He has assimilated for his own ends new elements which he employs with exceptional intelligence. He brings whatever he studies to life; he renders it with remarkable charm."

The Salon was the most important venue available for artists to attract attention that would sell their paintings. It was initiated in the seventeenth century as an exhibition for the students of the French Académie des Beaux-Arts. After the French Revolution, the Salon was opened to all artists, including those who were not French.

Paintings were judged by how closely artists adhered to academic standards. The finish had to be very smooth, with no sign of brushstroke to mar the illusion of reality. The Salon adhered to a strict hierarchy of "acceptable" subjects. Paintings of historical or mythological subjects were deemed the highest level. Genre paintings, portraits, landscapes, and still-life motifs were less important.

The walls of the Salon exhibition hall were crowded with paintings from eye level to the ceiling. Prominent artists whose works met academic standards were hung "on the line" (at eye level) where they were easily seen. Paintings by lesser-known artists were usually "skyed" (hung at the top of the wall near the ceiling), like Pissarro's 1869 painting.

A group of avant-garde artists, including Pissarro and his friends, gained notoriety from their participation in the Salon des Refusés in 1863. That year, the Salon jury rejected more than 3,000 paintings, and artists whose works were excluded raised loud protests. Responding to their dissent, Emperor Napoléon III established the Salon des Refusés, an alternative exhibition in an annex to the regular Salon. Although the show generated much derision and scorn, it became a cause célèbre for artists who did not follow academic mandates. It united them in a common cause—the right to have their work seen and evaluated by the general public.

Unlike academic artists, Pissarro and his friends were working outdoors *en plein air* and painting rapidly to capture the elusive effects of light and atmosphere. The artist's touch, apparent in the brushstrokes, was easily visible on the canvas. Their paintings were generally landscapes, and they painted what their eyes actually perceived—not the perfect image that the mind would expect. Their motifs were modern, depicting everyday life, with recent developments such as trains and factories. Despite their objections, the radical young artists had no other choice than the official Salon.

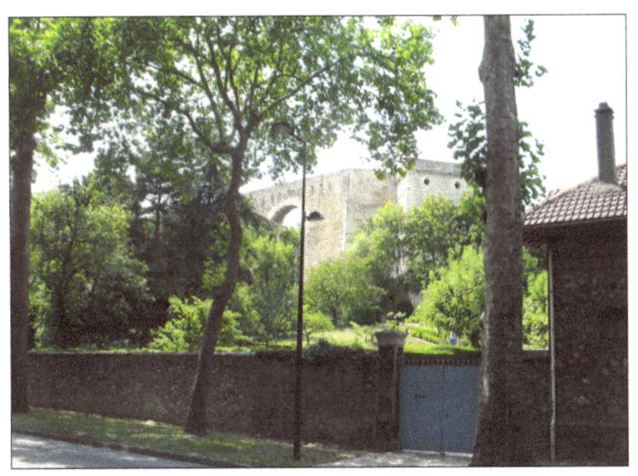

This close-up view of the aqueduct was painted by Sisley.

The Franco-Prussian War

Any benefit Pissarro might have gained from having his paintings chosen for the Salon of 1869 was wiped away within months. In July 1870, simmering tensions erupted into the Franco-Prussian war, and enemy soldiers immediately invaded France. As the Prussians came closer to Paris, Pissarro and his young family fled to Montfoucault, in the Pays de la Loire region of western France, to the home of their friends Ludovic and Adèle Piette. They left everything behind, including all of Pissarro's paintings and drawings—all of his life's work to that point. (See chapter on Montfoucault.)

The Prussian troops reached Paris in mid-September, and, within a few days, they had encircled the city. During the siege, the French resistance used hot-air balloons to rescue people and send mail to the provinces. Return mail was brought back to Paris by carrier pigeons. Suffering from famine and cold, Paris surrendered on January 28, 1871.

As the Prussian troops extended their occupation of France, the Pissarro family fled again—this time to London where Pissarro's mother had already taken sanctuary with relatives. (See chapter on London).

After the war, in late June 1871, Pissarro and his family finally returned to Louveciennes. Letters from Julie's sister and a neighbor had prepared them for the sad homecoming. Their home was totally uninhabitable. For almost four months, Prussian soldiers had occupied the house, keeping horses on the ground floor while they lived upstairs. A fire in the bedroom had damaged a beam in the roof. The landlord had salvaged some things—"two beds, but no mattresses, your wardrobe, wash stand, desk, about forty paintings, the small wooden bed."

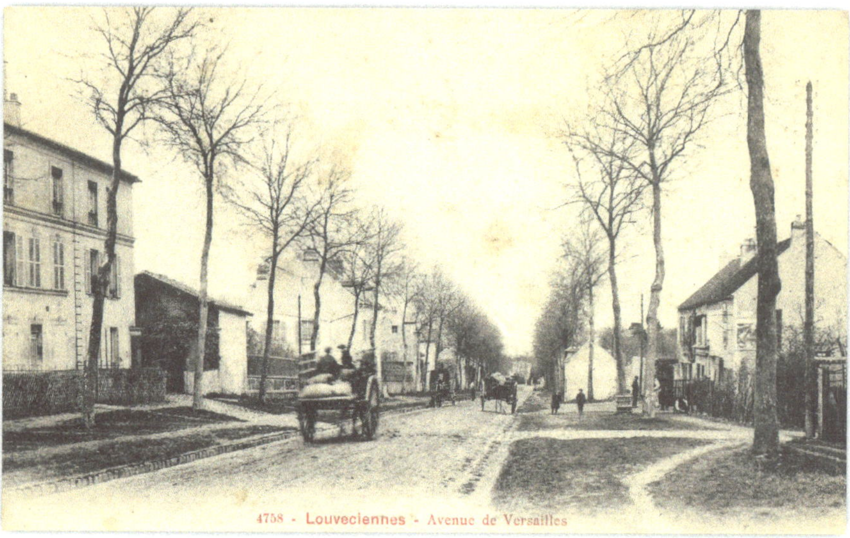

This historic postcard shows Pissarro's house on the left. The small building next door served as his studio.

Prussian soldiers had used Pissarro's painted canvases as aprons when they butchered poultry and rabbits. Other paintings were laid over muddy places in the garden. Pissarro estimated that he had lost about 15,000 works. This must have included all the drawings and sketches he made as a young man in St. Thomas, drawings and paintings from Venezuela, early paintings from his first years in Paris, and paintings from his first visit to Montfoucault. Even if his number was exaggerated as some scholars believe, this was an inestimable loss. He received an indemnity from the French government of only 835 francs.

After the War

Following his return from London, Pissarro began painting immediately, turning again to familiar motifs. He made another painting of the Route de Versailles, essentially the same view as the painting of 1870, which included his home. This painting is very different from the earlier ones. The tall trees that had lined the road were cut down during the war by soldiers for firewood, an injury that would not be remedied right away.

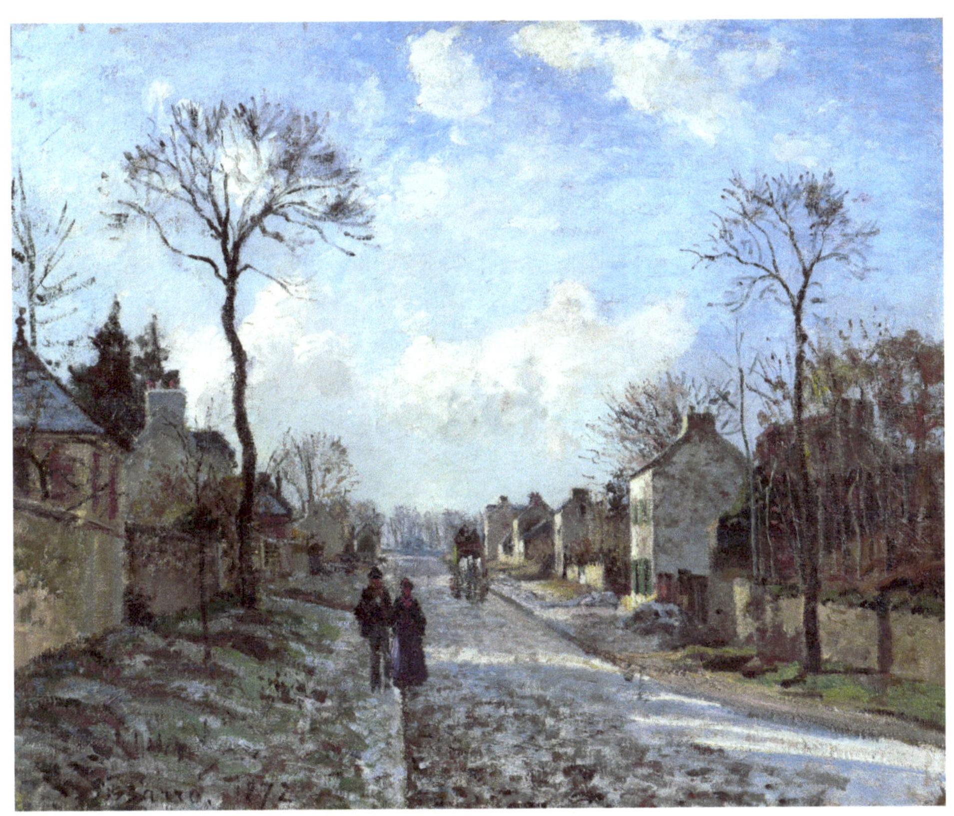

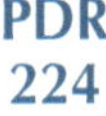

PDR 224

Route de Versailles, Louveciennes

1872

Musee d'Orsay, Paris

PDR 224

When the Franco-Prussian War ended, Pissarro came back from London to Louveciennes. He returned to the motif he had painted just two years earlier, the familiar scene of the Route de Versailles. Though the view is essentially the same as in 1870, it looks very different. The tall trees that had lined the road before were cut down by the Prussian army, an injury that would not be remedied right away.

The low winter sun slants through the trees and illuminates the fronts of the houses, but it provides little warmth to the chilly scene. Patches of snow and ice cover the frozen ground. Though people are on the road, the scene suggests stillness and a passive numbness.

Pissarro's life resumed, and his family grew larger with the birth of his second son Georges on November 22, 1871. When the baby suffered from convulsions, Dr. Paul Gachet, a homeopathic physician, came to help and the baby gradually recovered. Dr. Gachet was friendly with all the young artists. He himself was an amateur painter, and he sometimes borrowed Pissarro's paintings to study the technique. He also developed a large collection of Impressionist paintings, many of them works of Pissarro.

In 1872, Paul Durand-Ruel, an art dealer whom Pissarro met in London, began buying his paintings, acquiring a total of 22 that year. At last, Pissarro's paintings received recognition, and at the age of 42, the artist was financially independent for the first time. There are approximately 70 paintings remaining of those Pissarro made in Louveciennes.

The little group of artists did not remain in that area very long, but the concepts and techniques that they developed there solidified into a new form that would change the art world forever.

Pontoise

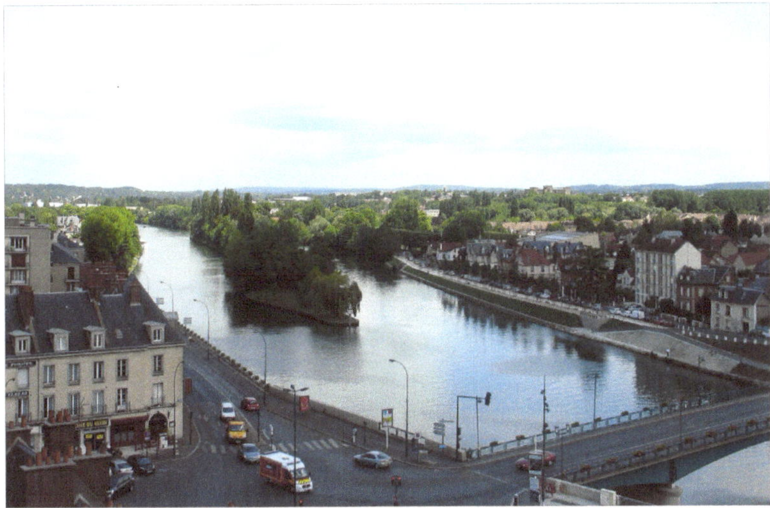

Pontoise and the bridge (*pont*) over the beautiful River Oise

The Pivotal Years

The Impressionist movement came into being during the nearly two decades Pissarro lived in Pontoise and Louveciennes, 1866–1884. There were eight Impressionist exhibitions in all, and seven of them were held during those years. It was in Pontoise that Pissarro worked side by side with Cézanne and taught Gauguin to paint in the Impressionist style. Pontoise provided a stimulating environment for Pissarro's artistic temperament and a painting laboratory for the many artists who came to work with him.

Although he stayed longer in Éragny, Pontoise may have been more of a real home to Pissarro than any other place outside

Paris. Pontoise was the birthplace of Pissarro's fourth child Félix (July 24, 1874) and second daughter Jeanne-Marguerite (August 27, 1881), called "Cocotte" in the family. His first daughter, Jeanne-Rachel (Minette), died on April 6, 1874, at the age of eight and was buried in Pontoise, just days before the opening of the first Impressionist exhibition. Despite all that happened while he was there, it was in Pontoise and the nearby countryside that Pissarro created some of his most memorable Impressionist paintings.

First Years in Pontoise – 1866–1868

The Pissarro family lived in Pontoise at two different times. When they first moved to Pontoise in 1866, Pissarro and his companion Julie had two young toddlers: Lucien, three, and Minette, not quite one year old. They were struggling financially and needed a home where they could live comfortably but less expensively than in Paris.

Pontoise was linked by railroad with Dieppe, Rouen, and Paris, making travel to Paris easy for Pissarro. Commerce in Pontoise was dominated by numerous markets—the poultry market, grain market, and herb market, all of which drew large throngs of people from the surrounding agricultural area.

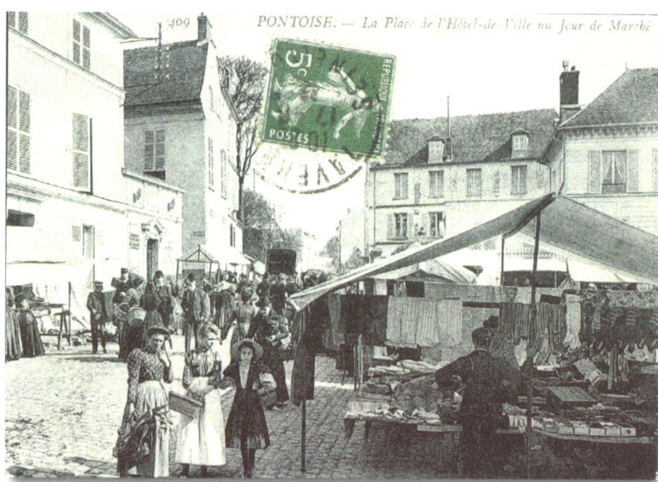

There are still markets at Pontoise several days a week.

The family settled, not in the city center, but on the outskirts in a suburb called l'Hermitage. The name of the neighborhood came from a group of hermits who had lived in the surrounding hills at the end of the fifteenth century. By the time Pissarro moved there, the steep hillsides of l'Hermitage were covered with vegetable gardens and vineyards. The vineyards are now gone, but vegetable gardens still cover the hillsides.

Pissarro was working hard to gain recognition as an artist and sell his paintings. His father, who was contributing to the family's

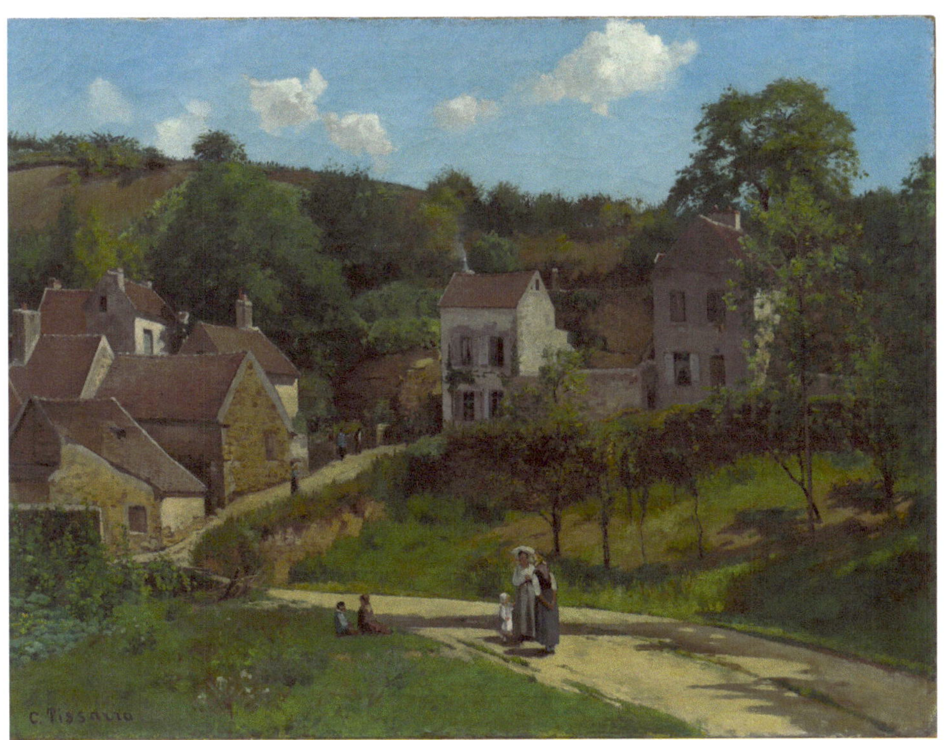

The Hills at l'Hermitage, Pointoise

c. 1867

Solomon R. Guggenheim Museum, New York, NY

PDR 121

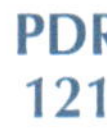

Always pushing the edge of creativity and inventiveness, Pissarro painted *The Hills at l'Hermitage, Pontoise* in 1867, seven years before the First Impressionist Exhibition. But it demonstrates all the elements of Impressionism—the light palette, a commonplace scene, and depiction of the weather.

It is the largest painting ever made by Pissarro; he may have painted it for submission to the annual Salon jury. The painting was bought from Pissarro by Paul Durand-Ruel, his agent, in March 1873 and sold the same day to Jean-Baptiste Faure, a famous operatic baritone who sang in Paris and London.

The people in Pissarro's paintings are integral to its composition, but they are not there to tell a story. In fact, they often raise questions that have no answers. In this painting, a woman and little girl are talking to another woman. Most scholars agree that they are in fact Julie, the painter's wife, and his daughter Minette. They are talking to a woman whose back is towards us, but we can see from her arms clasped behind her back that she has dark skin. This is especially noticeable because the skin of July and Minette are very light, almost pink.

Who is this dark-skinned woman and what is the conversation between these two women from obviously different backgrounds? Is she an African living in France or a Roma (gypsy) woman? As provocative as this question may be, the women are just two small elements in the painting. The disparity in skin-color is so subtle that it goes unnoticed by many viewers.

income, urged him to create paintings that would be accepted by the Salon. Generally speaking, the Salon jury favored paintings that were very large and depicted scenes of historical or mythological stories. Pissarro's landscapes, a category considered less important in the eyes of the Salon, depicted everyday life, not mythical or historical scenes. His palette was also lighter than that of many Salon paintings.

In 1867, Pissarro produced a large painting called *The Hills of l'Hermitage*. It was the largest painting he ever made. Records show that one of Pissarro's paintings, entitled "*l'Ermitage*," was shown in the 1869 Salon, and based on its large size, it may have been this one. We know that this painting was bought six years later by the art dealer Paul Durand-Ruel and sold the same day to Jean-Baptiste Faure, a popular opera singer who was an avid collector of Impressionist art.

Return to Pontoise – 1872–1882

After the difficult years in Louveciennes, with the disruptions of the Franco-Prussian War and exiles in Montfoucault and London (1869–1872), Pissarro returned to Pontoise. Camille and Julie were now legally married (See London chapter), and their family included a third child, Georges. This time, they lived in the center of Pontoise near Rue de Gisors, a busy city street. Pissarro made five paintings of the rue de Gisors, and three of them depict snowy scenes. This area of Pontoise has barely changed since Pissarro lived there [See PDR 284].

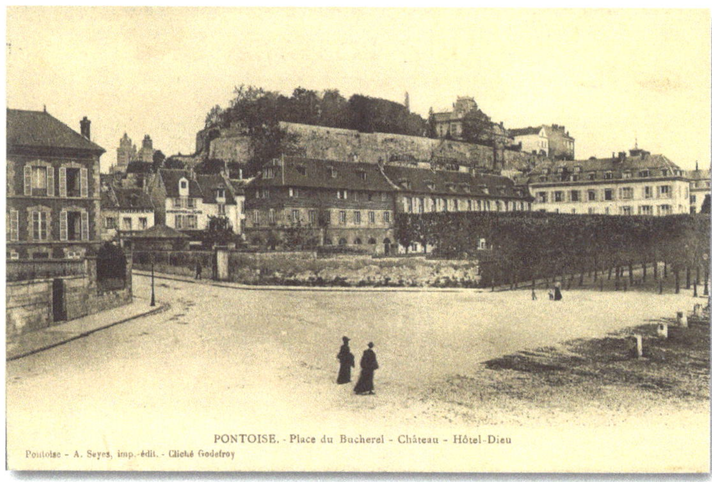

The chateau on top of the cliff is now the Musée Pissarro.

As he had done during his early years in Pontoise, Pissarro painted the banks of the Oise River. He included recent industrial additions, such as the railway bridge and the new factories at the river's edge. In 1872, a distillery and potash factory with a chimney more than 80 feet high was built across the river from Pontoise. Pissarro painted the factory several times, and its chimney is visible in many other paintings of the river [See PDR 300].

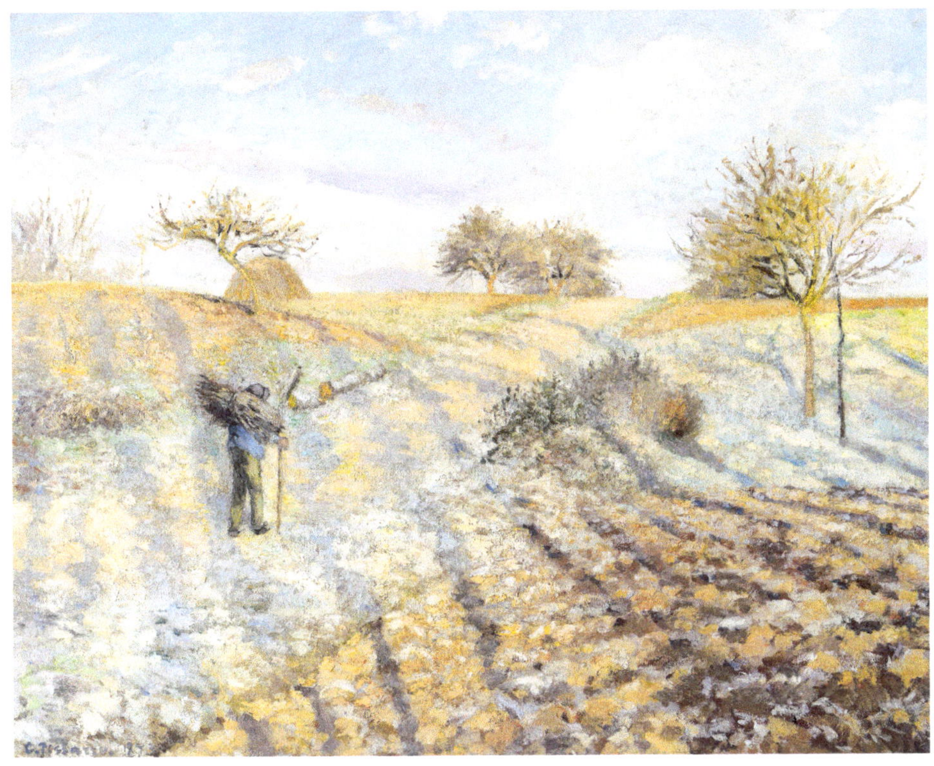

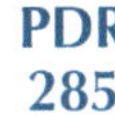

PDR 285

Hoar-Frost at Ennery

1873

Musée d'Orsay, Paris, France

PDR 285

One cold winter morning, Pissarro carried his easel directly north of Pontoise to the fields of nearby Ennery. The painting he made there, *Hoar-Frost at Ennery*, was shown in the first exhibition of the Impressonists at Nadar's studio in Paris in 1874.

Responses from some of the art critics of the time were extremely disparaging. One harsh critic pointed out what was considered one of the most serious mistakes of that era, showing shadows on the ground of trees that are not in the picture. Another proclaimed that the painting had "neither head nor tail, neither top nor bottom, neither front nor back."

Even to our eyes, the painting is dramatically different from other Impressionist paintings. The blue sky with its puffy clouds, the bare trees lining the horizon and the peasant walking through the field provide familiar reference points. But take those away, leaving only the patchwork of colors crisscrossed by parallel lines with a dark green anchor near the center, and the work could be that of a contemporary abstract artist.

As was his custom, Pissarro looked to his own neighborhood for motifs, generally those with generous hillside views and clusters of houses. In one of Pissarro's paintings, The Climb, we feel as if we could fall off the edge down a precipitous cliff [See PDR 405]. That path is now a street leading from l'Hermitage over a steep hill to the center of Pontoise, and the modern fence at the edge of the cliff gives us some measure of security not present in the painting. It is only by seeing the site in person that we can understand that Pissarro's vantage point is only halfway up the hill.

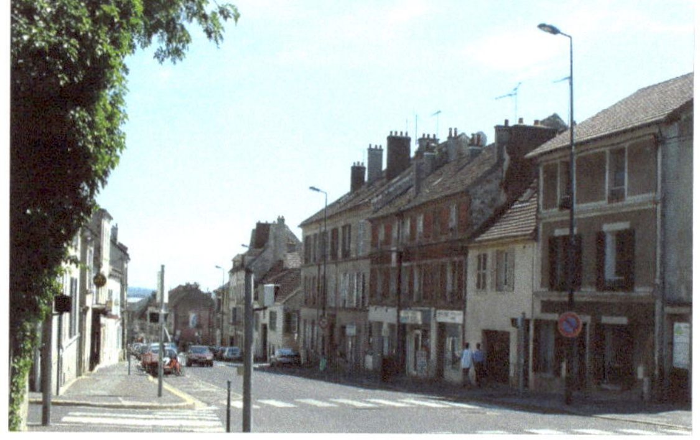

Current photograph of the site on Rue de Gisors painted by Pissarro in 1873

The Glory of Pontoise's Past

The Oise River is at the heart of the city's history and even its name. In the French language, Pontoise literally means bridge (pont) of the Oise, and the city's history spans more than 1,000 years.

Traces of Gallo-Roman settlements have been found where the old Roman road from Paris to Rouen (which still exists today as N-14) crossed the Oise River. By the ninth century AD, Pontoise was a prosperous town and active religious center with a weekly market. In 1090, the construction of what is now the Cathédrale Saint-Maclou was begun in the center of the town.

By the twelfth century, Pontoise was the capitol of the French Vexin (the ancient name given the large agricultural region to the north and east of the Epte River). Because of its strategic position on the tall cliffs by the Oise, it was the first line of defense against invasions from the Normans. Atop the natural lookout on the rocky cliffs was a fortified castle.

From the twelfth to the fourteenth centuries, Pontoise was an international commercial center, attracting foreign investments. A period of decline began with the Hundred Years' War in 1373, and continued through the French Revolution in the late eighteenth century when the considerable holdings of the Church were dismantled, and monasteries and convents were sold or

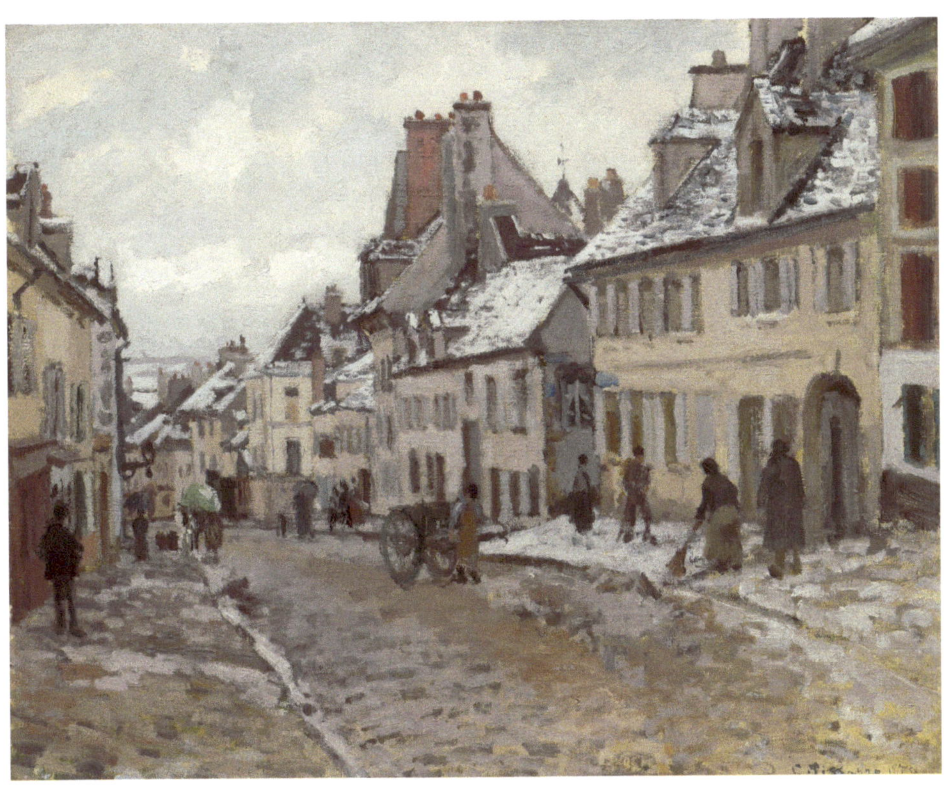

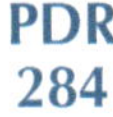

Rue de Gisors, Effect of Snow, Pontoise

1873

Museum of Fine Arts, Boston, MA

PDR 284

The overnight snowfall was still evident as Pissarro set up his easel on the side of the road. Just to the right of the two-wheeled cart, we can easily see the corner of the street where Pissarro lived.

This scene has hardly changed at all since Pissarro painted it. The pink building now has three stories, but the smaller buildings on that side are still the same and the tall angled roof is still there although it does not seem nearly as high as he portrayed it.

The people of the village are busy with their daily errands; a peddler pushes his cart as a woman sweeps snow off the sidewalk. Pissarro gives us an accurate sense of the gentle downward slope of the road with the decreasing levels of the rooftops. Even though the dominant colors of the painting are warm pinks and mauves, the cold crispness of the air suggested by the white snow on the roofs is intense. Pissarro's face and hands must have been numb as he mixed the colors on his palette.

destroyed. By the time Pissarro arrived, Pontoise was in the backwater of French history, no longer important.

Today, the spot on the high cliff where the castle once stood is occupied by a nineteenth century mansion. It is home to the Musée Pissarro, inaugurated in 1980 on the 150th anniversary of the artist's birth.

The Musée Pissarro

Pissarro and Cézanne Together in Pontoise

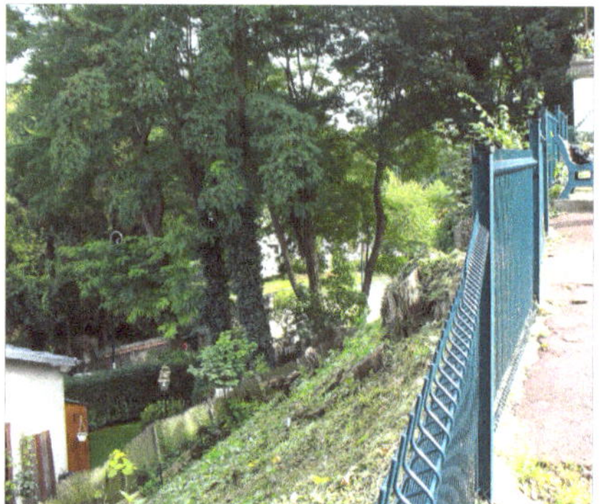
Current photograph of the site of Pissarro's 1875 painting, *The Climb, Rue de la Côte-du-Jalet*, Pontoise

Pissarro willingly shared his time with several artist friends who came to Pontoise to paint with him. One of his most frequent visitors was Paul Cézanne, whom he met in 1861 at the Académie Suisse. Soon Cézanne moved to the nearby town of Auvers-sur-Oise (the same town where Vincent van Gogh lived a few years later). Their friendship and artistic exchange continued for 20 years.

Joachim Pissarro, who curated a important exhibition about their artistic dialogue (*Cézanne & Pissarro: Pioneering Modern Painting*, 2005) described their working relationship: "While the two artists nudged each other in new directions, they mostly searched to define themselves.... Their individualities or differences become most evident in the paintings they executed side by side, recurrently working on the same motifs."

Gauguin and Pissarro

In 1874, Pissarro met Paul Gauguin, a young stockbroker interested in art and trying to learn to draw. Gauguin began to buy Pissarro's paintings and to arrange sales of his paintings to other businessmen. Gauguin began painting on the weekends, and in 1876, one of his paintings was accepted by the Salon. In 1879, Gauguin was permitted to exhibit a sculpture in the fourth Impressionist exhibition. That summer, he came with his family to Pontoise to paint with Pissarro. Although Pissarro taught and encouraged him, their friendship was never as close as the relationship between Pissarro and Cézanne.

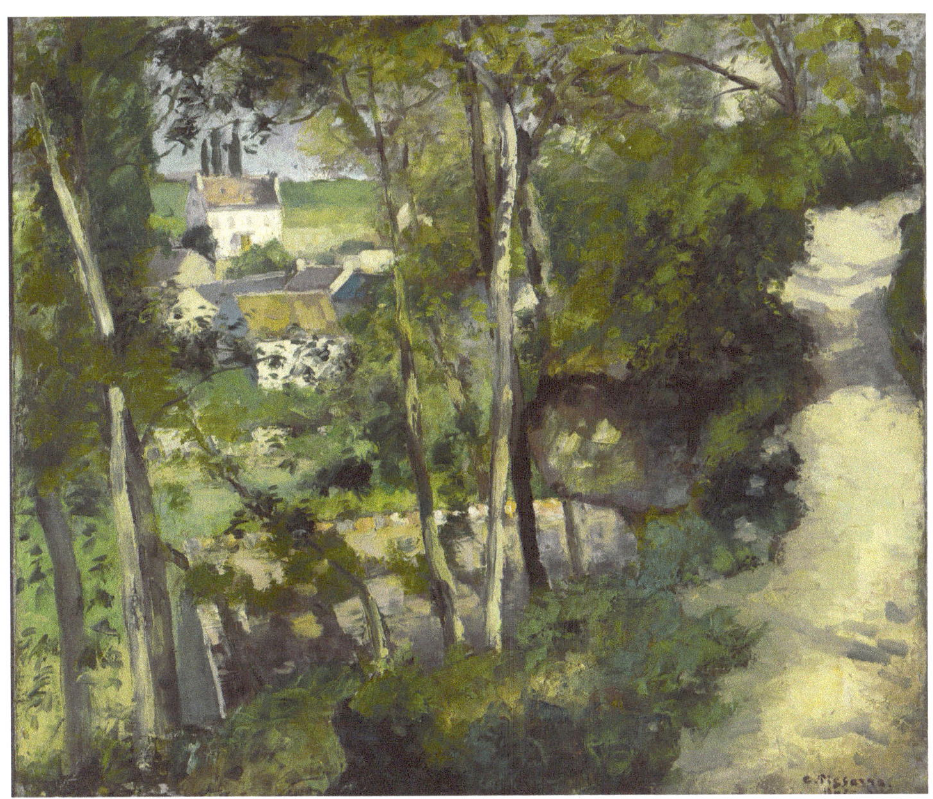

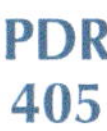

The Climb, Rue de la Côte-du-Jalet, Pontoise

1875

Brooklyn Museum of Art, Brooklyn, NY

PDR 405

Pissarro chose to paint a particularly complex view on the rue de la Côte-du-Jalet (now rue Victor Hugo) which looks back toward l'Hermitage. Although the houses on a nearby hill are visible, they can only be seen between the slender trunks of trees that line the edge of a very steep path. The artist was living at the time on rue l'Hermitage near the corner of this street. But to reach this site, he had to carry his easel and paints up a very steep incline. The site of this painting today is still remarkably similar to Pissarro's painting. In fact, he was only halfway up. The curve that leads off the right side of his canvas conceals the steep route to the top of the hill.

Pissarro ably depicts the steepness of the hill by leading the pathway straight up the right side of the canvas, with only the barest hint of a horizon line above it. We feel as if the roadway is falling away under our feet as we look down the sharp incline on the left. The painting is divided almost in half by two crisscrossed trees, one with a light trunk bathed in sunlight and one behind with a dark trunk. Everything on the right points up and everything on the left tumbles down. From this precarious perch, we look across a narrow valley to the adjoining hill and the houses with their multicolored roofs. And in case our eyes are tempted to rest in the distance, there are three tall trees that visually connect with the limbs of the trees on our pathway. Pissarro demonstrates his mastery of perspective by creating, on a flat canvas, a sense of instability that can only be experienced in three dimensions.

Realizing Impressionism

The discontent Pissarro and his artist friends felt with the state-sanctioned Salon had been growing ever since their participation in the Salon des Refusés in 1863. As early as 1867, the artists began discussing an alternative venue, a place where they could show their work without the arbitrary filter of an opinionated Academy jury. Finally, in the spring of 1873, Pissarro and Monet took action. With their friends and fellow artists, they organized an association to sponsor an independent exhibition. In a letter to Pissarro, Monet wrote, "Everyone definitely thinks it's a good idea, only Manet is opposed." And Manet remained true to his word; he never participated in any of the Impressionist exhibitions.

Pissarro wrote the charter for the new association, and in December 1873, the *Société anonyme coopérative des artistes, peintres, sculpteurs, graveurs, etc.*, was officially instituted. It allowed any member to show as many works as he liked without submission to a jury.

Their first exhibition opened on April 15, 1874, two weeks before the opening of the official Salon, at the Paris studio of the popular photographer, Félix Nadar. There were 167 works from 30 painters, including five recent paintings by Pissarro. More than 3,000 people visited the exhibition, and the event was covered by local journals. However, the reviews were generally unfavorable, and the exhibition was a financial failure.

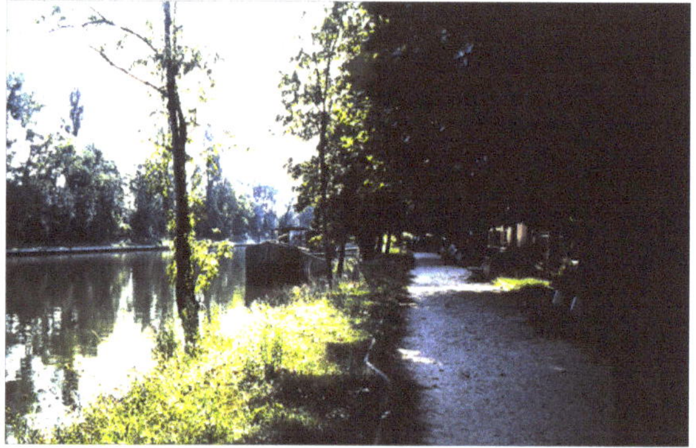
Barges still dock along the towpath of the River Oise.

It was two years before the artists could regroup to present the second Impressionist exhibition. This time, there were only 19 artists and 280 works were exhibited. Again, the reviews were vicious, with the exception of one or two. Émile Zola, a journalist and art critic who had written favorably about Pissarro's work in the past, said, "In his work, the notes take on a simplicity and clarity of the utmost ingenuousness ... there is very great talent in them [the paintings] and a very personal interpretation of nature."

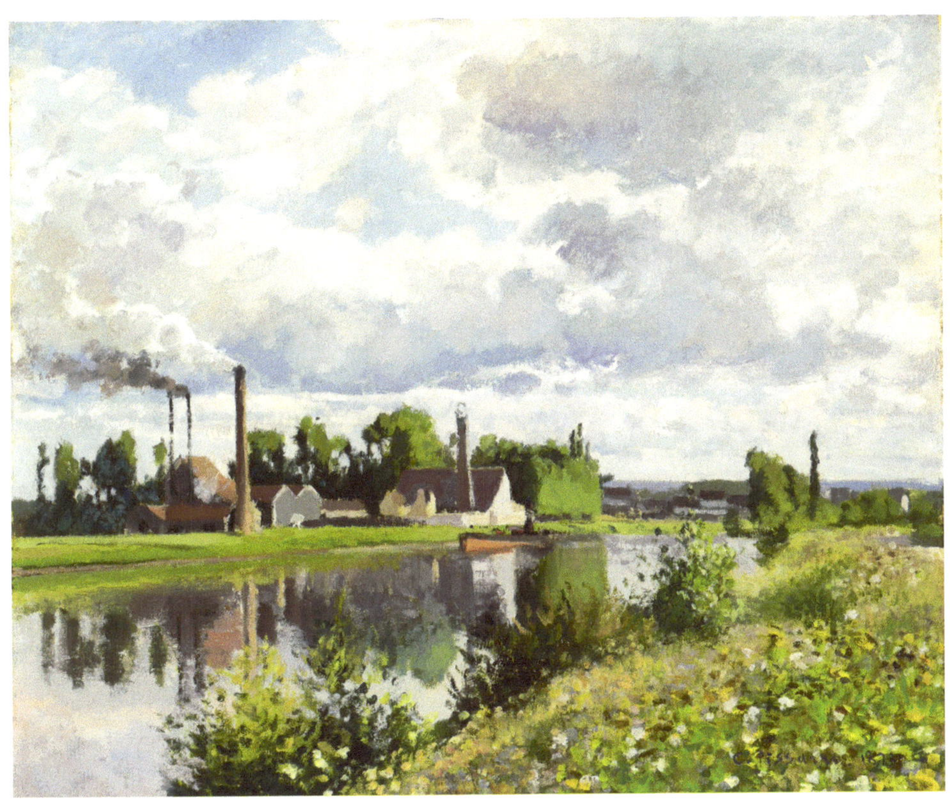

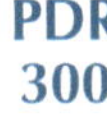

PDR
300

Factory on the Banks of the Oise, Saint-Ouen-l'Aumône

1873

Sterling and Francine Clark Art Institute, Williamstown, MA

PDR 300

One warm spring day, Pissarro took his easel to the banks of the Oise River and made a painting that is archetypical of the Impressionist movement. It contains nearly all of the characteristics commonly associated with the Impressionist style: the lavish portrayal of sunlight, the consciousness of the changing weather as gray clouds crowd the intense blue sky, the presence of modernity in the new factories lining the bank of the Oise River, and the immediacy of the scene that bespeaks *en plein air* painting.

The painting itself has a classic composition divided almost equally between the sky and the earth, with the river dwindling away on the right side. The water, still as a mirror, reflects the smokestacks and buildings on the other side and connects them with the freshness of the spring flowers in the right foreground. The factory, a distillery, had just been completed in 1872. The white building with the small smokestack is still there, along with a few of the small buildings.

During the time Pissarro lived in Pontoise, the Impressionists produced five more exhibitions: the Third in 1877, the Fourth in 1879, the Fifth in 1880, the Sixth in 1881, and the Seventh in 1882. (The Eighth and final Impressionist exhibition took place in 1886 after Pissarro moved to Éragny.) The list of participants was different each time. Pissarro was the only artist who participated in all eight Impressionist exhibitions.

Pissarro found an endless source of inspiration in Pontoise. While there, he completed some 300 oil paintings and innumerable pastels, gouaches, engravings, and drawings. His work in Pontoise included some of his most inventive and creative paintings. This group of paintings exemplify the beauty and mystery of Pissarro's œuvre—his insistence on pushing the limits of Impressionism, his restless innovative spirit constantly searching for a more profound way to express his sensations.

Montfoucault

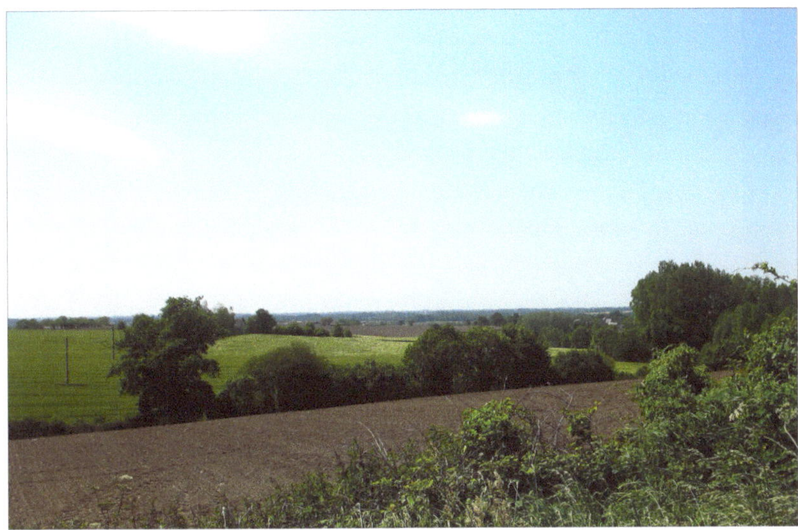

Expansive fields near Montfoucault

A Place That Time Forgot

In western France, where the Pays de la Loire meets Normandy and Brittany, we find Montfoucault, an intensely rural setting and certainly the most bucolic place Pissarro ever worked. This country estate has a magical quality as if it were the site of "once upon a time." Located on a dead-end road, it was, and remains today, isolated from the "worldliness" of nearby beach resorts and great cities. It is seemingly an unusual location for Pissarro, who enjoyed the refined cultural ambiance of Paris.

Montfoucault was the country home of Ludovic Piette de Montfoucault, a fellow artist whom Pissarro befriended in the late 1850s. Piette had inherited the large country estate from his family and made his home there after his marriage in 1862 to his wife, the former Adèle Lèvy. Pissarro visited this isolated rural setting five times and we know of 53 canvases he painted there. A strong bond developed between Piette and Pissarro that would nurture both artists until Piette's untimely death in 1878.

Pissarro's First Visit to Montfoucault–1864

It was at Piette's urging that Pissarro, Julie Vellay, and their 18-month-old son Lucien made the long journey to Montfoucault in the autumn of 1864. There he was presented with fresh motifs and new artistic challenges. Even more important, it provided a respite from the harsh financial realities of their everyday lives. It was a safe haven where the young family could live for several weeks without worries about money.

Only three paintings from Pissarro's first visit to Montfoucault are known. They portray the bleak winter landscape in colors reminiscent of the paintings of Charles-François Daubigny and Gustave, older artists that Pissarro admired.

One painting, a simple landscape with a woman walking along the road, has an inscription in Pissarro's hand on the back, stating that it had been pierced with a sword by Prussian soldiers during their occupation of the Pissarro home in 1871 and restored by his artist friend A. Gauthier. Since Pissarro was at Montfoucault for several weeks, we can imagine that he made more than three paintings. We will never know whether other paintings made during this 1864 visit were among those destroyed by the Prussian soldiers (See chapter on Louveciennes). As it is, our understanding of Pissarro's initial impressions of Montfoucault must rely only on these three paintings.

An Ancient Land That Has Barely Changed

The prehistoric monuments near Montfoucault remind us that this landscape was inhabited back through the far reaches of time. On a nearby farm is a menhir (a large stone standing

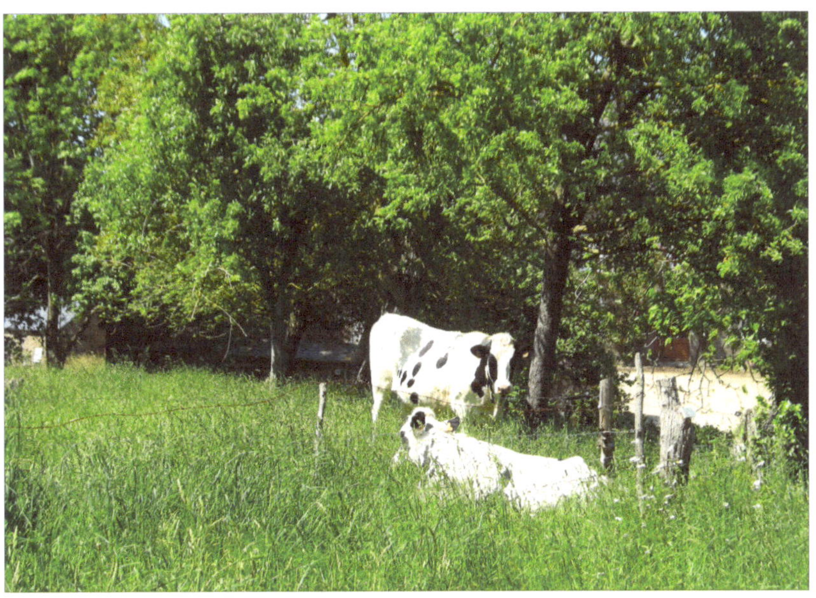

Fields and pastures near Montfoucault

upright) and in the other direction is a small dolmen (a flat stone placed on top of upright stones like a table top), similar to those at Carnac on the western shore of Brittany. If they were constructed around the same time, they would date to 4500 BCE.

Around 600 BCE, the Celts migrated into France and settled primarily in Brittany, mixing their culture with the pagan practices and superstitions. Montfoucault was not within the historical boundaries of Brittany, but it was near enough to be influenced by Breton customs and beliefs. In 56 BCE, Julius Caesar marched into this part of France with his soldiers, and the Romans ruled the region until their withdrawal in the fifth century AD.

After the Roman empire collapsed, Christian missionaries from England inundated the land to convert the people of Brittany. Catholicism rapidly gained a strong foothold in northern France, although some local superstitions rooted in ancient pagan rites remained. The priests added crosses to many of the pagan religious sites and adapted traditional holidays to their own celebrations.

Montfoucault is near Melleray-la-Vallée, a tiny village that also has deep religious roots. The town was established in 1134 by Catholic monks who built a small monastery and completed a church in 1183. Their monastic practices continued until 1791 when they were expelled from France. The monks returned in 1817 but were expelled again during the Revolution of 1830.

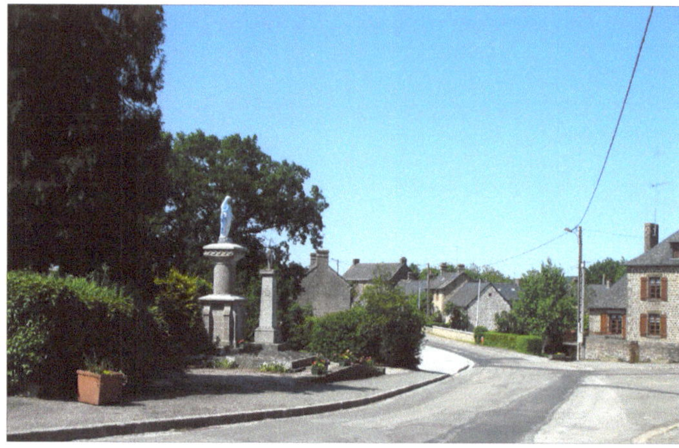
Melleray-la-Vallée

Although it was three decades later when Pissarro visited Montfoucault, the religious beliefs of the community were still strong, as evidenced by fervent conservatism. In a letter to Pissarro, Piette warned his friends that they would need to abide by certain "ground rules" during their visit. "You know, my dear Pissarro, that we have to live with wolves, living in a land of prejudice. I am forced to accept it in order to avoid gossips. Consequently, as the rule goes, I must pretend that you are married, and you have to let them believe it: this will cut short all the ramblings. I should think that you will agree with me, this is stupid but necessary."

The farmland surrounding Montfoucault is lush with apple and pear orchards. In summer, the sun shines heavily on the tree-edged fields as enormous cows graze in the pastures. Nearby is an old cider mill dating from the seventeenth century, now a museum, Musée du Cidre, Melleray-la-Vallée. It still has its original heavy millstones, an apple press, and distillation equipment for making Calvados, the apple brandy unique to northern France.

Not far away from the cider mill is a small country road ending in a cul-de-sac, surrounded by vast fields and wooded areas. From the end of the road, a narrow lane leads to a small pond on the right surrounded by bending trees, their branches almost dipping into the water. This is the pond that Pissarro painted so many times. In summer, he painted it with the trees and blue sky reflecting in the water. He also painted it in full autumn color and covered in winter's ice.

Farther down the road, we see Piette's large two-story stone farmhouse surrounded by a stone wall. Piette's house looks very much the same now as it did then, except for dormer windows that are no longer there. Several stone buildings are still clustered along the road, and vegetable gardens surround the old stone well just as they did in Pissarro's day.

Montfoucault–A Refuge from War

Pissarro and Julie returned to Montfoucault six years later under vastly different circumstances. In July 1870, the Franco-Prussian war began, and by the end of summer, the Prussians were already marching toward Paris. By September, Pissarro and Julie, who now lived in Louveciennes just west of Paris, were in grave danger. Prussian forces had occupied nearby Mont Valérien and aimed their guns at the small village.

Pissarro and Julie (who was seven months pregnant at the time), their seven-year-old son Lucien, and their five-year-old daughter Minette fled to Piette's home in Brittany. They found safety in the isolation of Montfoucault. With all of his farm workers away at war, Piette immediately drafted Pissarro to help him bring in the fall harvest of pears, apples, grapes, and chestnuts.

It is little wonder that there are no known paintings from that trip. The short stressful visit included several life-altering events. A few weeks after their arrival at Montfoucault, Julie gave birth to their third child, a little girl whom they named Adèle-Emma. The infant acquired an intestinal infection and died just three weeks later, on November 5. Piette and his wife offered a burial place for the baby in their family vault in Melleray.

During that time, Pissarro wrote a letter to his mother asking her permission to marry Julie. Certainly, this question had been addressed before, and it is unclear why it should arise at this particular time. Perhaps the occupation of Paris and his home at Louveciennes reminded Pissarro that if he were to die, Julie would inherit his estate only if she were officially his wife. At first, his mother wrote back giving permission, but she quickly rescinded that decision and asked him not to do it.

It seems strange that a forty-year-old man would need his mother's permission to get married. In fact, Article 173 of the French Civil Code introduced in 1803 gave parents the right to oppose a wedding and prevent its taking place. The law could be invoked for the simple reason that the parents considered their child's choice of spouse inappropriate. Surprisingly, this law is still on the books today, though it is seldom invoked.

With Prussian troops advancing nearer to Montfoucault in early December, Pissarro and his family fled again to London, where the couple married without his mother's permission (See chapter on London).

Winter of 1874–1875 at Montfoucault

Pissarro's next trip to Montfoucault was four years later, when he and his family were beset by misfortune. In April of 1874, their daughter Minette had died at the age of eight, just days before the First Impressionist Exhibition. The exhibition had been a financial disaster and had resulted in harsh criticism from journalists and collectors alike. Durand-Ruel, the agent for Pissarro and other Impressionists, withdrew much of his support to the artists, buying only four of Pissarro's canvases that year. The birth of their third son Félix that July was no doubt a happy event, but it also added to Pissarro's financial burden.

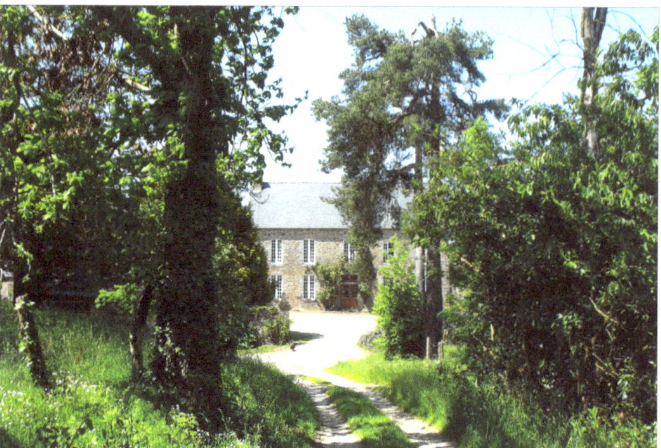

Piette's house is just as beautiful today as it was when Pissarro visited there.

In mid-October 1874, Pissarro and his family went to live at Montfoucault until February of the following year. This lengthy stay at Montfoucault gave them a breather from financial worries. By then, Lucien was 11 years old and Georges-Henri (born in November 1871) was almost four years old. Having two young boys in the house must have been enjoyable for Ludovic and Adèle, who had no children of their own.

During this long visit, Pissarro had time to create a substantial body of work. These paintings reflect an intimacy with the place that was not present in the paintings he made in 1864. As he did in Pontoise, Pissarro depicted local scenes that included farm workers busy at their daily tasks—fetching water from the well, gathering hay, tending animals, and spinning wool.

The winter must have been harsh because a number of Pissarro's paintings show Montfoucault blanketed with snow and the pond

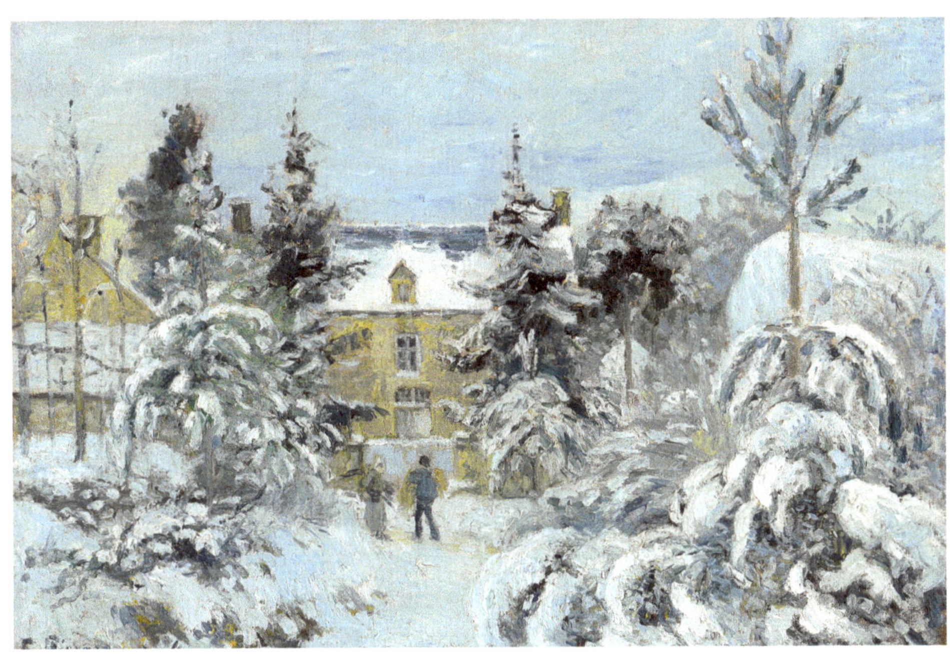

Piette's House at Montfoucault, Effect of Snow

1874

Sterling and Francine Clark Art Institute, Williamstown, MA

PDR 389

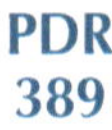

PDR 389

In this horizontal painting, layers of snow weigh heavily on the dark green branches of the massive evergreen trees. The entire scene appears to be white snow, but a closer look reveals that the white is a multitude of pale blue and peach tints. Behind the gate, the yellowish stone of the large house is the only large block of warm color in the painting, suggesting the warmth inside.

Overhead, the clouds are heavy in the darkening sky. White brushstrokes in the sky reveal darker blue-gray underneath, and unite the winter sky with the snow on the ground. The overall effect is of the threat of more snow and numbing cold.

Two figures carrying burdens approach the closed gate. The wide-legged stance of the man suggests that his load is heavy, and we can imagine that he is anxious to finish the tasks and retreat to the warmth indoors. If Pissarro set up his easel in the snow, his nose and fingers must have been freezing.

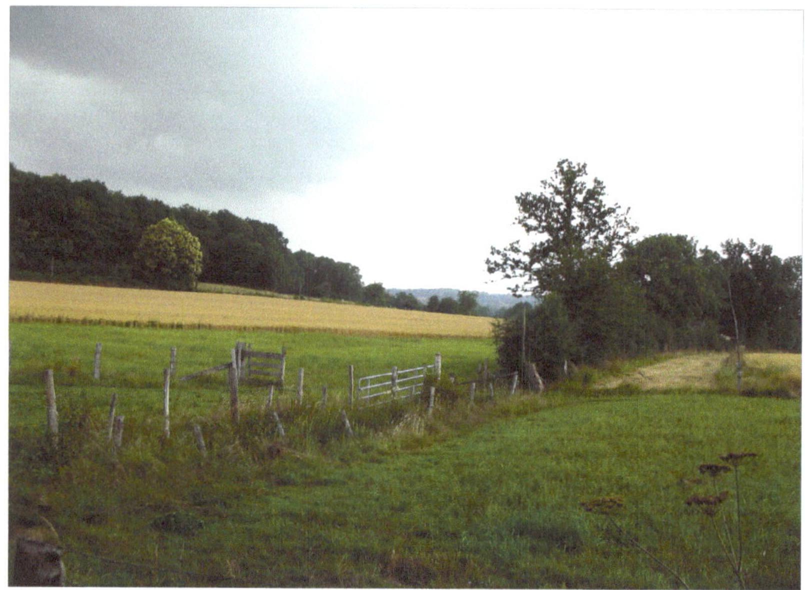

Fields near Montfoucault

covered with ice. One of the most beautiful paintings of this group is Piette's House at Montfoucault, Effect of Snow. We wonder if he set up his easel in the snow and painted *en plein air* despite the weather, or if he sketched the scene outside and finished the painting inside. It would have been difficult to produce all those pale shades of color in the snow unless he was in the bright outdoors, given that the light inside the big stone house was probably dim, especially on short winter days. After all, he had made paintings in the snow in previous years in Louveciennes [See PDR 389].

Autumn of 1875 at Montfoucault

The Pissarro family's next visit to Montfoucault took place later that year, in the autumn and winter of 1875. Again the Pissarro family was desperate for money. During the few weeks they were at Montfoucault, Pissarro made eleven paintings. This time, Pissarro seemed intent on painting figures of people and animals. His friend Théodore Duret had written him, "I urge you to push further and further along the path you've been exploring lately, the association of man and animals in an open-air landscape. That is the modern path, and it is there that you will find the best use for your distinctive qualities."

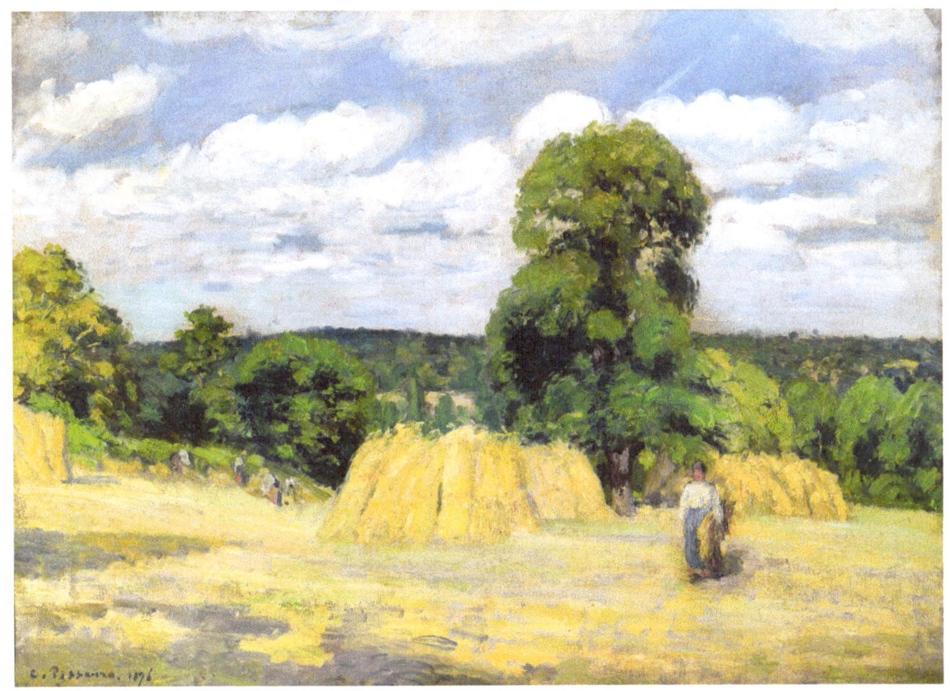

Harvest at Montfoucault
1876
Musée d'Orsay, Paris, France
PDR 465

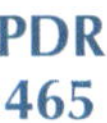
PDR 465

Pissarro captured the rural essence and isolation of Montfoucault in this painting completed during his last visit, in 1876. This expansive depiction of the haystacks at Montfoucault is somewhat reminiscent of previous landscapes at Pontoise in that it includes a broad view of the fields among the surrounding hills. The striking difference is that the Pontoise paintings included the houses of l'Hermitage. This painting is totally agricultural, showing only fields against a heavily wooded area, which emphasizes its total isolation.

Our eyes are immediately drawn to the large haystacks in the center front, anchored at the right by a large tree, whose tall branches lead the eye upward into the billowy clouds and bright azure sky. Another haystack to the right forms what is practically an isosceles triangle, making the composition symmetrical and providing a sense of stability.

The strength of the sunlight, evident in the golden grain scattered across the field, is intensified by the long lavender shadows in the lower left, which suggest the coming sunset. The palette takes a slice from the color wheel, advancing from yellow-gold in the foreground to the lush green of the tree and the forest in the background, to the deep azure blue of the sky. The progression is interrupted only by the painterly clouds whose puffiness sets up a rhythm in the sky contrasting the solidity of the triangle below.

The woman in the foreground bears little resemblance to the virtuous gleaners depicted by Millet. She looks out at the viewer with no expression to suggest her mood or any religious or moral allusion. She does, however, provide a human scale for measuring the height of the haystacks, and the blue in her skirt reflects the color of the sky. At the far left, a straggling group of workers appears to be leaving the field, leaving the lonely woman as a metaphor for the isolation and loneliness of the place.

Several of the works Pissarro completed during that visit were painted near the small pond at Montfoucault. He saw the colorful fall foliage and warm sunshine reflecting on the pond, and he stayed long enough to see the very same scene in winter's icy grip, the pond frozen and snow covering the ground.

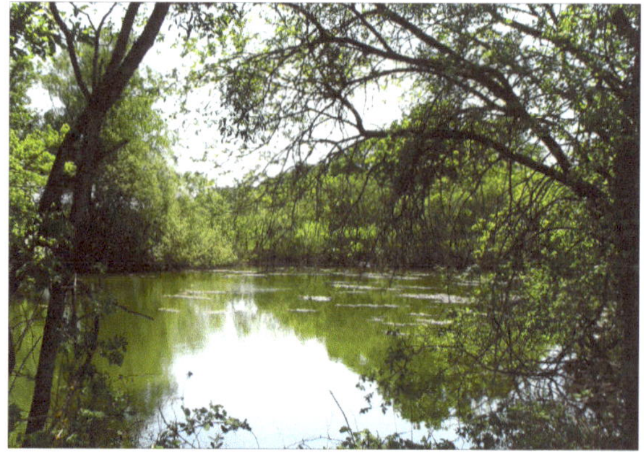

Pissarro made several paintings of this pond near Montfoucault.

Last Visit–Autumn 1876

With money in short supply, Pissarro along with Julie, Lucien, George, and Felix went to Montfoucault for a few weeks in the autumn of 1876. Of the paintings Pissarro made during this visit, five depict the hay harvest, showing the fields and a threshing machine. Perhaps he wanted to record the use of modern agricultural implements in France. Or maybe he was simply intrigued by the geometric angles of the bright green machine set against the golden yellow of the hay. It was that year that Pissarro made one of his loveliest Montfoucault paintings, *Harvest at Montfoucault*, which captures the distinctly rural nature of the area [See PDR 465].

Pissarro and Piette were kindred spirits. Piette was a competent artist, but he always knew that he could not keep pace with his friend. In a letter to Pissarro, Piette said, "Haven't we travelled the same hard road together, side-by-side? And together we left it to tread another, pleasanter one, only you will go much further than me ... [you] will sink a deeper furrow, thus making it more fertile. I am joyfully certain of this."

The death of Piette from cancer on April 14, 1878 must have been a terrible loss to Pissarro. Thanks to his deep friendship with Piette, Pissarro was able to experience several periods of time that were free of financial constraints in a place that offered new and interesting pictorial challenges. Although Montfoucault was in fact very different from any other place Pissarro encountered, he faithfully portrayed its unique location and character.

London

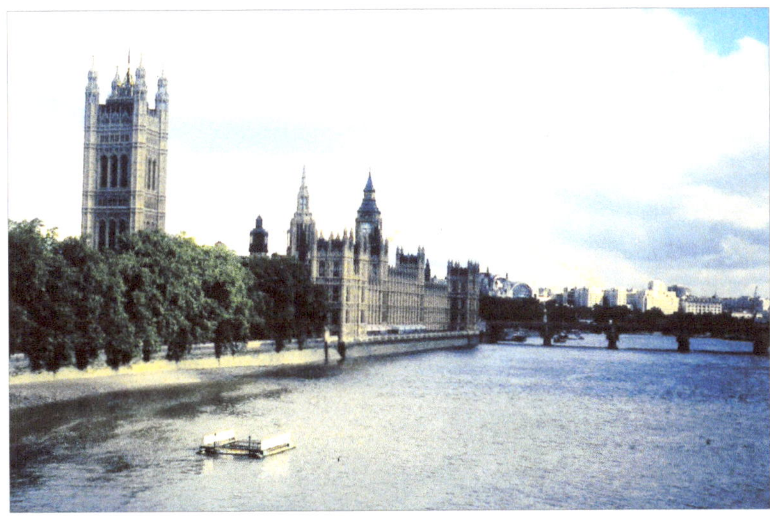

The Houses of Parliament on the River Thames

A Love Affair with London

Pissarro would have liked to make his home in London. He said so in 1894 in one of his letters to Lucien, his oldest son, who lived there. *"If we hadn't made the mistake of buying the Éragny Castle, how easy it would have been for all of us to stay in England! ... I felt it at the time! But this is between the two of us!"*

During his four visits to London, Pissarro painted many urban and suburban places. In other cities, he tended to stay away from sites that were well-known. In London, however, he made exceptions, creating many enchanting views of places familiar to local people: the Crystal Palace, Kew Gardens, Charing Cross Bridge, and the Serpentine in Hyde Park.

Refuge in London–1870

Pissarro's visit in 1870 was not a matter of choice, but of necessity. London provided a safe haven for Pissarro and his small family as they escaped the advance of the Prussian army into the heart of Normandy (See chapter on Montfoucault).

His mother Rachel had already fled Paris and was staying with family in London, along with Pissarro's brother Alfred and his wife and son. Pissarro, Julie, and their two young children, Lucien, 7, and Minette, 5, sailed to England in early December 1870. They rented lodgings in Lower Norwood, a suburb south of London. They soon moved to Canham's Dairy, Westow Hill in Upper Norwood and finally settled at 2 Chatham Terrace, Palace Road in Upper Norwood. This modern suburb south of London, a working-class neighborhood with parks and open spaces, had grown rapidly after railroad service began in 1839.

Pissarro was comfortable in London, but the exile was very difficult for Julie, who did not speak English and was not able to learn it. Julie was a strong and self-reliant woman, and we can imagine that she hated having to depend on her husband for translations.

Moreover, Julie disliked being so far away from her own family in France. To make matters worse, Pissarro's family ignored her existence because they disapproved of her. (The two young people had met when Rachel hired Julie as a maid in their Paris home. See chapter on Paris.) The Pissarro family also objected to the fact that Julie was not Jewish. Although Rachel was pleased to see her grandchildren, she had little to do with Julie.

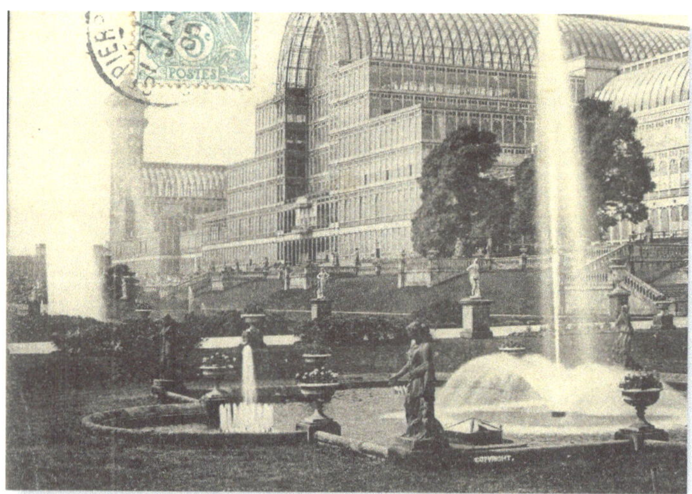

While the Franco-Prussian War raged in France, Pissarro and his family lived in Lodon near the massive Crystal Palace.

On the positive side, the art scene in London was extraordinarily active during this period, with many French artists seeking refuge from the war. In January 1871, Pissarro got together with Charles-François Daubigny, an older French artist who was instrumental in getting Pissarro's paintings accepted by the Salon.

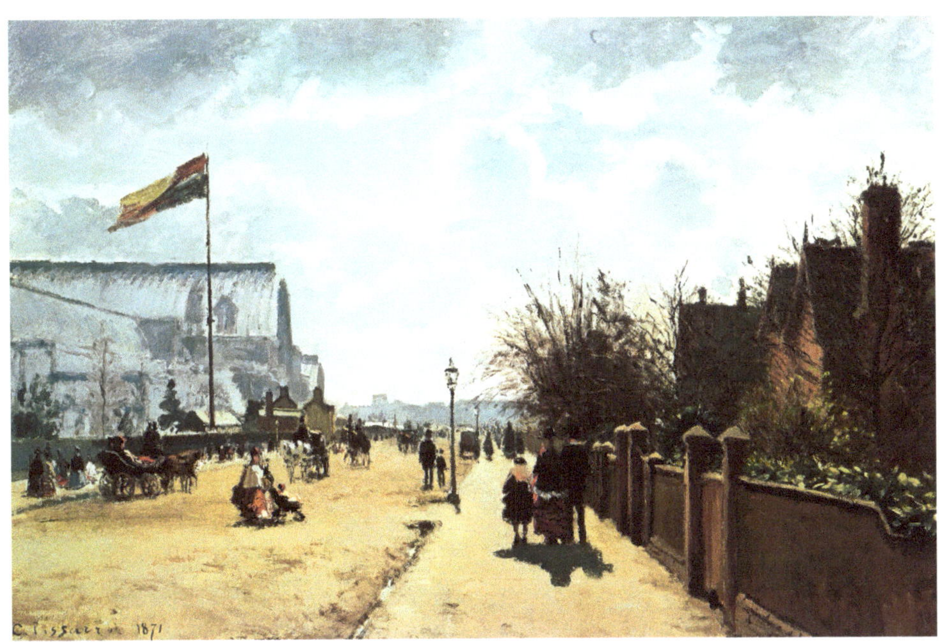

Crystal Palace Viewed From Fox Hill, Upper Norwood

1871

Art Institute of Chicago, Chicago, IL

PDR 183

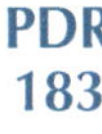

The Crystal Palace painting is a poetic balance of colors, contrasting dull brick homes with the shiny glass structure across the street. As he sometimes does, Pissarro divides this painting in the middle, using an inconspicuous street light in the lower center of the canvas to separate the two sides. On the left, preeminence is given to the massive Crystal Palace, a shining specter stretching from canvas edge to the vanishing point. Pissarro depicts the sky's reflection in the shiny glass, a controlled repetition of patterns in various shades of icy blue-gray. The dazzling structure suggests a place of make-believe and fantastic illusion.

In contrast, the substantial brick homes on the other side, the epitome of solidity with their peaked roofs, large chimneys, and tall garden walls, depict the everyday world. Overhead, puffy clouds fill the pale blue winter sky, but fail to block the sunlight that carves strong shadows on the ground. A woman pushing a baby carriage across the road unites the two sides. On the sidewalks, lines of people head toward the main entrance, suggesting the popularity of that day's main attraction.

This relatively small canvas is one of the best known and most loved paintings by Pissarro and demonstrates that he had already perfected the techniques of Impressionism even before the movement's birth.

Daubigny introduced Pissarro to the art dealer Paul Durand-Ruel, who bought two of Pissarro's paintings and gave him the London address of his friend Claude Monet, also exiled in London by the war.

Monet and Pissarro visited museums in London and studied the works of the English artists Turner and Constable. We can imagine that Pissarro rode the train into the city to meet Monet, who was living in Kensington. From there, they could have taken the Tube, which already had stations operable on the Circle Line to the National Gallery. (The Metro in Paris was not opened until 1900.)

Both artists began painting London sites. Monet worked in the parks in Kensington near where he lived, while Pissarro explored the neighborhood of Upper Norwood. Pissarro continued to experiment with the light palette and loose brushstrokes that would characterize the Impressionist movement.

In a departure from his usual practice of focusing on commonplace scenes, Pissarro painted the Crystal Palace, a popular tourist attraction in south London. Originally located in Hyde Park, the Crystal Palace was the centerpiece of the Great Exposition of 1851 and showcased English leadership in the Industrial Revolution. After the exposition ended, it was moved to a park near Sydenham where it housed cultural exhibitions and entertainment. It was a popular attraction, featuring such amazing acts as tightrope walkers, until it burned down in 1936.

In Pissarro's painting, the flagpole bears the Royal Standard, used to announce the presence of Queen Victoria. This is an interesting nod to English monarchy from a young French artist who usually ignored governmental references. Or maybe Queen Victoria was actually there that day, and he simply painted what he saw [See PDR 183].

Although he accomplished spectacular work in London, Pissarro was disappointed by the lack of acceptance of his paintings. Both Monet and Pissarro submitted paintings to the Royal Academy and were refused. However, their work was shown at the International Exhibition of Fine Art in South Kensington and was also included in exhibitions at Durand-Ruel's London gallery on Bond Street. Pissarro wrote his friend Théodore Duret, a French journalist and art critic, that the English did not appreciate his painting: *"What a difference here, where one meets with nothing but scorn, indifference and even rudeness; among colleagues there is the most self-centered jealousy and mistrust. Here, there is no art, everything is a question of business."*

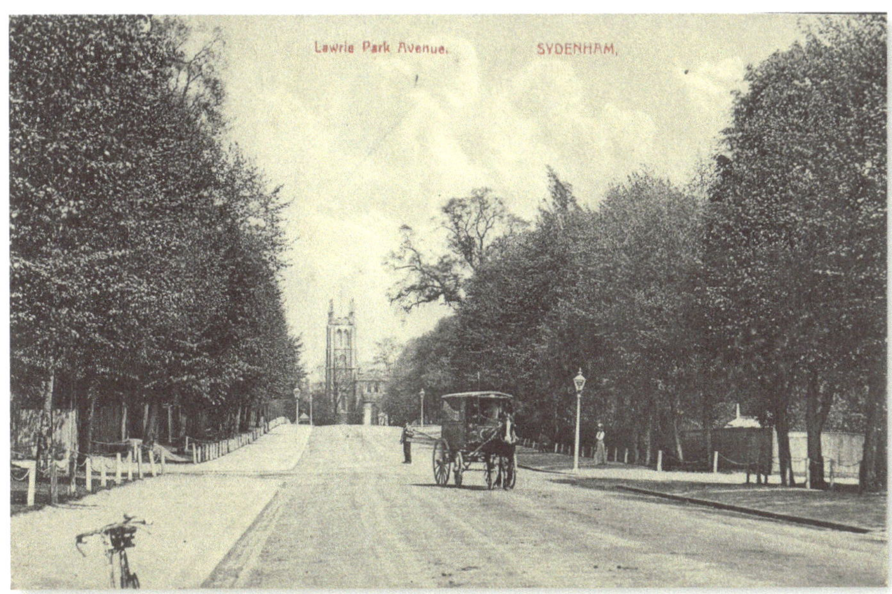

Pissarro painted this view in 1871 of Sydenham, a town in south London. The site looks almost exactly the same today.

On June 14, 1871, shortly before their return to Paris, Camille and Julie Pissarro were married without the permission of his mother at the Register office in the village of Croydon. No one from either of their families was present. As a wedding gift, Pissarro gave Julie a particularly lovely painting, *View of Alleyn Park, West Dulwich* [See PDR 190]. Nine days later, the family headed back to France to pick through what remained of their belongings after the occupation of the Prussian army.

London –The Emergence of a Modern City

Pissarro seemed to enjoy the energy of London, which had experienced phenomenal population growth fueled by the Industrial Revolution. At that time, London was the biggest city in the world, and by the middle of the nineteenth century it was the biggest city that had ever existed.

The London that Pissarro knew is similar in many ways to the London we know today. Founded around 43 AD by Roman troops, it had grown by the third century into a city of 30,000. The Romans built the first bridge across the Thames, and it lasted until 1209 when it was replaced by the legendary London Bridge, which was in use until 1832.

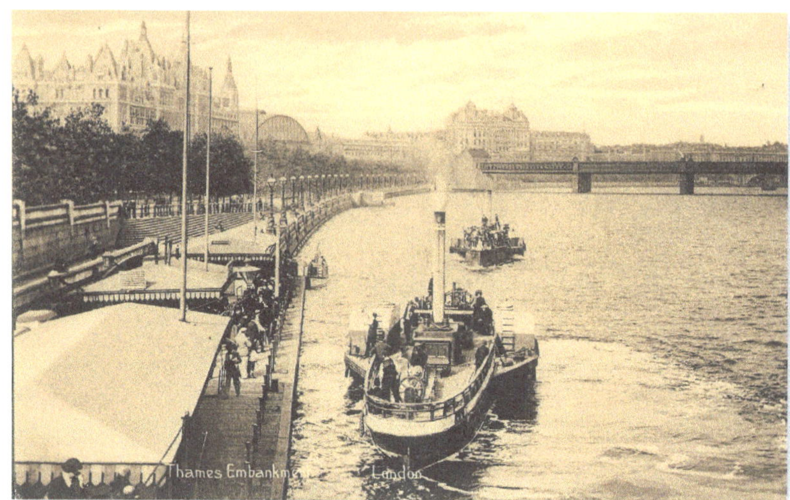

This historic postcard shows a close view of the odd-shaped paddle-wheeled ferries that Pissarro included in his painting of Charing Cross Bridge.

As the Industrial Revolution continued into the mid-nineteenth century, London became increasingly crowded with warehouses, offices, and stalled traffic. Along with urbanization came the poverty and squalor described by Dickens in his novels. Streets were filled with horse-drawn omnibuses, carriages, and even cattle being driven to slaughter. The massive use of coal fires for heating, cooking, and manufacturing filled the air with soot. Combined with fog, it created a dense black smog that covered the city for days on end.

The first intercity steam train to carry passengers began operating in 1830, and people flocked to nearby suburbs for a cleaner, healthier lifestyle. The Tube was inaugurated in 1863, and by 1870 stations were operable on the Circle Line route.

London – Twenty Years Later in 1890

Two decades passed before Pissarro returned to London. In 1890, he and his oldest son Lucien went to London to visit his second son, Georges, who was living there with his cousins. Pissarro had told one of his dealers, Théo Van Gogh, that he expected to "*come back with some new things*." He was depending on his London visit to "*rekindle*" his sensations.

In between visiting museums, Pissarro began six paintings, which he ultimately finished at home in his studio. Paintings made during this trip reveled in large spaces. Two were panoramic views of bridges across the River Thames, and one depicted the Serpentine,

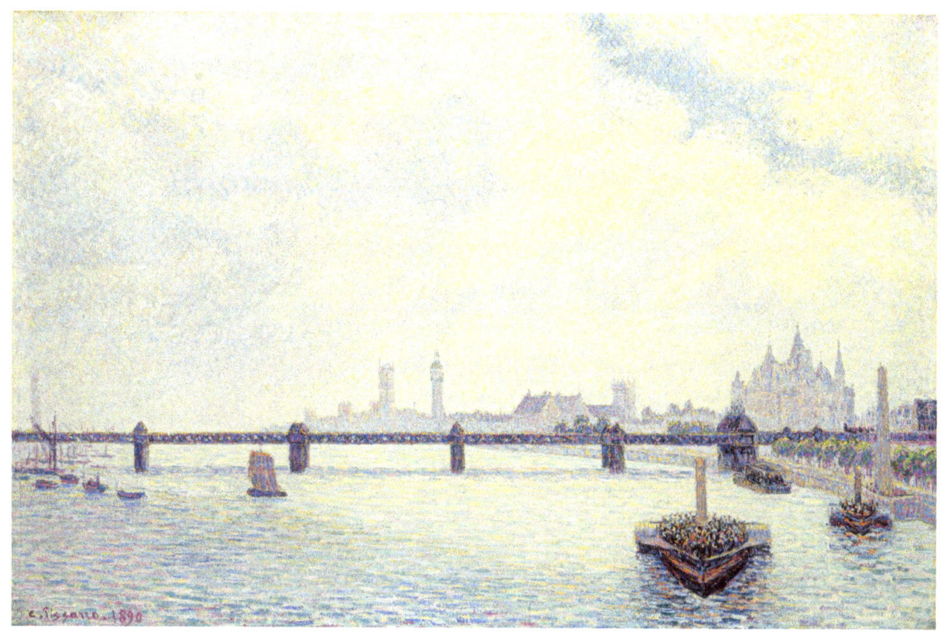

Charing Cross Bridge, London

1890
National Gallery of Art, Washington, DC
PDR 884

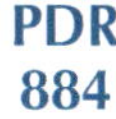

Pissarro emphasizes the expansiveness of Charing Cross Bridge by choosing a canvas half again as wide as it is high. The bridge is just a narrow band through the center of the painting. Even though the Houses of Parliament, Westminster Abbey, and other important buildings are in the background, they are subdued into pastel silhouettes. Even Cleopatra's Needle, the ancient Egyptian obelisk on the right, is subdued into anonymity.

The big boats are all placed on the right side, with one large passenger boat heading straight into view. On the left is one small sailboat with a string of tiny crafts disappearing into the canvas edge. The center of the canvas contains nothing more than a span of water reflecting the sky. In the background is the Clock Tower, known as Big Ben, which was completed in 1859. Pissarro was concerned that well-known landmarks be correct, and as he was finishing this painting in his studio in Éragny, he wrote to his niece Esther Isaacson in London to confirm the exact placement of various details.

The sky dominates more than half the painting. What appear to be white puffy clouds are made up of pale pinks, blues, and mauves in tiny comma-like strokes. The colors are the same ones seen on distant buildings. Only one sliver of blue sky is visible cutting across the right upper corner of the canvas. The river reflects the same colors, the pinks, blues, and mauves, laid down in wavelets.

The ferryboat plowing through the water in the lower right foreground was powered by a steam-driven paddle wheel, a model not yet used in France. The deck was loaded with passengers, who according to Pissarro created a *"mass of dots that give these boats their characteristic appearance."* The following year in his studio, Pissarro painted another version of this scene on a less-expansive canvas, moving all the boats closer to the center.

a lake in Hyde Park. The other three reflected his enchantment with English parks and delight in the vast open areas enjoyed by the public.

His bridge paintings, Battersea Bridge and Charing Cross Bridge, emphasized the expansiveness of the view, extending the panorama outside the canvas on both sides. Both paintings are essentially two horizontal stripes, one of the sky above and the other of the reflective water below, separated by the bridge, a narrow band in the center. The buildings that appear over the surface of the bridge are clearly secondary to the composition [See PDR 884].

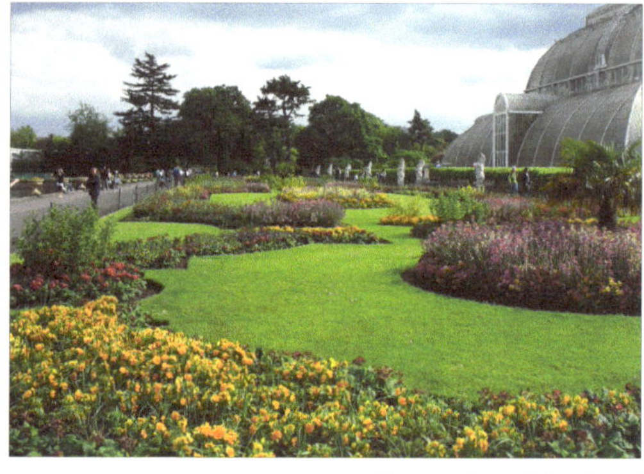

Current photo of the view of Kew Gardens painted by Pissarro. He did not include the large glass Palm House in his painting, but the steps are visible at the edge of the canvas.

Intervention on Behalf of Lucien–1892

Encouraged by his highly successful exhibition at Durand-Ruel's Paris gallery in January of 1892, Pissarro was soon itching for new motifs that would give him a fresh perspective. *"I've been seized these last few days with an appetite for working directly from nature. It takes hold of you like that from time to time, like a need for renewal, something you want and which seems absolutely necessary,"* he wrote to his friend Octave Mirbeau, a journalist and art critic. While he was contemplating a visit to Rouen or Beauvais, family considerations gave him a reason to travel again to London.

By this time, Lucien had been living in London for nine years. It was only natural that he turned to his father when faced with seemingly impossible obstacles to getting married. Lucien had fallen in love with Esther Bensusan, the daughter of an Orthodox Jewish family. They would approve the marriage only if Lucien converted to Judaism. Even though his father was Jewish, Lucien was not considered Jewish because he was born of a Gentile mother.

Pissarro could well understand his son's anguish. No doubt he remembered his own childhood when his parents had defied Jewish law and the whole family suffered harsh consequences (See chapter on St. Thomas). Anxious to assist his son, Pissarro went to London to intervene with Esther's father. Although this attempt failed, Pissarro stayed in London until August 1892, when Esther and Lucien were eventually married without her parents' permission.

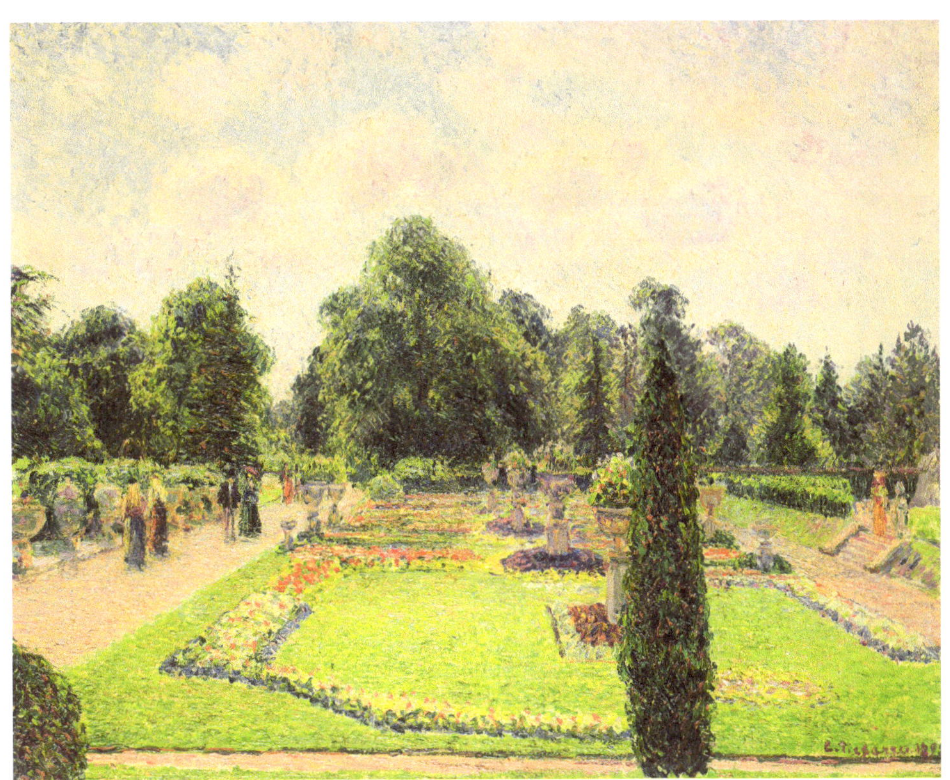

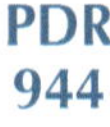

Kew Gardens, London, the Path to the Large Glass House

1892

Yamagata Museum of Art (on long-term loan), Yamagata, Japan

PDR 944

The Royal Botanic Gardens at Kew, which was nearly 150 years old in 1892, became Pissarro's inspiration for this visit to London. He wrote Julie that the motif he was working on was "*a promenade with square patches of lawn, small flower beds, pointy pine trees, and tall trees in the background, it looks like the garden at Versailles.*" On the right are steps leading up to the Palm House, but there is little hint of the massive Victorian glass and iron structure itself.

Pissarro must have been painting at midday because the shadows from the numerous strollers are minimal. The intensity of the sun is evident in the green grass flecked with yellow. Even the "*pointy pine tree*" has speckles of red, which heighten its deep green.

It is interesting to speculate why Pissarro chose this particular viewpoint instead of a view of the front of the Palm House. It is all about perspective. By setting his easel to the left of the pine tree, he can capture the giant flower-filled urns that parade down the garden's center and correspond to the walkways. The shape of his almost square canvas easily accommodates all the verticals and still provides enough room for blue sky and white billowy clouds. Today, the garden is much the same as when Pissarro painted it.

After spending a month with his sons, Pissarro found separate lodgings at Kew, a village on the southwestern edge of London. During that visit, he made eleven paintings of Kew and two of London. Pissarro was quite pleased with his Kew paintings, and his dealer Durand-Ruel bought several of them later that year.

Pissarro's Last London Visit–1897

Once more, Pissarro went to the aid of his son Lucien, who in May 1897 suffered a stroke-like illness that caused paralysis. Pissarro stayed in London until July 19, providing assistance to Lucien's wife Esther and helping care for their daughter Orovida.

As Lucien's health improved, Pissarro began to paint the motifs around him. Lucien and Esther had just moved to a new home on Bath Road. A one-story building adjoined the house in the back, and its roof provided a flat terrace overlooking fields and what was at that time the Hammersmith railway line. Five of the seven paintings Pissarro produced during this visit were created from this rooftop.

He painted cricket matches and a local celebration of Queen Victoria's Diamond Jubilee. He also made a painting of Esther and Orovida in the garden of their home on Bath Road. Its composition and style are very similar to a painting he made of his wife Julie and their daughter Minette in Louveciennes 27 years earlier. Pissarro remained in London until October, when Lucien's health significantly improved.

In November of that year, Pissarro's third son, Félix, became gravely ill with tuberculosis. This time, it was Julie who rushed to London to care for him. He died within the week at the age of 23 and was buried in Richmond cemetery in London.

Lucien and his family remained in London, and Pissarro's granddaughter Orovida lived her entire life there. Lucien eventually became an English citizen. Their attachment to England resulted in a bequest to the Ashmolean Museum at Oxford of a vast treasure of Pissarro paintings, drawings, and family archives.

SAINT THOMAS

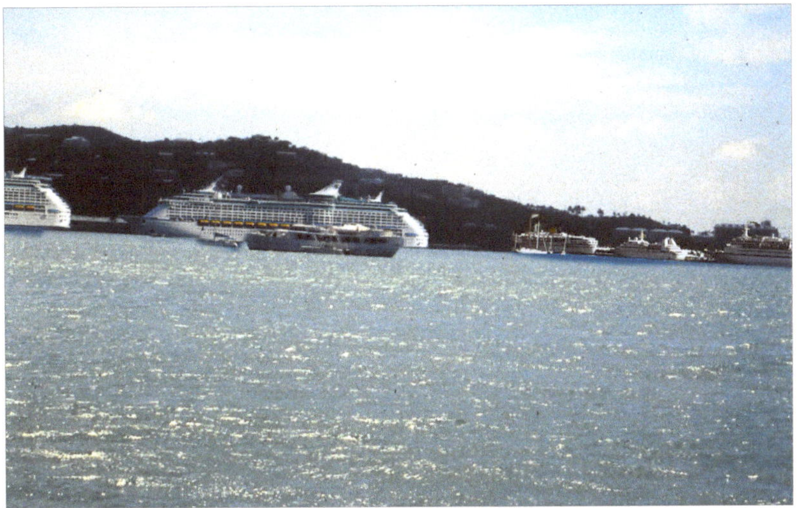

Long Bay, a familiar landmark drawn and painted by Pissarro.

Pissarro's Roots in the West Indies

By the standards of the French art world, Pissarro's path to an artistic career was completely unconventional. He was not born in France. His artistic education did not revolve around the prestigious Paris art schools, although he attended some ateliers for short periods. He also disdained the Salon, the French government's system of recognizing artists, even though some of his paintings were accepted for the Salon and exhibited.

A strange set of circumstances brought about the birth of Camille Pissarro on July 10, 1830 in the Virgin Islands. And this is why he would for his entire life be a Danish citizen. To get the full picture, we must look back to previous generations.

Family Ties in France

The story begins in the city of Bordeaux, France, with two Jewish families—the Petits and the Pissarros. The Petit family had a successful mercantile business, which included commercial ventures on the island of St. Thomas. One of the sons, Isaac Petit, was sent to Charlotte Amalie to manage the family business.

The Pissarro family, originally from Braganza, Portugal, had fled to Bordeaux in 1769 to escape the oppression of Marranos, the name given to Spanish Jews who were forced during the Spanish Inquisition to convert to Christianity but continued to covertly practice their Jewish faith. Within the relatively safe haven of Bordeaux, the Pissarro family built a successful import-export business with contacts in Europe and the Americas. The Petit family and the Pissarro family were united by the marriage of Isaac's sister Anne-Félicité to Joseph Gabriel Jean Pissarro (Camille's paternal grandfather). In 1802, they had a son named Frédéric (Camille's father).

On the Island of St. Thomas

In Charlotte Amalie, Isaac Petit married Esther Manzana-Pomié, a young woman from a French-Jewish family that had fled to St. Thomas from Saint-Domingue (now the Dominican Republic) during the Haitian revolution in 1791–1793. When Esther died at an early age, Isaac married her sister Rachel, who was 21 years younger than he.

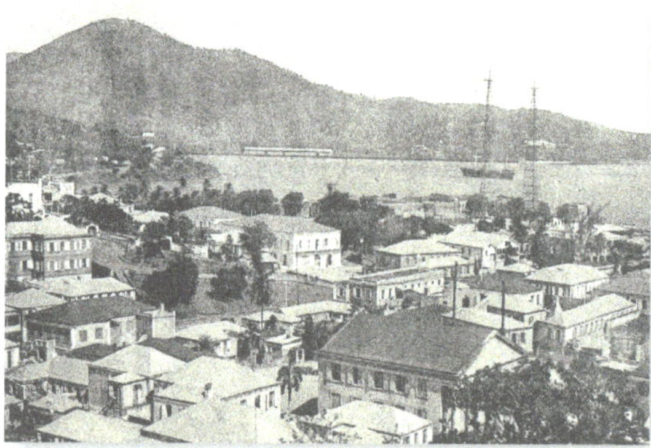

Charlotte Amalie, the principal city on the island of St. Thomas at the beginning of the 20th century

Rachel and Isaac had three children together, and she was pregnant with their fourth child when Isaac died in 1824 at the age of 50. At the age of 29, Rachel was left alone with three small children and a fourth on the way. There was no one to respond to the ever-expanding demands of the family business. By this time, Frédéric Pissarro was 22 years old and already a successful businessman in France. Among the family in Bordeaux, he was the obvious choice to go to St. Thomas and sort things out.

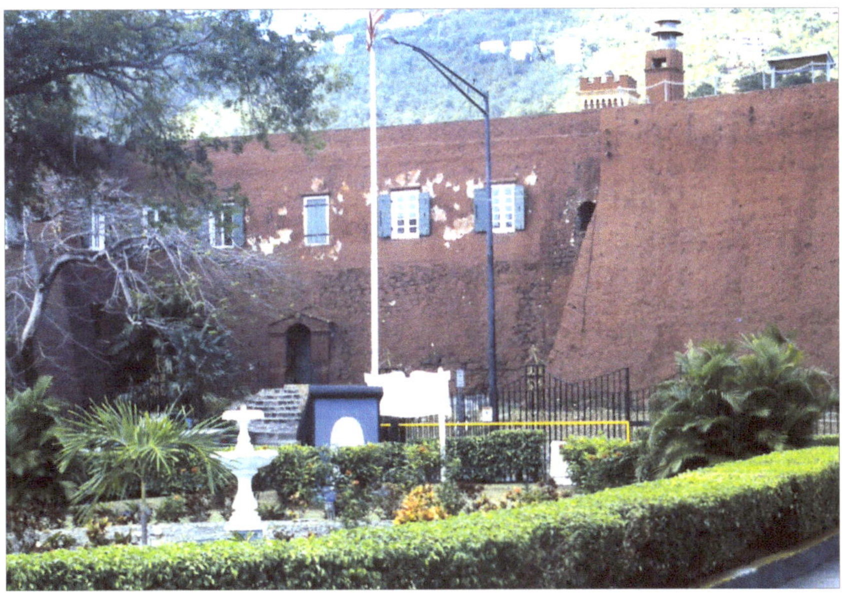

Fort Christian, built by the Danes in 1666 to defend the island, was the subject of early drawings by Pissarro.

International Commerce in the Caribbean

Frédéric Pissarro arrived during the glory days of commerce in the West Indies. Ships crossing the Atlantic Ocean in all directions stopped for provisions at the tiny island of St. Thomas, only 13 miles long and 4 miles wide. Merchants and shippers found refuge in Charlotte Amalie's natural deep-water harbor protected by small islands. Along the docks were long wooden warehouses, built to store merchandise. Extending up the steep hillside were businesses and private homes.

The island of St. Thomas, colonized by Denmark in 1672, was declared a free port in 1764. By 1800, Charlotte Amalie was a bustling international port and trading center. Between the years of 1831 and 1840 (when Camille was 10 years old), 35 ships from the United States stopped there, as did 14 ships from Denmark, 18 from Great Britain, 11 from France, and 22 from other countries.

During that period in St. Thomas, slave trading was a brisk commercial business. Because of the island's steep mountains, there were few plantations. However, large numbers of slaves were brought in, sold at the local slave market, and exported to other countries.

Large Jewish Presence in St. Thomas

Because St. Thomas shared the religious tolerance of the Danish government, it became a welcome haven for large numbers of Sephardic Jews, who settled there as early as the 1700s. They were free to work as traders and merchants, and in 1814, the Danish government granted them full civil rights.

In 1796, the Jewish congregation founded a synagogue, Kahal Kadosh Beracha VeShalom (the Holy Congregation Blessing and Peace). The second-oldest synagogue in the Western Hemisphere, it has continuously maintained an active congregation since its founding. Even today, the synagogue's floor is covered with the fine white powdery sand of the island, a tradition believed to be rooted in the practice of the Marrano Jews, who used sand to muffle the sounds of their secret meetings during the Inquisition. This synagogue played a central part in the life of the Pissarro family.

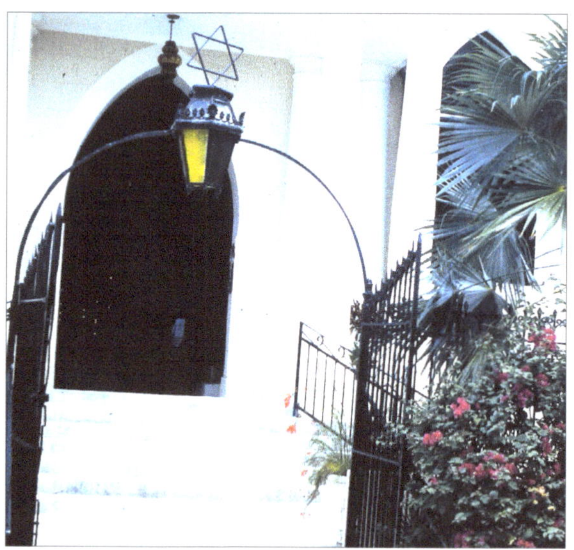

Camille Pissarro's father donated funds to construct this synagogue after the previous building burned.

The Story of Frédéric and Rachel

Frédéric Pissarro came to Rachel's rescue, taking over the family business and helping her raise the four children of Isaac Petit. After a couple of years, the two young people found that they were going to have a child together. They tried to arrange their marriage at the synagogue, but were refused. A union between them would, the elders said, constitute violation of Jewish law, which does not allow a man to marry his uncle's wife, even if she is his aunt by marriage. Furthermore, Jewish law does not allow a man to marry a woman who is still breastfeeding a child under the age of two.

Frédéric and Rachel appealed to the king of Denmark, who agreed that they should marry. The wedding took place in the presence of a minion, a group of ten Jewish men. When they

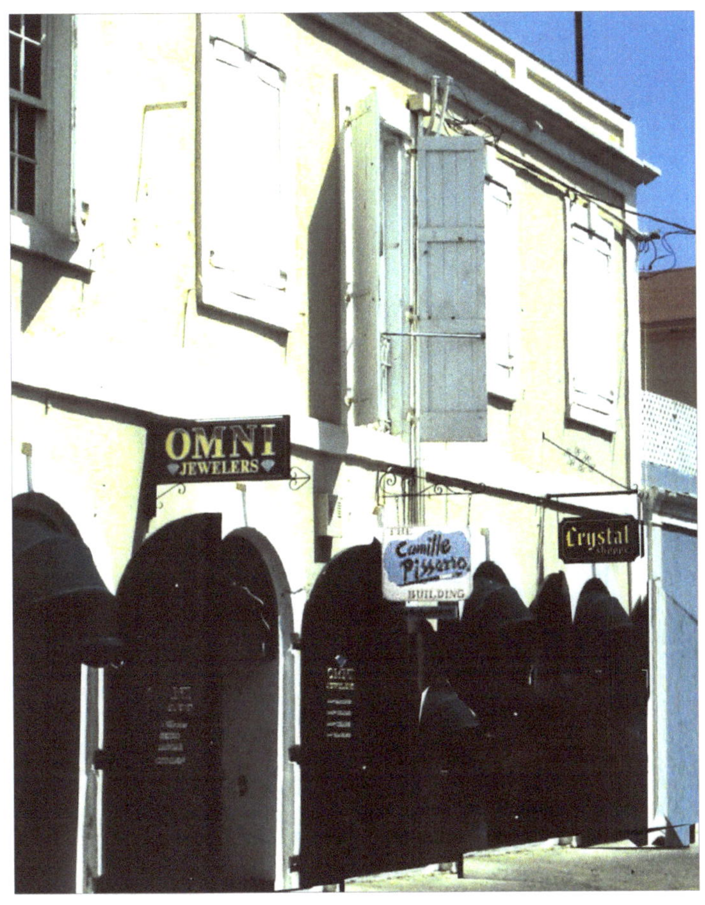

The house on the main street of Charlotte Amalie where Camille Pissarro was born on July 10, 1830

announced their marriage in the newspaper, the elders of the synagogue responded immediately, denouncing the legitimacy of the marriage. This erupted into a scandal that caused the Jewish congregation and even ministers of the white Protestant congregations in St. Thomas to disassociate themselves from the young couple.

Camille Pissarro was the third son of Frédéric and Rachel, who had four children together, all boys. Despite the synagogue's refusal to recognize the marriage, all four children's names were inscribed in the records of the synagogue. Finally, in 1833, after the birth of their fourth son, the synagogue recognized the marriage and the Pissarro family achieved some measure of acceptance in the community.

It must have been important to Pissarro to have his birth recorded accurately because years later after he was living in Paris, he took steps to set the record straight. He asked his older brother Alfred, still in St. Thomas, to make corrections in the synagogue's records which listed his name as Jacob Pizarro, son of Abraham Pizarro and Rachel Petit. He asked that the spelling of the last name be changed to Pissarro and that Camille be added to his name. He also asked that Pissarro be added to his mother's name.

Growing Up in Charlotte Amalie

The house where Camille Pissarro was born, a two-story stone and stucco building, is located at 14 Dronningens Gade, the main street of Charlotte Amalie. The ground level housed the family business, which included a haberdashery, ship's store, and general merchandise. The family occupied a spacious apartment upstairs. It was here in the front bedroom on what was most likely a hot July day that Camille Pissarro was born.

The house is still there. A small blue sign hanging outside marks it as the Camille Pissarro Building. The arches along the front lead to a small courtyard surrounded by several boutiques. An art gallery occupies the space upstairs where the family once lived.

As soon as he was old enough, Pissarro went with his brothers to the Moravian school, along with the children of slaves and free black people. Perhaps it was easier for the Pissarro children to go there than the local public schools, where they may have encountered insults because of the scandal surrounding their parents' marriage. This childhood experience of being among black people must have influenced the impressionable young boy. He grew up speaking French, English, and Spanish, all of which were in common use on the island.

To School in France

Most of the well-to-do people on St. Thomas sent their children back to Europe to private schools to give them a proper education. Such was the case with Pissarro's family, and, at the age of twelve, young Camille traveled to France to attend school at Passy, a suburb of Paris (See chapter on Paris). His six-year course included drawing lessons, and by the time he returned to St. Thomas at age eighteen, he was already a skilled draftsman.

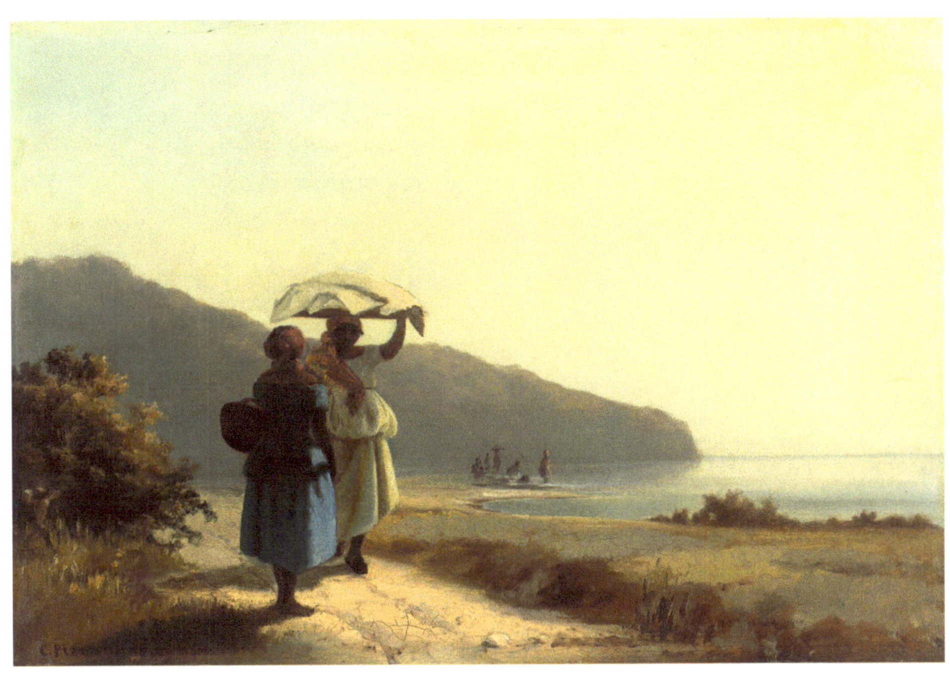

Two Women Chatting by the Sea, St. Thomas
1856
National Gallery, Washington, DC
PDR 23

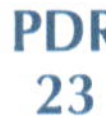

The motif for this painting, *Two Women Chatting by the Sea*, is a familiar location in St. Thomas—Long Bay, where today huge cruise ships with multitudes of tourists dock. The location is easily visible from the waterfront in Charlotte Amalie, particularly near Fort Christian, a historic red brick fortress with a clock tower that appears in some of Pissarro's drawings of St. Thomas.

At the edge of the beach in the distance is a group of people, perhaps women washing clothes, a motif Pissarro painted many times during his career. In the foreground are two women on a small road, one with a large flat bundle balanced on her head. The native women frequently carried burdens of various kinds on their heads, and Pissarro enjoyed drawing and painting them.

The brilliant tropical light is very much like a powerful spotlight shining on the two women. Its intensity is depicted by the darkness of the shadows on the first woman's back and the sparkling white sand. The ocean is totally still and the sky is rosy, suggesting late afternoon.

During the years he spent in St. Thomas and Venezuela, Pissarro made countless drawing of the people around him. This painting confirms his early interest and skill in portraying the human figure.

His father expected that he would take on some of the responsibilities of the business. It was soon apparent, however, that Pissarro had little aptitude for or interest in the complexities of the mercantile trade. He much preferred the intricacies of creating images with light and shadow, form and volume. Pissarro was already committed to an artistic career.

The Young Artist in St. Thomas

In 1848, the same year that Pissarro returned to St. Thomas from six years of school in Paris, he witnessed the emancipation of slaves in all of the Virgin Islands. We can only wonder what impact this had on the young man, who until the age of twelve had attended school with the black children of the community. This and the isolation of his family imposed by the religious communities during his childhood in Charlotte Amalie must have been pivotal in shaping his adult views of religion and human rights.

Although he was already committed to an artistic career, Pissarro took his place in the family business in St. Thomas. While he supervised the loading of merchandise onto cargo ships, he sketched the activity on the docks and at local sites, such as the historic Ft. Christian. After he returned to France in 1856, he used one of his sketches of Long Bay to make an oil painting [See PDR 23].

When Pissarro was 21, he met Fritz Melbye, a Danish painter, who had come to the Caribbean to paint exotic landscapes for European collectors. Their friendship grew as Melbye shared his professional skills and experience with Pissarro.

Breaking Away

Just two years later, the artists traveled together to Venezuela. Knowing that his father would never sanction his actions, Pissarro left without telling his family, leaving them a note of explanation. Later he wrote, "*I was in St. Thomas in 1852, a well-paid shop clerk. But I couldn't stand it, so without giving it a thought I dropped everything and ran off to Caracas, to break the mooring that tied me to bourgeois life. What I suffered is incredible, of course, but I lived.*"

Melbye had previously visited Venezuela, following in the footsteps of numerous artists and scientists who went there to explore the tropical wilderness. Pissarro was probably intrigued by his friend's descriptions of the lush landscape with its forested mountains.

Discovered by Christopher Columbus on his third trip to the Americas in 1498, Venezuela became the site of large plantations worked by African slaves who were shipped there as early as the mid-sixteenth century. Despite its stormy political history, Venezuela was the first Latin American country to declare its independence in 1811. Spain finally recognized Venezuela's independence in 1821, although its civil wars continued to rage until 1870. However, things were relatively calm when Pissarro and Melbye arrived in November 1852, and there is no evidence of civil unrest during the nearly two years of their stay.

Melbye and Pissarro sailed on the French vessel Varaqueña, almost directly south to the port of La Guaira on the Caribbean Sea. This section of Venezuela's northern coast is fringed with a range of mountains, an extension of the Andes to the west.

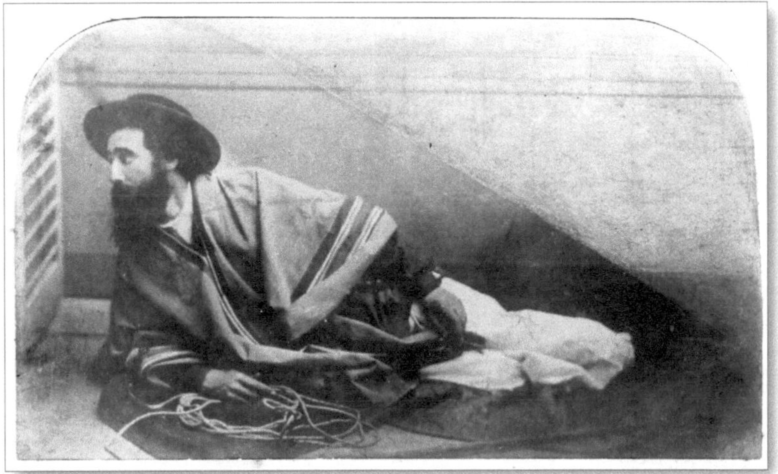

A photograph of Camille Pissarro as a young man in a gaucho costume. Lionel and Sandrine Pissarro Archives

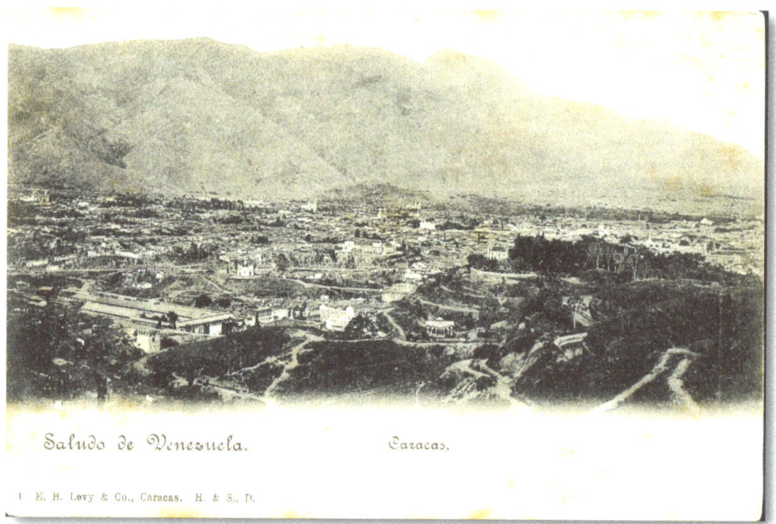

Caracas, surrounded by steep mountains, was already a large city when Pissarro lived there.

The town of La Guaira, still the major port for Caracas, clings to a narrow strip of land where the mountains plunge into the sea. For more than a month, the artists stayed in a boarding house and worked in the open air, directly from nature. Pissarro's drawings from that time include views of the seaside town, the steep mountain slopes by the sea, tropical vegetation including cacti and palm trees, and a crude road up the mountain that had been constructed just a few years earlier.

Discovering Caracas

The rugged road in Pissarro's drawing was the one that he and Melbye used to travel to the city of Caracas, located more than 3000 feet above sea level. There, the temperatures were cool and the climate moderate. Originally named Santiago de León de Caracas, the city was established in 1567, and in 1577, it was made the capital of Venezuela. In 1595, it was burned by pirates, and was twice destroyed by earthquakes, first in 1641 and then again in 1812. After the second earthquake, the city was slow to rebuild, and some of the remaining ruins are visible in drawings made by Pissarro during his visit in 1852 [See Bridge at Caracas-Watercolor].

The two artists rented a large house in the center of the city on the Plaza Mayor (now Plaza Bolívar), overlooking the

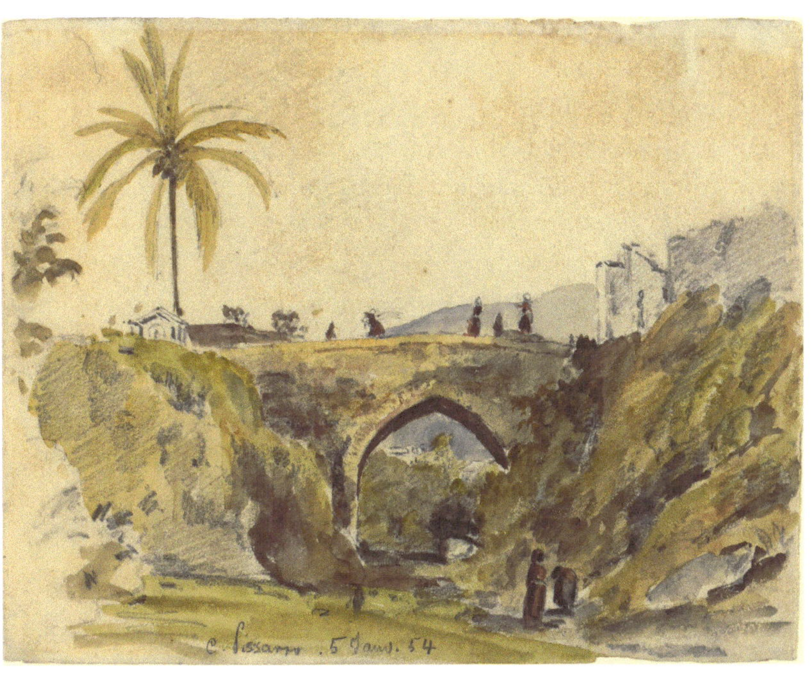

Bridge at Caracas
1854
National Gallery, Washington, DC
Watercolor

site of the daily market. Near the plaza is the Cathedral of Caracas, built in 1666, with its tall white campanile (bell tower), which appears in two of Pissarro's Caracas paintings.

The large studio, shown in a drawing by Pissarro, shows Melbye seated at an easel on the left and Pissarro, with dark hair and a small goatee, talking to a child. To make money, they taught art lessons and sold their paintings to private collectors.

At that time, Caracas was a lively intellectual center with a university, a college, theaters, and drawing and music academies. The city had a population of about a quarter million people, including a large group of Europeans. The two men rapidly became involved in the city's many cultural activities. To Pissarro, it must have seemed far more exciting than the little town of Charlotte Amalie.

It was also here at the beginning of his career that Pissarro identified many of the motifs that he would explore for the rest of his life. He pictured city scenes around him, nearby villages and lively markets. Already, the subjects of his paintings were working-class people going about their daily tasks, not members of the middle or upper classes. He also depicted houses clinging to mountains and lush tropical foliage. Even at this early stage, his work reveals sophistication in the portrayal of light and shadow, and a remarkable ability to create perspective. His drawings and paintings demonstrate that he had already developed the ability to create believable landscapes and portray human and animal figures.

Along with other artists and friends, Pissarro and Melbye made many excursions into the surrounding hills and mountains. Pissarro's sketches and paintings document one trip to the waterfalls at Galipan, a village high on the mountain of Avila.

Once again, Pissarro witnessed the emancipation of slaves when the Republic of Venezuela finally abolished slavery in 1854. His work from this period includes many figure studies of black people, who are pictured with the same grace and dignity he would later impart to the farmers and working people of France.

After a little more than a year and a half in Caracas, Pissarro agreed to return to St. Thomas to help out so that his brother Alfred could take a holiday in Paris. Those 13 months would be the last time he spent working in the family's business.

Beginning an Artistic Career in Paris

When Pissarro was finally free to return to Paris in 1855, he was already an accomplished artist committed to his life's work. He brought with him many of the drawings and watercolors he had made in St. Thomas and Caracas and used them to execute oil paintings.

Because relatively few works are available from that period, it is difficult to chart Pissarro's progress during the early years in St. Thomas and Venezuela. Some 1500 of his works were destroyed in Louveciennes during the Franco-Prussian war when soldiers occupied his home. Many of those may have been sketches, watercolors, or paintings from those early years in St. Thomas and Venezuela.

Éragny

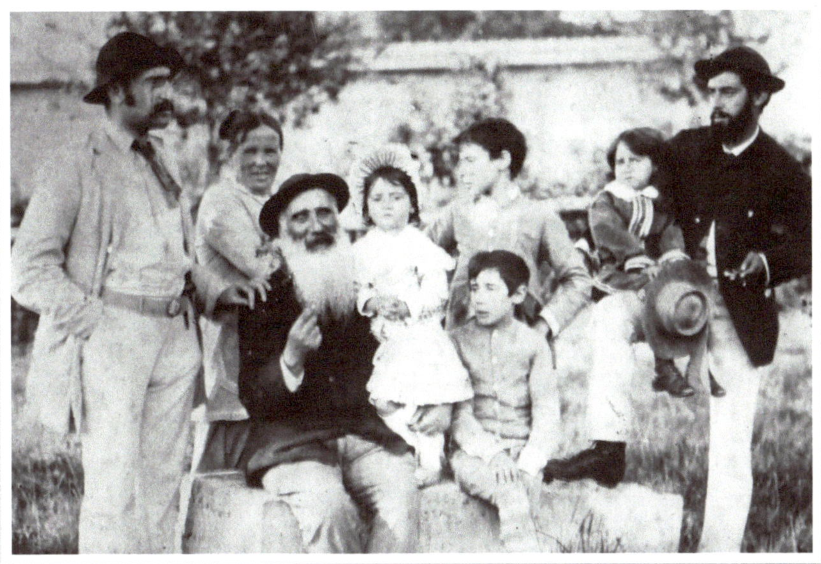

The Pissarro family at Éragny (left to right): Alfred Isaacson (a cousin), Julie Pissarro, Camille Pissarro with Cocotte in his arms, Georges (standing), Félix (sitting), Ludovic-Rodo and Lucien. Photograph c. 1884 Lionel and Sandrine Pissarro Archives

At Home in Éragny

The provincial village of Éragny, on the border of Picardy and Haute-Normandie, seems an odd choice for a cosmopolitan man like Pissarro. In fact, he was not ready to leave Pontoise, but it was becoming too expensive to live there any longer. "*I have to leave Pontoise much to my regret, as I cannot find a house there that is well-located and reasonably priced. It is much to my regret, because it seemed to me that Pontoise suited me from every point of view…,*" he wrote his friend Monet.

Before settling on Éragny, Pissarro and his family moved temporarily to nearby Osny and began to search in earnest for a new home. It had to meet many requirements: the house must be

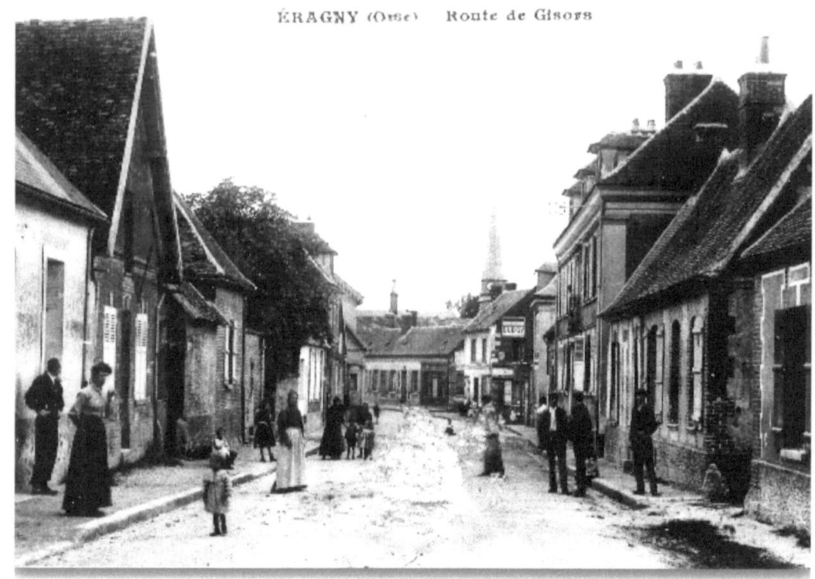

The main street of Éragny, now called rue Camille Pissarro, looks much the same today as when Pissarro lived there.

large enough to contain his growing family, and the rent must fit within his small budget. Most important, the surrounding countryside must be interesting, with many new motifs.

After visiting a number of towns, he wrote Lucien, *"I've been chasing about all over the place in search of a house. I spent three days in Gisors. We didn't visit it properly together. We didn't see all the wooded part in the public gardens: superb woods, with extraordinary undulations, the ruins of the château de la Reine Blanche in the garden between big trees, and old towers covered with vegetation. In the distance are church towers, it's superb. A few old streets, three little rivers, full of picturesque motifs. The countryside is superb as well."*

It was near Gisors, in Éragny, that Pissarro finally found a suitable home. The house, less than two miles north of town, was a substantial brick dwelling with plenty of room outside for the children to run and play. In addition, the gardens, orchards, and meadows offered a variety of motifs for Pissarro to paint. He described it to Lucien, *"Yes, we've settled on Éragny-sur-Epte. The house is superb and not expensive: a thousand francs, with garden and meadow. It's two hours from Paris."*

When the Pissarro family moved to Éragny in April 1884, the trees and meadows were covered in the delicate green of springtime. Paulémile Pissarro, the couple's final child, was

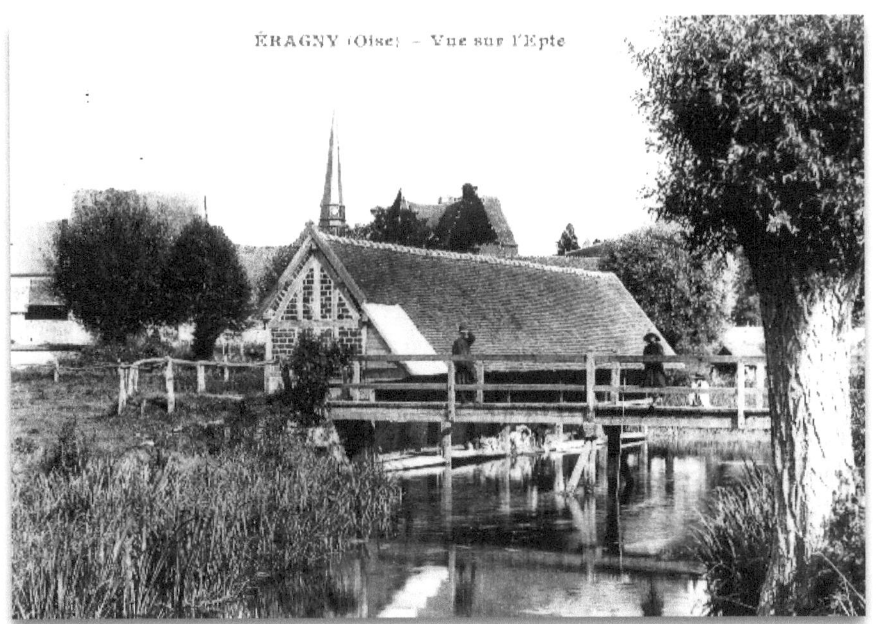

The bridge over the Epte River at the turn of the 20th century

born soon after on August 22, 1884. During that first year in his new home, Pissarro made two paintings depicting the main road entering the village, which is now called rue Camille-Pissarro. These Éragny paintings are quite similar to two paintings of rue de l'Hermitage, the street where Pissarro lived during his first year in Pontoise. There is an even more striking resemblance between these Éragny paintings and five paintings of la route de Versailles, the street in Louveciennes where Pissarro lived. They, too, were painted during his first year in residence. Perhaps making these paintings was Pissarro's way of orienting himself to his new environs—of putting himself into this new place.

Pissarro was excited by the abundance of new motifs, all of them distinct from those of recent years. The area around Éragny was more rural than Pontoise or Louveciennes, but not nearly as isolated as Montfoucault. He wrote, *"I haven't been able to resist painting, so beautiful are the views all around my garden. So I began work yesterday, eager to resume my daily routine."*

During that first year in Éragny, Pissarro stood in his own orchard and painted the view of the nearby manor house and church. The large manor house dates from the sixteenth century and was built for the Lord of Éragny. By the time Pissarro lived there, it was no more than a large farmhouse, but it figured prominently in many of his paintings.

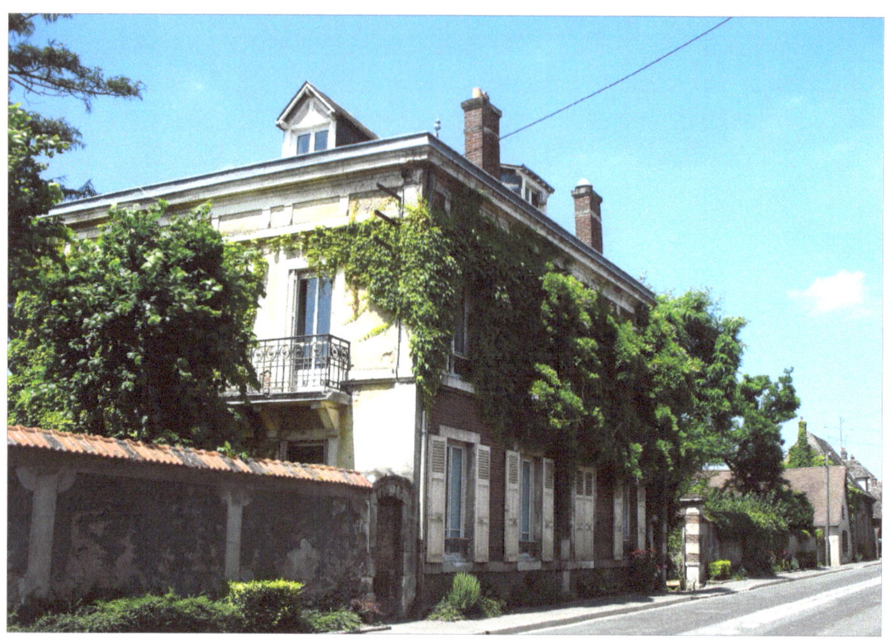

The Éragny home of Camille Pissarro, now privately owned

Painting at Éragny

Pissarro painted everything in sight in every season, depicting the big walnut tree bare of leaves in winter, apple trees blooming in spring, the lush green grass of the meadow in summer, and apple picking in the fall. He returned to these motifs time after time, always finding something new and fresh. In all, he made some 350 oil paintings at Éragny, along with countless gouaches, pastels, watercolors, and prints.

For several years, Pissarro was content painting the orchard and garden of his new home and the neighboring fields and meadows. He also painted views of the nearby hamlet Bazincourt and the tiny River Epte, which separates the two communities. (This is the same River Epte that runs past Monet's home and feeds the lily pond in Giverny, just before it empties into the Seine.)

Éragny today is not much different than it was when Pissarro lived there. We can clearly see what inspired his paintings, especially during spring and summer. In 1880, there were 467 people living in Éragny. More recent population figures in 2007 showed an increase to 577.

Pissarro and Pointillism

During this period, Pissarro embarked upon one of the most dramatic experiments of his artistic life—Pointillism. It seemed to him a natural progression from the experiments he had been making with color. Pissarro had been studying and experimenting with various color theories being proposed at the time. Michel Eugène Chevruel, a chemist at the Royal Manufacturers at Gobelins, had previously published research showing that colors appear lighter or darker depending on the color beside them.

In 1881, the American scientist, Ogden Rood, updated color theory by shining light through colored transparencies onto white or colored surfaces. Rood demonstrated that color in light was different from color in painter's pigment (which Chevruel had used in his experiments). Rood put complementary colors of light side by side and created strong contrasts, which on canvas made an image appear more brilliant and vibrant.

In 1885, Pissarro met Paul Signac, a young artist about the same age as his eldest son. A few months later, Signac introduced Pissarro to Georges Seurat, who was putting Rood's theories into practice, using the complementary colors of light and pure colors, rather than mixed pigments. Instead of conventional brush strokes, Seurat applied paint in small dots, close together but not touching. This new technique, called Pointillism, seemed to fuse Pissarro's own experiments with color and Rood's new scientific information.

Always eager to push beyond the traditional methods of painting, Pissarro eagerly embraced Seurat's style. He enthusiastically applied the new technique to all his familiar motifs at Éragny, experimenting with different ways of using the dot. One of Pissarro's most famous Pointillist paintings depicts the crooked apple tree in his orchard surrounded by apple pickers. The multitude of tiny colored dots produces a surface shimmering with light [See PDR 850].

Last Impressionist Exhibition–1886

Four years had passed since the seventh Impressionist exhibition in 1882. Pissarro was eager to bring together the original Impressionist artists with the younger artists painting in the Pointillist style—Seurat, Signac, and his son Lucien Pissarro. It was difficult to get agreement among the artists who had participated previously. Many of them were intensely opposed to the new Pointillist paintings and would not accept the new generation of artists. Monet, Renoir, Sisley, and Caillebotte, who vigorously opposed the inclusion of the Pointillist paintings, chose not to participate.

However, Mary Cassatt, Edgar Degas, Armand Guillaumin, and Berthe Morisot, all of whom had participated in previous exhibitions, stood by Pissarro. Because the Pointillist paintings were being included, Degas insisted that the word "Impressionist" be excluded from the name of the event. It was simply called the "Eighth Exhibition of Paintings."

To secure agreement among the participating artists, it was decided that the Pointillist paintings would be hung separately from the Impressionist works. Accordingly, when the exhibition opened in Paris on May 15, 1886, the paintings of Seurat, Signac, Pissarro, and his son Lucien were presented in a separate room. One of the art critics, Félix Fénéon, was enthusiastic about Pointillism and gave the artists the name "Neo-Impressionists." This was the last group exhibition of the Impressionists. Even though Pissarro was listed as a Neo-Impressionist in this exhibition, he was the only artist who participated in all eight exhibitions.

His fellow artists were not the only ones who failed to understand or appreciate the new Pointillist technique. Durand-Ruel, his primary art dealer, told Pissarro that he liked the paintings but not the style of execution. According to Pissarro, *"Durand prefers the old execution, however he grants that my recent paintings have more light—in short, he isn't very keen."*

Even Pissarro's wife, Julie, was not enamored of the new technique. Pissarro wrote Lucien that, *"Your mother wanted me to do a painting for her, but, as ever, not in my new manner. It would be impossible for me to do one in my old manner..."*

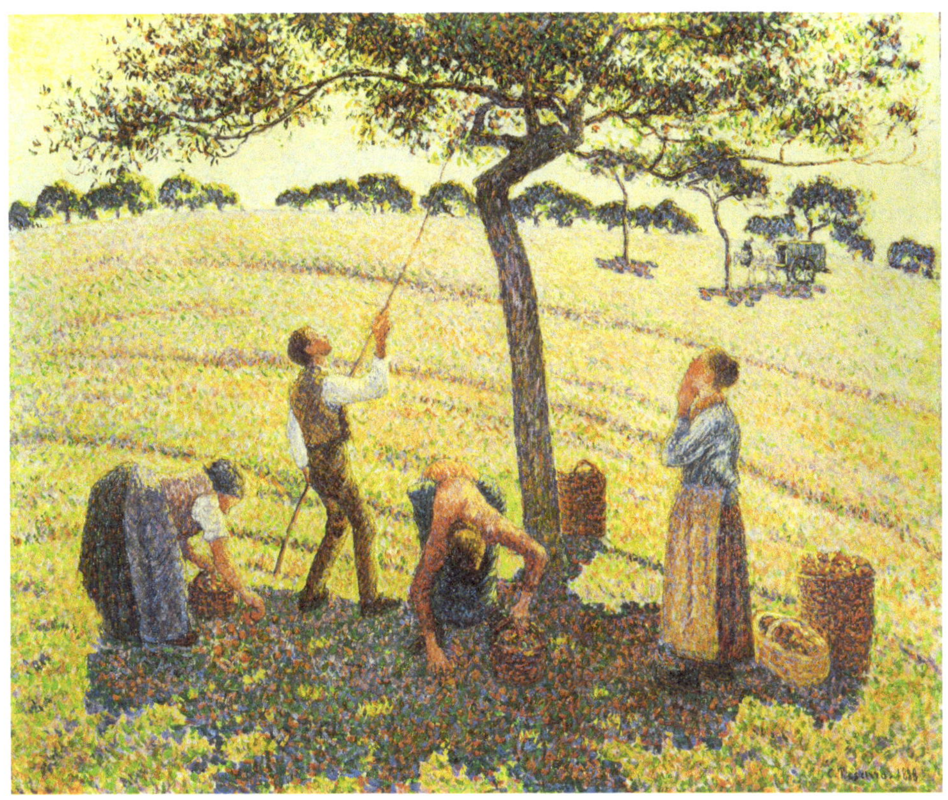

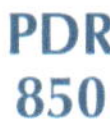

Apple-Picking, Éragny
1887—1888
Dallas Museum of Art, Dallas, TX
PDR 850

This is one of the most famous of Pissarro's Pointillist paintings. It clearly demonstrates the technique of painting with dots or "points" that Seurat was using. The painting is dominated by a bent apple tree. On the ground are the fallen apples—hardly bigger than the red dots that contrast with the blue-green dots of the shadow. Was Pissarro using the red apples as a gentle pun on the red dots? He did have a keen sense of humor.

This painting was carefully planned, involving several preparatory sketches, and executed with every line and surface molded by the mixture of contrasting dots. It is fascinating to examine the different colors Pissarro used to make the dark shadow, and it is equally interesting to look beyond the tree to see the many colors he used to portray the sunlight on the grass. To show the field receding into the distance, he gradually altered the shades of colors and accented the perspective by the size of the horse and wagon.

The effect is one of shimmering brilliance, a fitting portrayal of the sun-filled autumn day. When we are close to the painting, we see multitudes of dots, but as we move back, the retina of our eye mixes the dots to create pure color. We can only imagine how long it took Pissarro to create this small canvas filled with countless dots.

Despite his enthusiasm for the theories of Pointillism, the new technique required Pissarro to spend much more time on each canvas. By 1887, he was feeling constrained and wrote Lucien that his painting was taking much too long. *"Perhaps, I will be compelled to return to my old style? That would be very embarrassing! We shall see. Anyway, I will have learned to be more precise."* In the end, the Pointillist manner proved to be too frustrating for Pissarro. He expressed his concerns to Lucien: *"How is one to combine the purity and simplicity of the dot with the full-bodiedness, suppleness, freedom, spontaneity and freshness of sensation of our Impressionist art? That is the question, it preoccupies me a lot, for the dot is meager, lacking in body, diaphanous, more monotonous than simple."*

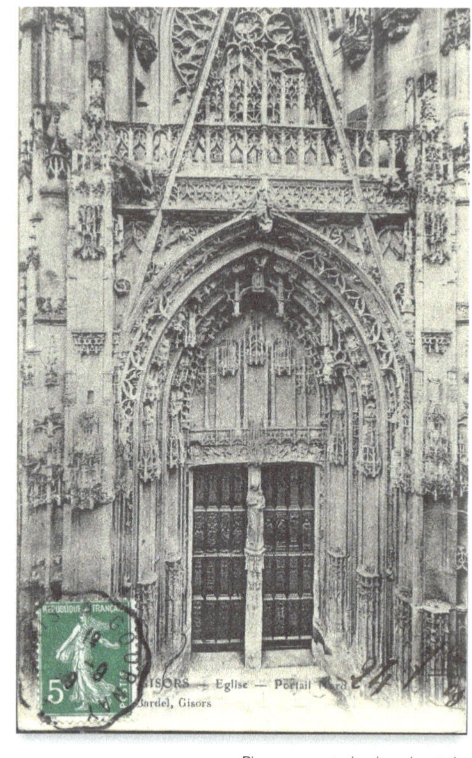

Pissarro wrote Lucien about the intricately-carved doors of the cathédrale in Gisors.

In response, he altered the technique somewhat, adapting more of a small curved stroke, like a comma. But he retained the division of color, which makes the paintings of this period some of his most luminous.

As the years progressed, Pissarro gradually moved away from Pointillism. After five years of experimentation, he wrote Lucien in 1891 that three new canvases were progressing rapidly and one was almost finished. *"It's no longer the dot, which I've entirely abandoned, returning instead to the division of pure colors, without waiting for the paint to dry, which had the drawback of cooling the sensation. I'm much happier that way, and I can assure you that the colors are every bit as delicate and freer in sensation, more personal."*

Seeking New Sensations

For several years, Pissarro had concentrated on Éragny and his immediate surroundings. Now he needed a change of scenery. In 1891, he even thought of moving away from Éragny, possibly back to Pontoise. He could have found more diverse motifs in Gisors, just a short distance away. Shortly after moving to the region, he made just a few paintings of the hills and prairies surrounding Gisors, the busy Monday market, and the church tower as viewed from the city gardens.

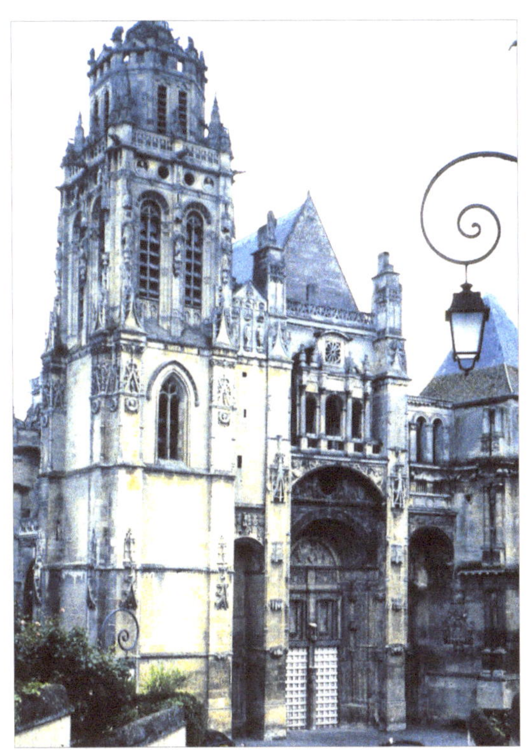
The cathédrale in Gisors

As usual, Pissarro did not paint the local landmarks, although he raved about the art treasures in Gisors in a letter to his son Lucien: "...*Gisors has art treasures that should delight a tourist with taste; tell her [Lucien's wife Esther] about the diversified style of the church, about the wooden doors of Jean Goujon, about the stairways, the genealogical tree, the French frescoes (rare) [his emphasis], and the basin which I almost omitted from my list.*"

Indeed, the church that Pissarro described, Saint-Gervais-Saint-Protais, had been declared a historic monument by the French government in 1862, long before Pissarro moved to the region. The original church was consecrated in 1119 by Pope Callistus II, but the Romanesque nave was destroyed by fire four years later. It was rebuilt in the flamboyant Gothic style with a much higher vaulted ceiling, and a Gothic choir was added in the thirteenth century. The first organ was placed in the church in the fifteenth century, and in the sixteenth century, the Renaissance façade was added, framed by two large towers.

During the 1940 World War II bombing of Gisors, the entire church roof and organ were destroyed by fire. The building was restored in 1957, and in 1982, a new organ was installed.

Another Gisors landmark that Pissarro did not describe is equally interesting, the Château de Gisors. Built in 1097, it was the site of numerous battles between English and French forces. The medieval fortress, constructed on a huge earthen mound, is an octagonal stone tower surrounded by high stone walls. Between 1158 and 1160, Gisors was put in the custody of the Knights Templar, a Catholic military order that fought during the Crusades. (This historic fact led to speculation after World War II that they had hidden treasure in Gisors, but no treasure was ever found).

Éragny Castle

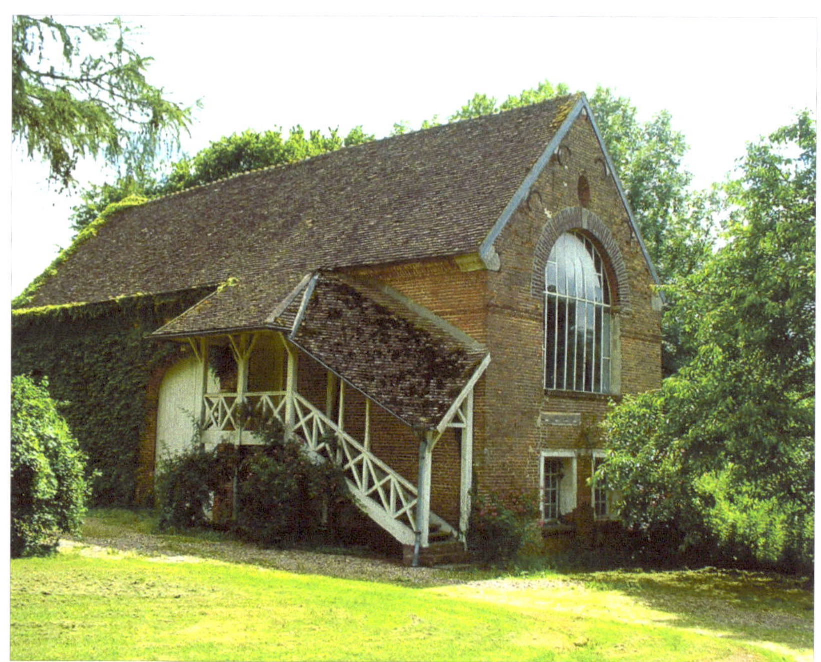

Pissarro converted his barn to a studio at his home in Éragny.

While Pissarro was in London in 1892, the owner of their rented house decided to sell it. The Pissarro family would therefore have to move or buy the property. Without consulting with Pissarro, Julie went to Claude Monet and asked if he would loan them enough money to buy the house. After living in Éragny for eight years, she had made it her home. She was well-liked in the neighborhood and had much in common with the local residents because she had come from a small community. The loan was arranged, and even though Pissarro was reluctant to invest in property, he became a landowner.

The following year Pissarro took quick action to convert the barn behind the house into a studio. The large upper floor provided ample space for his work. A local carpenter made extensive repairs and installed a fireplace. Pissarro also had a large arched window inserted in the north end from which he had an excellent view of the church and manor house. On the west side, he installed large windows. When he stood in front of the opened glass panels, he had expansive vistas of the meadows, the Epte River, and Bazincourt.

Pissarro was ambivalent about having a studio. He recalled how in the past, he had painted outdoors in any kind of weather. Despite the convenience, he worried: "*The studio is splendid, but I often ask myself what is the point in having a studio? In the past, I would do my painting anywhere. In all seasons, in sweltering heat, rain, biting cold, I managed to work with enthusiasm…. Will I be able to work in this new environment??? Surely my paintings will feel the effects? My painting will put on gloves, I'll become official, damn it!!!*"

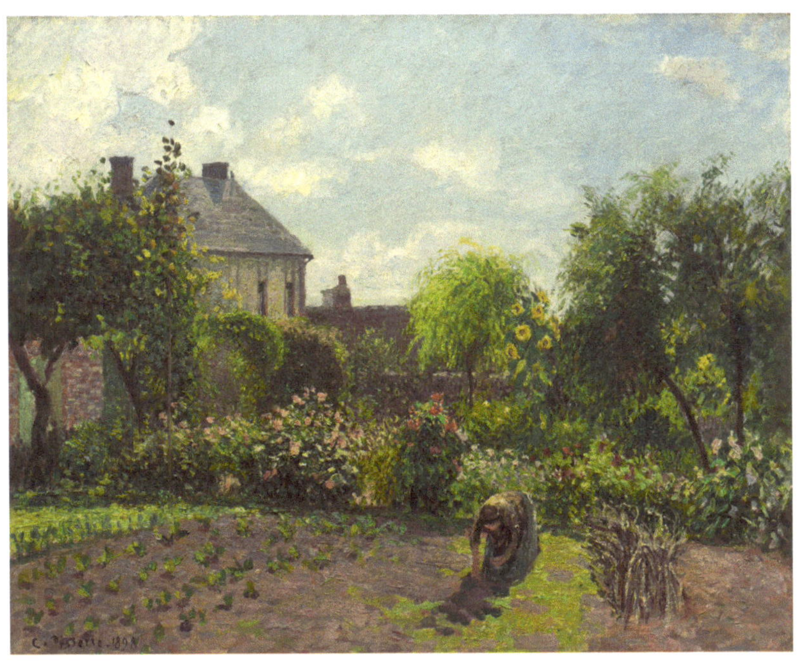

The Garden, Éragny

1898

National Gallery of Art, Washington, DC

PDR 1215

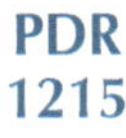

This lush painting is a symphony of color and light. With its careful composition and delicate arrangement of colors, it is a fitting tribute to the family home at Éragny.

The brilliance of the summer sun is so strong that it fades the pinks and dark reds of the glorious flowers bordering the tidy vegetable garden. The diagonal of the roof of the neighboring house stands out sharply against the blue sky. Our eyes follow its line down to the red flowers and the focal point, a woman hard at work tending the young plants. She may be Julie, the painter's wife. Although we cannot see her face, her light brown hair is fastened up in a bun on the back of her head in her usual style. Her dark shadow is clearly delineated on the ground in front of her.

One of the benefits of having the studio was that Pissarro was finally able to purchase a printing press and pursue the art of making lithographs and etchings. Then, rather than entrusting the plates he prepared so carefully to someone else, he was able to execute the prints himself.

In fall of 1895, Pissarro wrote, "*And I really want to go to Paris and see what is happening there. Despite a great sweep of work, I am very bored in Éragny.... Is it anxiety about money, the fact that the coming winter already makes itself felt, weariness with the same old motifs, or my lack of data for the figure paintings I am doing in the studio?*"

Near the end of 1898, Pissarro rented a flat in Paris and brought his family to stay with him for the winter. After that, they spent their winters in Paris, and Éragny became a summer home.

Over the years, the property became known to Pissarro and the children as "Éragny Castle," and the family welcomed a host of visitors, including many prominent Impressionist artists, dealers, and collectors. Éragny remained home to the Pissarro family until Julie's death in 1926.

Rouen

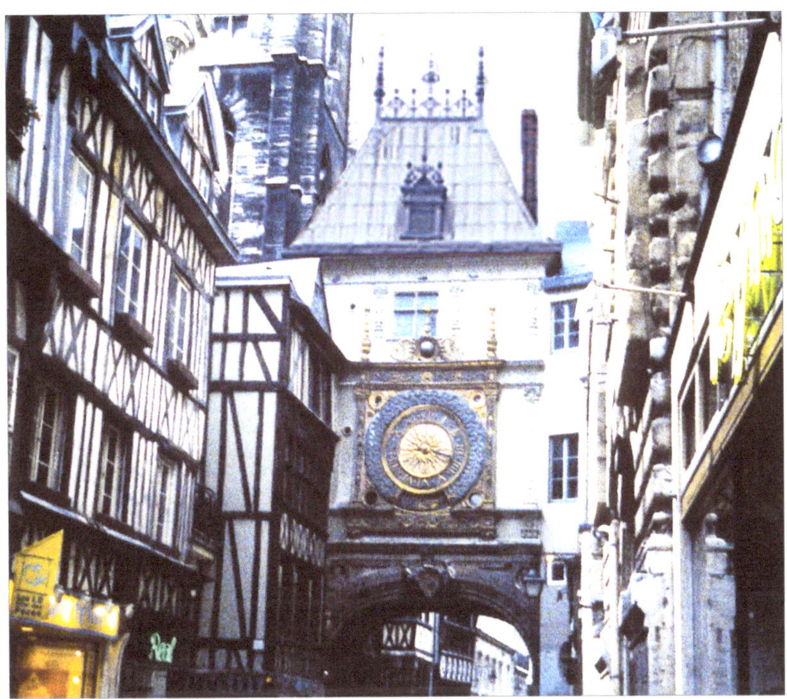

Pissarro sketched the 14th century Gros-Horlage (large clock), but made no paintings of the landmark.

Pissarro's Rouen

The Rouen that Pissarro visited in the nineteenth century was a rich, colorful tapestry of history, culture, and art laced with new construction. Much to the artist's dismay, medieval buildings were being replaced by newer structures. The Rouen we see today is still an uneasy mix of the very old with the startlingly new. Narrow medieval lanes are crowded with half-timbered houses whose upper stories reach out over the street, whereas banal 1950s apartment blocks fill nearby streets.

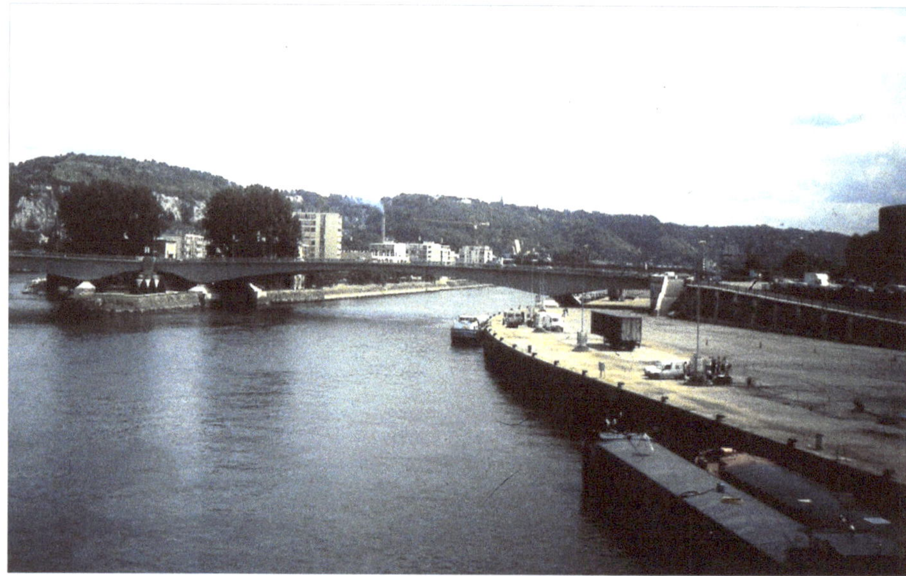

Current photograph of Pissarro's 1883 painting

Pissarro in Rouen–1883

During his visits to Rouen, Pissarro made numerous drawings, sketches, and watercolors of historic sites. But when it came to painting canvases, he turned his attention to the River Seine and its commercial boats and quays. One of the most interesting paintings from his first visit to Rouen is *Place Lafayette, Rouen,* which he painted from the quay across the river from Rouen [See PDR 724].

In fact, this painting appears to be a continuation of his youthful interest in drawing boats and harbors in the Caribbean. In both cases, his paintings portray docks crowded with boats, mules transporting cargo, and workers loading and unloading freight. Interestingly, they are set against a high hill topped by a small building. *Place Lafayette, Rouen* hung in Pissarro's home and is shown in the background of a still life, *Bouquet de Fleurs,* which he painted in 1898. At Pissarro's death, the Rouen painting was inherited by his son Georges.

The Charm of Rouen

Much of the appeal of the city is its location. To simply say that Rouen is situated on the Seine is to diminish its allure. It is nestled at the bottom of large hills that gently fold like a voluminous skirt into

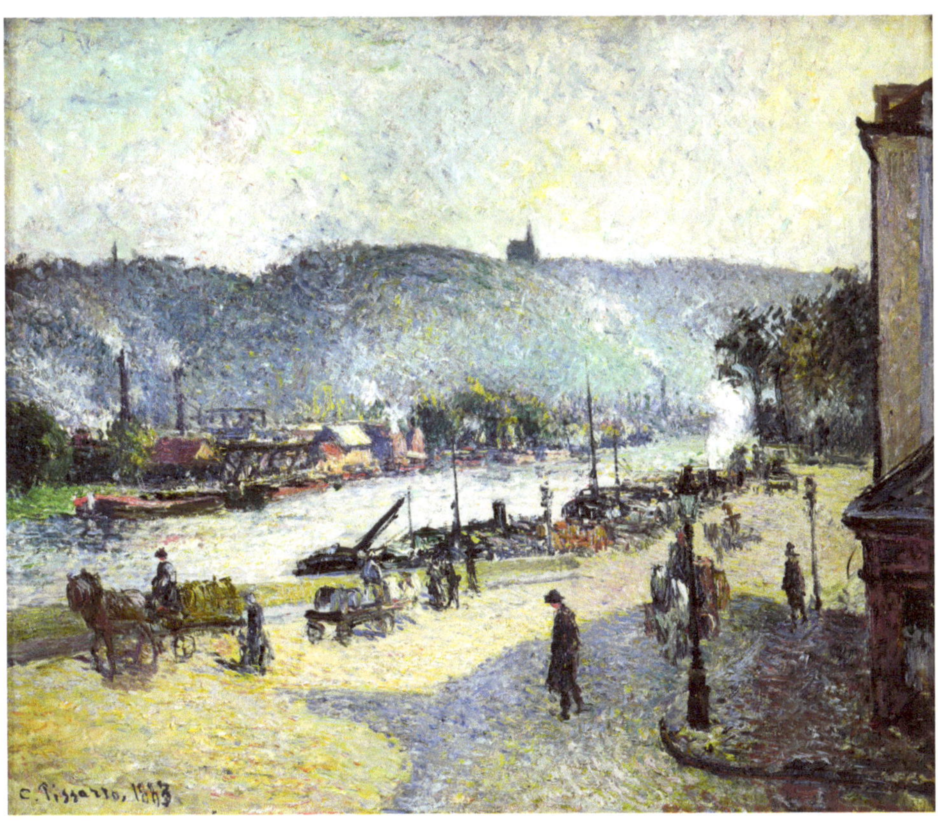

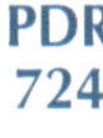

Place Lafayette, Rouen

1883

Courtauld Institute Galleries, London, UK

PDR 724

Place Lafayette, Rouen pictures the lively commercial activity on the quay of the Rive Droite (right bank of the Seine). Across the river on top of the hill of St. Catherine is the tiny basilica of Notre-Dame-de-Bon-Secours. The scene is enclosed on the right, but the activity on the river and the wagon heading down the quay moves our eyes into the open space on the left.

The palette is mostly primary colors, with blue hills, a small amount of red in the factories, and the yellow quay, broken only by silver reflections in the river and white wisps of smoke from smokestacks and steamships. The blues and mauves of the large shadow complement the golden glow of the paving stones. The brushstrokes are tiny, setting colors close together. This technique exemplifies how advanced Pissarro's experiments with color theory were, and how they foreshadow the Pointillist technique he developed later.

What makes this painting truly remarkable is the juxtaposition of the large blue shadow with the tiny church steeple across the river. The church steeple points upwards, but this shadowy spire points to the river, punctuating the movement of the water, the traffic, and the people.

the river. The city spills over on the Île Lacroix, which also serves as a pier supporting the bridge to Saint-Sever. Moving north away from the quay on the Rive Droite, the streets make a steep climb up the hillside.

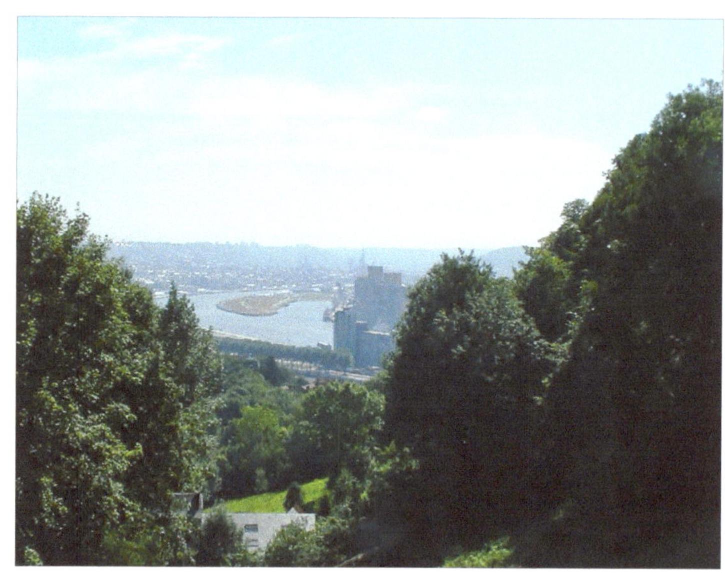

The view of Rouen and the Seine from Canteleu, still a popular place for local artists.

Approaching Rouen from either direction, the road descends in hairpin curves, providing spectacular views of the city and the river spread out below. To the east of the city is the hill of St. Catherine and the nineteenth century Basilica of Notre-Dame - de-Bonsecours with its small steeple. The approach from the other side is from the hilltop village of Canteleu, which offers another spectacular vista. In the small park by the church, artists still gather to sketch or paint, as they have done for centuries.

During his sojourn in Rouen, Pissarro was visited by his Impressionist colleague, Claude Monet, Monet's son Jean and brother Léon, along with the art dealer Paul Durand-Ruel and his son Joseph. Pissarro wrote Lucien, *"The day was beautiful and we went to Canteleu, a village on the outskirts of Deville, on a high hill. We beheld the most wonderful landscape a painter could hope to see. The view of Rouen in the distance with the Seine spread out as calm as glass, sunny slopes, splendid foregrounds, was magical. I will decidedly go to this village to paint next year, it is marvelous."*

Pissarro never painted that magical place, but he did not forget its beauty. Later in 1892, when Pissarro's son Lucien took his wife Esther on a honeymoon trip to Rouen, he offered his son some advice: *"Don't forget to show Esther the splendid view of Rouen from the heights of Canteleu; it is so grand that I still regret not having made a study of it."*

During his first painting campaign in Rouen, Pissarro stayed at the Hôtel du Dauphin et d'Espagne, owned by his friend Eugène Murer and located near the river on the Place de la République facing the Pont Corneille and the Île Lacroix.

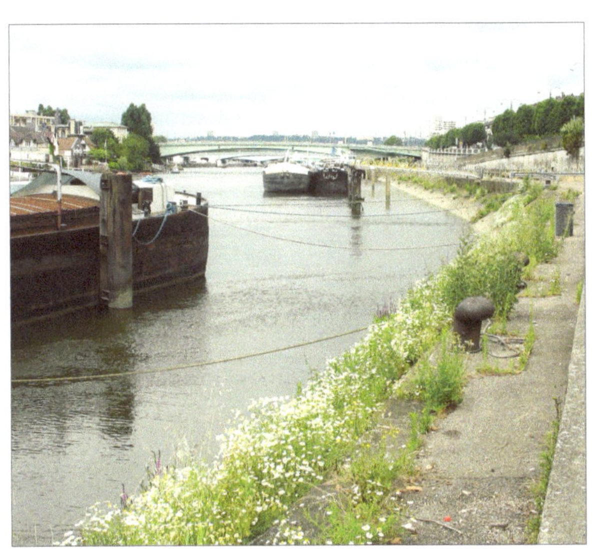

Barges are tied along the Seine just as they were in Pissarro's day.

Pissarro wrote to Lucien, *"I began a motif on the edge of the river (actually the quay de Paris on the right bank) moving up towards the church of Saint-Paul; looking towards Rouen, you have on the right all the houses on the quays lit up by the morning sun, in the background the pont de Pierre [or the pont Corneille], on the left the island (the Île Lacroix) with its houses, factories, boats, rowing-boats, on the right, a cluster of big barges of all colors."*

During that visit, Pissarro made 17 paintings, and only three were done from his hotel window. Most were painted *en plein air.* He carried his easel and paints from his hotel room to the riverside. Apparently people gathered round to watch him paint. In a letter to Pissarro, Gauguin referred to the "crowd packed in front of the painter...."

Pissarro was uncertain of the work he had done there and wrote Lucien, *"I look at them often; I myself, who made them, find them horrible at times. I understand them only at rare moments, long after completing them; when I've forgotten them, on days when I feel kindly disposed and fairly indulgent to the poor artist. At times, I am horribly afraid of turning a canvas round: I'm always frightened I'll find a monster instead of the precious jewel I thought I'd made!"*

Despite Pissarro's misgivings, his art dealer, Durand-Ruel, was very pleased with Pissarro's output and bought seven of the paintings. During this first visit to Rouen, Pissarro had two major advantages. He was only 53 years old and still able to paint *en plein air* in all kinds of weather. As he had done in Pontoise, he shouldered his easel and canvases and walked long distances on both sides of the river to find his favorite motifs. When he returned to Rouen in 1896, he was 66 years old, and carrying a heavy load was more difficult and tiring. Because of his eye inflammation, he had to find hotel windows in strategic locations to avoid the wind and cold weather.

When Pissarro was in Rouen, he made numerous sketches and watercolors of scenes he did not paint at the time. Five years after his first visit, he used a sketch and watercolor to make one of his most important paintings in the Pointillist manner, *The Seine at Rouen, The Île Lacroix, Effect of Fog* [See PDR 855].

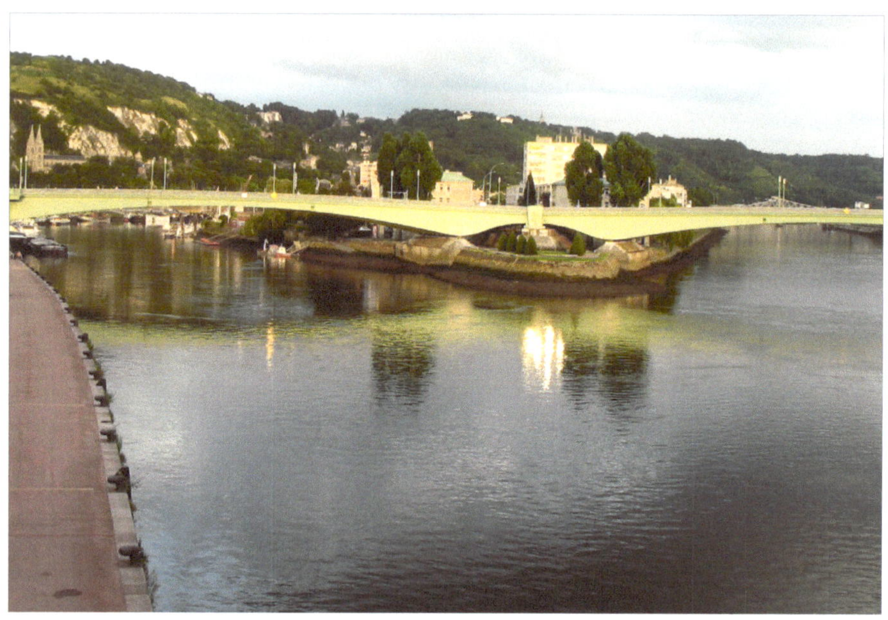

The site of Pissarro's painting of Île Lacroix is the channel on the left side of the island, visible beneath the bridge.

Historic Rouen – A Magnet for Artists

Pissarro was not the only artist who found attractive motifs in Rouen. Indeed, a number of prominent artists worked in Rouen over the centuries, including Turner, Bonington, Corot, Théodore Rousseau, J.S. Cotman, Gauguin, and Monet. In 1883, Pissarro wrote, *"It is strange that Turner chose just this motif. That's the way it is in Rouen, you are always struck by the same places. Yesterday I made a drawing of the rue de la Grosse Horloge. I had scarcely finished it when I saw a lithograph of the same street done in 1829 or 1830 by Bonington."*

The medieval half-timbered houses in the old city only hint at Rouen's long history. People were living in this area of France as long as 9000 years ago. Roman soldiers saw its potential as a port and founded their city here in the first century AD.

In 841, the Vikings attacked Rouen and made it the capital of Normandy. During the centuries that followed, control of the area switched back and forth many times between England and France. It was while the city was under English control on May 30, 1431, that Jeanne d'Arc was tried and burned at the stake in the Vieux-Marché. By the end of the fifteenth century, Rouen was firmly in the hands of the French. In 1843, the railroad came to Rouen, speeding the pace of the Industrial Revolution and the city's economic growth.

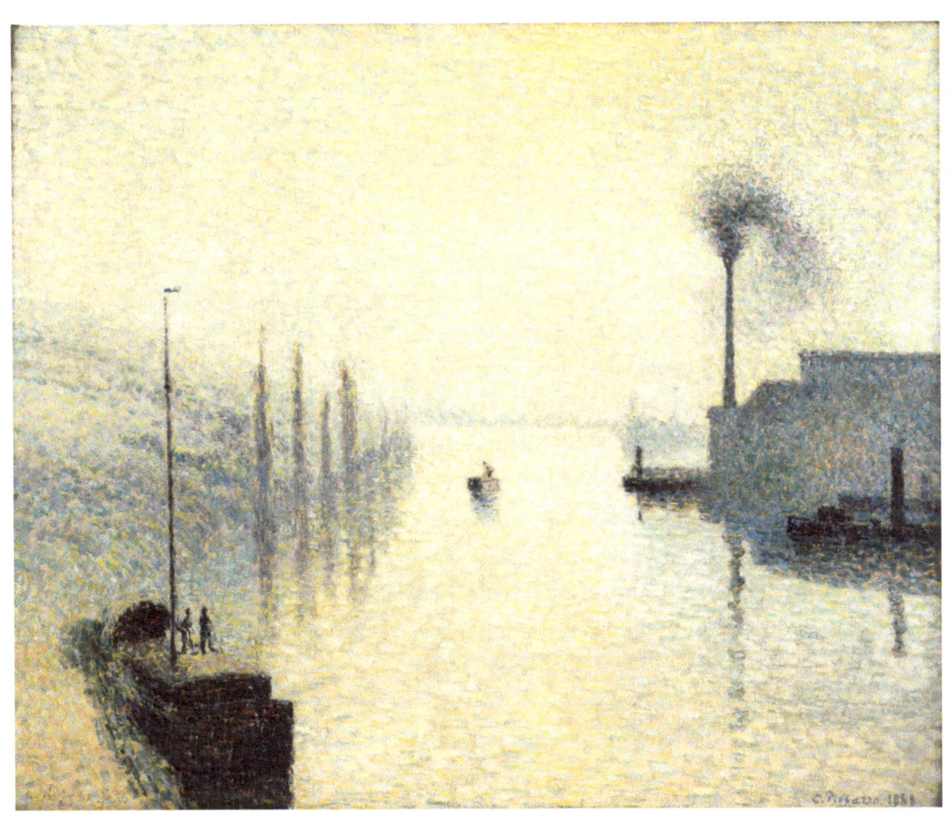

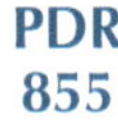

The Seine at Rouen, The Île Lacroix, Effect of Fog

1888
Philadelphia Museum of Art, Philadelphia, PA
PDR 855

During the time Pissarro was working in the Pointillist manner of Seurat and Signac, he made paintings from several sketches and watercolors from his first Rouen campaign. Although he does not totally replicate Seurat's technique of separating small dots, this painting is one of Pissarro's best works in the Pointillist style. Its luminous pearl-like finish masterfully captures the luster in the atmosphere created by the fog.

Pissarro places small patches of paint close together, using contrasting blues and reds to create the shadowy form of the gas-works. The composition perfectly balances the mill with the shore and a barge on the left. The vacant foreground is reflected in the bare sky, and they merge almost seamlessly on the empty horizon. On both sides, there are verticals reaching into the sky, and for each one a reflection down into the water.

A few years later, Pissarro admitted that he had grown impatient with the Pointillist technique. He wrote Lucien in 1891, *"It's no longer the dot, which I've entirely abandoned, returning instead to the division of pure colors, without waiting for the paint to dry, which had the drawback of cooling the sensations. I'm much happier that way, and I can assure you that the colors are every bit as delicate, and freer in sensation, more personal."*

However, what he discovered about color during this period would illuminate his painting for the rest of his career.

Pissarro could never have envisioned the widespread devastation that occurred just a few decades after his visits when the bombs of World War II destroyed most of Rouen, along with the important industrial center across the river at Saint-Sever.

Thankfully, the cathedral and many ancient buildings escaped total demolition, and were ultimately restored. Over time, the tangle of railroad tracks and the factory smokestacks of the old Saint-Sever that Pissarro painted were replaced by gigantic, boxlike glass and concrete buildings. Also gone from Rouen's riverfront are the working docks. These have now been relocated upriver, leaving the riverside quays to walkers and cyclists.

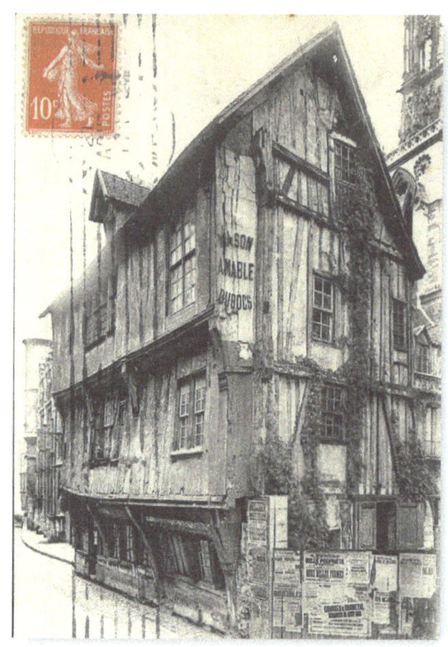

Pissarro supported local conservationists in saving the Old House on rue de Romain.

Pissarro in Rouen – January to March 1896

Except for a short visit in 1895 to plan his next painting campaign, Pissarro did not return to Rouen for 13 years. But in January 1896, he returned to the city ready to work. At that time, he was financially strapped, and there was not enough money for lodging in Rouen's better hotels. So Pissarro stayed at the Hôtel de Paris on the Quay de Paris, where he paid only five francs a day for a room on the second floor and another on the third to use as a studio. Though he thought the view was beautiful, he was cold. The rooms were *"so draughty, the wind blows from all sides and we heat ourselves with large open fireplaces and wood for fuel…Oh well, one makes do with what one has."*

On his arrival in Rouen, Pissarro was introduced to François Depeaux, a well-known industrialist who collected the modern art of the Impressionists. Depeaux had purchased an earlier Pissarro painting from Durand-Ruel in 1892. Knowing that Pissarro was painting the docks and quays, Depeaux offered to build a cabin for Pissarro in the dockyards to use as a studio. Pissarro admits to some stubbornness on his part in refusing the offer: *"I am too crotchety to accept, I am too afraid of colds. If this were summer it would be perfect.... But I am not thirty years old now, I have to be satisfied with a hotel window."*

There were now many more steamboats on the Seine than there had been on Pissarro's first visit. The quays were lined with steam-driven cranes. In his paintings, he captured the frenzied commercial activity of the place on canvas, mixing the smoke from the steamboats and cranes with that of the factories and blending their colors into the clouds.

Everything in Pissarro's paintings is in motion—the people, the boats, the smoke from the steamboats and factories, the wagons and horses, the cranes unloading the ships, boats chugging their way upriver, the clouds in the ever-changing sky, and the river itself flowing to its estuary at Le Havre. The ripples on the water show that even the wind is moving, and the movement of the sun is visible in the river's reflections.

Since Pissarro's previous visit, a new bridge had been built upriver from the Pont Corneille, which he had painted during his first visit. The new Pont Boieldieu had been opened in 1888 to take the place of an old suspension bridge. The modern new bridge captured Pissarro's imagination: *"...the one I'm most interested in is a motif of an iron bridge in rainy weather with a great commotion of carriages, strollers, stevedores, boats, smoke, haze in the distance, full of life and movement."*

Turning his gaze from the river to the city behind him, Pissarro found another unique motif, and his excitement is almost palpable: *"I shall stay here until the end of March, for I found a really uncommon motif in a room of the hotel facing north, ice-cold and without a fireplace. Just conceive for yourself: the whole of old Rouen seen from above the roofs, with the Cathédrale Notre-Dame, St. Ouen's church, and the fantastic roofs, really amazing turrets. Can you picture a canvas about 36 x 28 inches in size, filled with old, grey, worm-eaten roofs? It is extraordinary!"* The painting that Pissarro made from this view is generally considered to be one of his masterpieces [See PDR 1114].

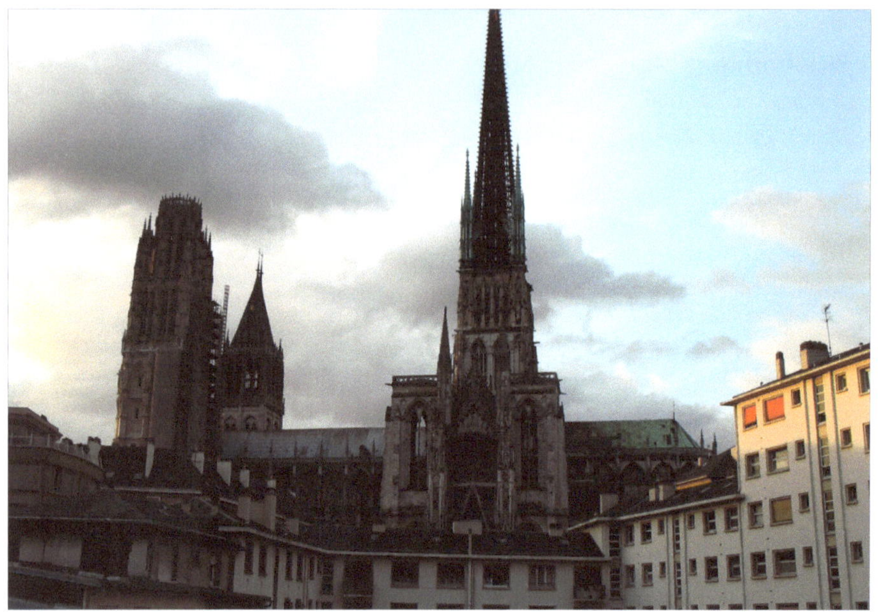

A current view of the cathédrale similar to Pissarro's painting. All of the old houses were destroyed in World War II and replaced with modern buildings.

Pissarro had agreed to sell the *Roofs of Old Rouen* to Depeaux, but the deal fell through. According to Pissarro, *"Well, then Depeaux doesn't care for the sky! I think I shall keep the picture for us."*

What Depeaux objected to is unclear. Might he have asked Pissarro to change the gray winter clouds to a brighter sky? To do that, Pissarro would have to change all the colors of the painting. The blue slate roofs would fade, the red tiles would look garish, and shadows would be falling from every turret and gable. Pissarro knew he had it right. He kept it for the rest of his life, and his wife Julie inherited it at his death.

During this painting campaign, Pissarro was under pressure to produce new canvases for his upcoming exhibition in April at the Durand-Ruel gallery in Paris. He met his deadline, completing 15 paintings. Of those, Durand-Ruel bought ten.

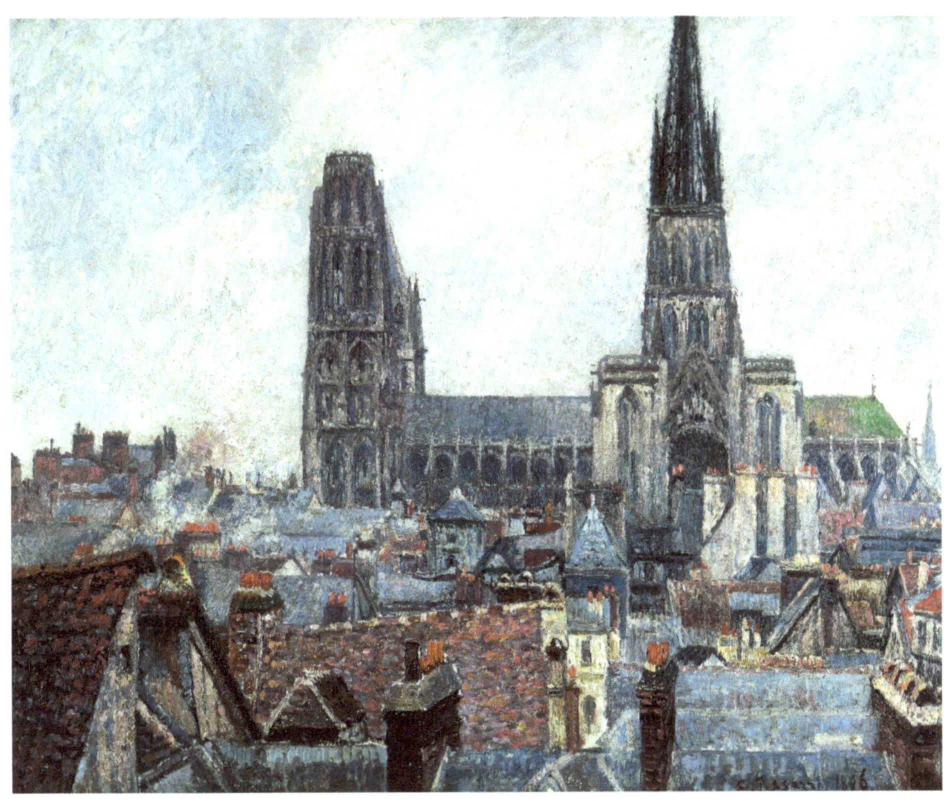

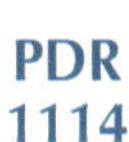

The Roofs of Old Rouen, Cathédrale Notre-Dame, Overcast Sky

1896

Toledo Museum of Art, Toledo, OH

PDR 1114

This painting presents a real challenge to our eyes, offering them no place to rest. Looking out the hotel window with Pissarro, we see slate blue roofs topped with red chimney pots in the immediate foreground. Beyond is a sea of red-tiled roofs punctuated by turrets and chimneys. Rising above the clutter of roofs is the Cathédrale Notre-Dame de Rouen, the Butter Tower to the left, and the great iron steeple piercing the top of the canvas. Beyond that to the right is Saint-Ouen's Church, its reddish-blue roof carving a different angle in the sky. Above is a cloudy winter sky, variegated with misty mauves and off-whites.

Some artists paint cathedrals as watchful guardians over the city. But this cathedral clearly is not the most important element in the painting. Only an upper slice is visible: the top of the steel tower is cut off and the lower level is hidden by the multitude of roofs and turrets. Unlike most of Pissarro's cityscapes, there are no people visible, but smoke coming out of the chimneys confirms their presence. The roofs themselves are alive with reds, rosy pinks, and mauves. The foreground is a jumble of different geometric shapes: triangular gables, square turrets, slim chimneys, and rectangular roofs that predict how Cubist paintings of the future will look.

Pissarro in Rouen – September to November 1896

In the fall of that same year, Pissarro returned to Rouen and stayed at the Hôtel d'Angleterre, with better accommodations than in his previous visit. From his window, he could see all three bridges crossing the Seine and on the opposite bank, the Saint-Sever district with its new train station, the Gare d'Orléans.

Pissarro was clearly concerned that historical buildings in Rouen were being destroyed. Although he painted what was modern in Rouen, he made numerous sketches and drawings of old Rouen.

In 1896, he wrote Lucien, *"I had zinc plates sent with [a] layer of powdered limestone to make lithos of Rouen, I began several sketches of old streets that are being demolished.... If you see the rue Saint-Romain, it's wonderful, I hope that it will have a certain interest."*

Although he was only a visitor to the city, Pissarro sent a donation to the Société des Amis des Monuments Rouennais, along with a letter of support. *"Dear Sir, I have received your kind and friendly letter in which you announce the decision...concerning the old and picturesque rue Saint-Romain, which, it seems, disturbs their love of the banal. You ask if you have my support in your protest against this appalling vandalism. Dear Sir, I join my poor and vain protestation to yours, certain that we will be shouting into the void! Poor Rouen, this admirable and venerable old city, it is being defaced from day to day to the great joy of the municipalities!! If my feeble voice can do anything to prevent this desecration, I shall join it to yours!!"*

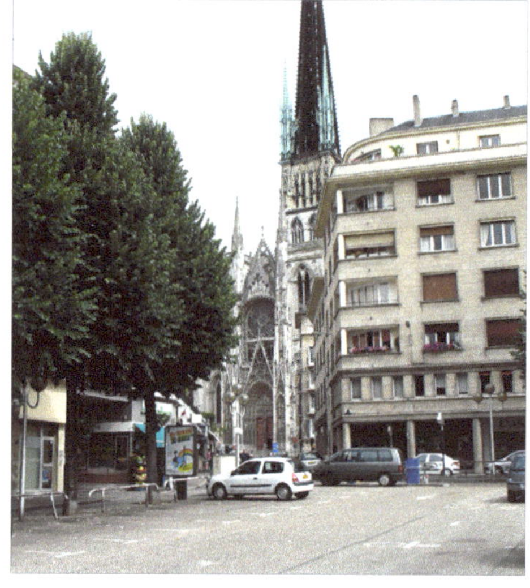

Current photograph of rue de l'Epicerie. Modern buildings now surround the cathédrale.

Pissarro in Rouen – July to October 1898

In 1898, Pissarro returned for his last painting excursion and took rooms at the Hôtel d'Angleterre. During this visit, he painted 19 canvases. In a letter to Lucien, Pissarro said, *"Yesterday I discovered an excellent place, where I hope to paint the rue de l'Épicerie and even the market, a really interesting one, which is held there every Friday. Unfortunately there was thunder and rain today."*

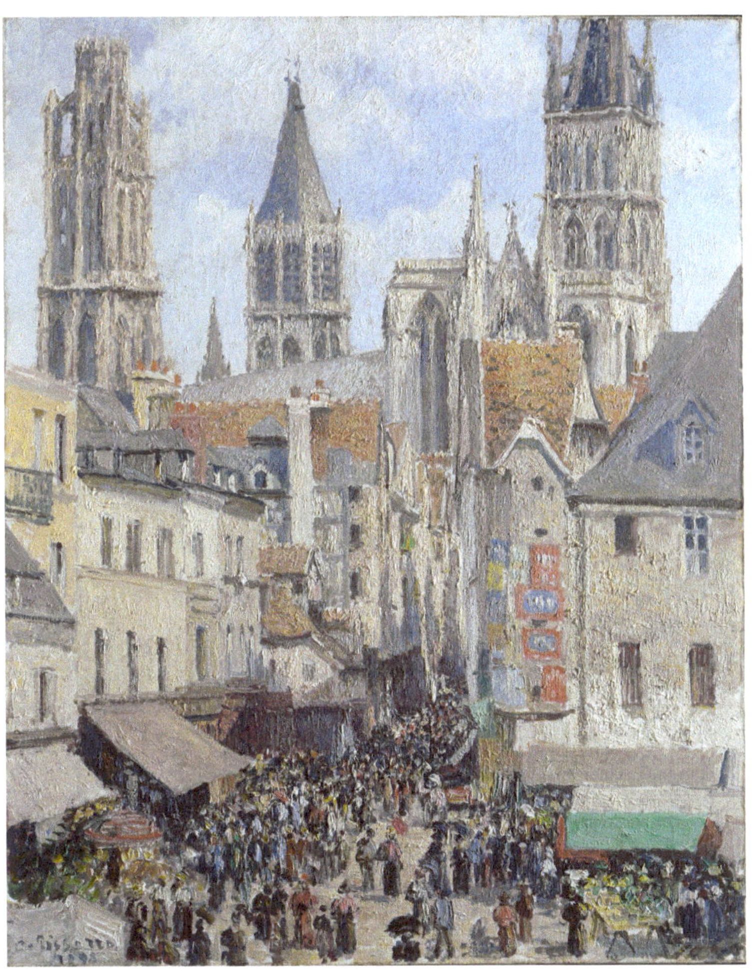

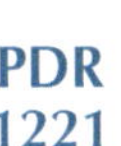

Rue de l'Épicerie in Rouen, Effect of Sunlight

1898

Metropolitan Museum, New York, NY

PDR 1221

Pissarro made three paintings of the rue de l'Épicerie, all of which look directly down the street to the cathedral façade. This one, depicting a bustling market scene, was probably painted on Friday, market day.

The rue de l'Épicerie, which ends at the south side of the Cathédrale Notre-Dame, is one of Rouen's oldest streets. When Pissarro painted it, it was lined on each side by sixteenth-century gabled houses. A market had been held continuously in that place since the thirteenth century. During World War II, the historic buildings on the street were destroyed. During the rebuilding process, the old marketplace became a public parking area. But even now, it is possible to experience the general contour of the motif that Pissarro painted.

Pissarro made three paintings of the rue de l'Épicerie. He chose a bright, sunny day to make his market painting, *Rue de l'Épicerie in Rouen, Effect of Sunlight.* He painted one canvas on a rainy morning, and another one in late afternoon, where he demonstrates his virtuosity in dealing with the deep shadows cast by the setting sun. Seeing all three of them together (or even reproductions) reveals Pissarro's expertise at capturing light in different weather conditions.

In his visits to Rouen, Pissarro focused on the new and modern, the bustling urban center that was the heartbeat of Rouen. As he fondly described it, *"just conceive the new section of Saint Sauveur [Saint-Sever] right opposite my window, with the Gare d'Orléans always new and shining, and a mass of chimneys from the gigantic to the diminutive with all their smoke. In the foreground, boats on the water, to the left of the station, the workers' quarters which extend along the quays up to the iron bridge, the bridge Boieldieu, you should see all this in the morning when the light is misty and delicate.... It is as beautiful as Venice...."*

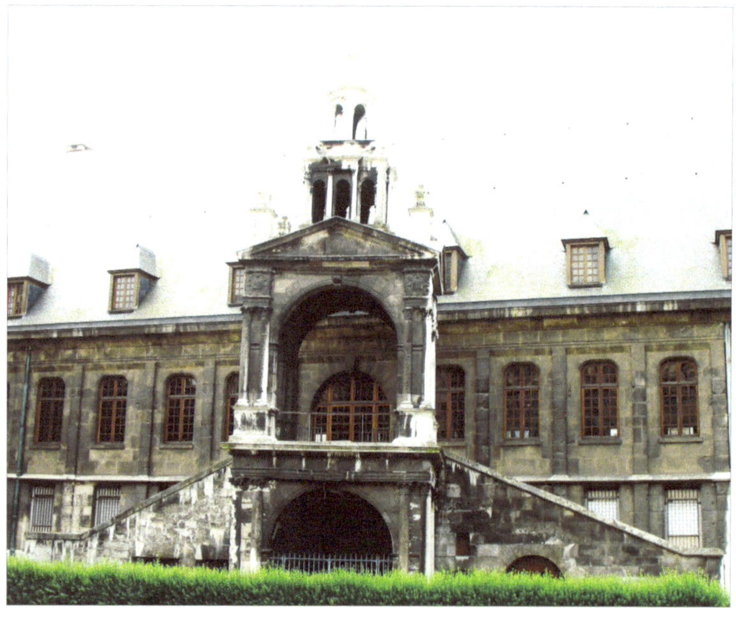

While painting rue de l'Épicerie, Pissarro may have stood here, at the Chapelle de la Fierte de St. Romain, a small elevated chapel built in 1542. According to legend, St. Romain saved Rouen from a monster with the help of a criminal. Beginning in 1210 on Ascension Day, the Cathedral was allowed to release a prisoner who then carried the saint's relics up to the chapel and raised them three times before the crowd of people. The practice ended in 1790 during the Revolution. The historic chapel remained safe during World War II bombings though the building behind it was damaged heavily.

Belgium

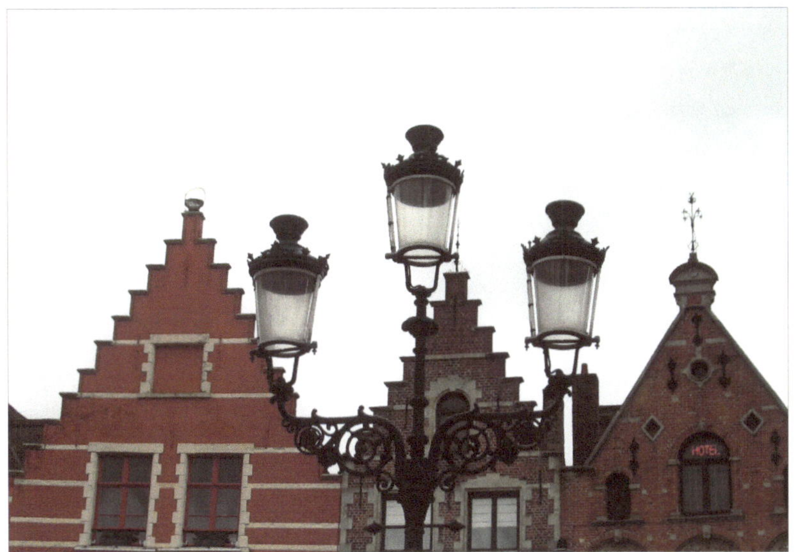

Picturesque Bruges

Family Trip to Belgium

There were many reasons for Pissarro to go to Belgium in 1894. About ten years earlier during his experimentation with Pointillism, Pissarro met an artist from Belgium, Théo van Rysselberghe, and the two became friends. In 1887, van Rysselberghe invited Pissarro and his Neo-Impressionist colleagues to exhibit their Pointillist paintings in Brussels with Les Vingt, a group of Belgian artists. Pissarro did not attend the exhibition, but was told that his works were well-received. Although Pissarro abandoned the Pointillist technique after a few years, he remained friendly with van Rysselberghe.

In the spring of 1894, van Rysselberghe and his wife invited Pissarro to visit them in Belgium. The trip offered multiple benefits. He and Julie could visit their friends and see Brussels for the first time. They could also find a suitable home for their son Félix, whose rambunctious nature could no longer be contained in the small village of Éragny. Now a twenty-year-old artist, he could pursue his artistic endeavors in Brussels under van Rysselberghe's watchful eye.

But most important, Pissarro had heard that Belgium offered some interesting motifs: *"I talked with Lecomte [Georges Lecomte, journalist and art critic] who told me that Bruges, an extraordinary city near Brussels, would be a gold mine for landscapists because it is an old town which has remained unspoiled by any modernism, and above all it is gray and sad,"* Pissarro wrote his son Georges.

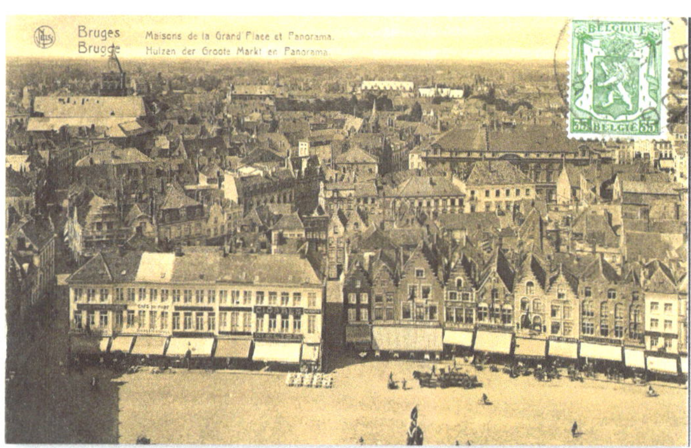

Panorama of the Grand Place in Bruges

Pissarro, Julie, and Félix took the train from Paris to Brussels, and he later wrote Lucien that *"while on the train, we saw some dazzling motifs."* After a week in Brussels with van Rysselberghe, the group traveled to Ghent, Knokke, and Bruges. Though he concentrated on watercolors in the few days he spent in Bruges, he painted a canvas, *Le Pont de la Clef à Bruges, Belgique,* which carries two dates: 1894 and 1903. It was probably composed in Belgium as an oil sketch and reworked nine years later in Pissarro's studio in Éragny, so it is a combination of his immediate sensation on site and the memory of his impressions [See PDR 1034].

The Old City of Bruges

It would have been hard for Pissarro to escape the old and antique in Bruges. When this historical city was still a Gallo-Roman outpost, it enjoyed access to the North Sea. In the ninth century, the port was fortified to protect against the raids of Vikings. Coins and documents confirm its importance as a center of trade. A severe flood in 1134 reshaped the coastline and cut off Bruges' ocean access. The city's commercial growth was renewed when a canal was built from Bruges to a neighboring town that had a deep channel to the ocean.

In the twelfth century, Bruges was a major center of the wool weaving industry. By the fourteenth century, it was part of the Hanseatic League, a powerful group of European trading cities. The lively international trade required complex negotiations, and Bruges developed into a sophisticated financial market.

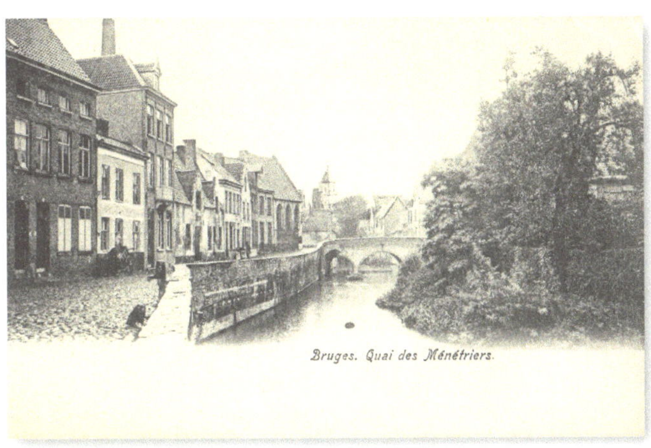

This postcard shows the exact location of Pissarro's painting in Bruges.

The wealth continued into the fifteenth century with the construction of many impressive late-Gothic buildings and churches. The city attracted important artists such as Jan van Eyck and Hans Memling. Pissarro was well aware of the art legacy there and wrote, *"I will avail myself of this opportunity, so long awaited, to see the beautiful collections of the Flemish school."*

The glory years of Bruges ended when silting of the channel finally cut off the link with the sea forever. The city slept in poverty and neglect until the early nineteenth century, when its treasure trove of medieval buildings was rediscovered.

In 1892, just two years before Pissarro visited Bruges, a Belgian writer wrote a gloomy novel set in Bruges that described its well-preserved antiquities. Perhaps Pissarro read the book and that may be why he described Bruges as "gray and sad." But there is no sadness in his sun-drenched painting of the bridge and the canal.

Unexpected Exile

Pissarro never intended to stay in Belgium for nearly four months, but that's what happened. The day before Pissarro and his family traveled to Belgium, June 24, 1894, the President of France, Sadi Carnot, was assassinated by an Italian anarchist. Police ordered house searches of people thought to be anarchists, and many people were arrested, even those who were friends of anarchists. The French National Assembly immediately adopted new laws to suppress freedom of the press and to arrest anyone who expressed opinions that opposed the government. Pissarro was afraid that he would be arrested if he returned to France during this unsettled period.

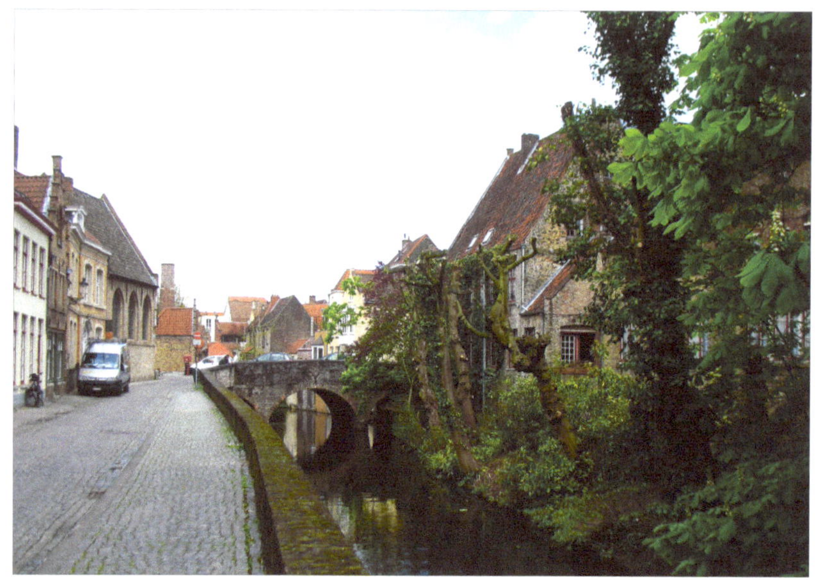

The site of Pissarro's painting is much the same as when he was there.

Pissarro had always proclaimed himself to be an anarchist and throughout his life he read the works of important philosophers who articulated those principles, including Pierre-Joseph Proudhon, Peter Kropotkin, and Élisée Reclus. As a movement, anarchism had gained popularity in the late nineteenth century. In France, where frequent revolutions seemed inevitable, many people believed that the next one would result in a better way of life ensuring freedom and equality for all.

Richard Brettell, renowned Impressionist scholar, provides the best explanation of Pissarro's involvement in anarchy: "He had been attracted to anarchist ideas and writings in his early life, and his earliest close friend in France, Ludovic Piette, was involved in left-wing and even radical French politics by the late 1850s.... Throughout his life, Pissarro was an idealist who actually believed that society could—and would—be completely transformed, and that such a transformation would come as the result of cooperative action following a large-scale revolution."

Because he subscribed to the anarchist newspapers, "Le Père Peinard" and "La Révolte," and supported them financially, Pissarro was considered by authorities to be an anarchist. He had a police record, which noted that "Pissarro, in Éragny (Oise) is the well-known Impressionist painter. His political opinions are not known

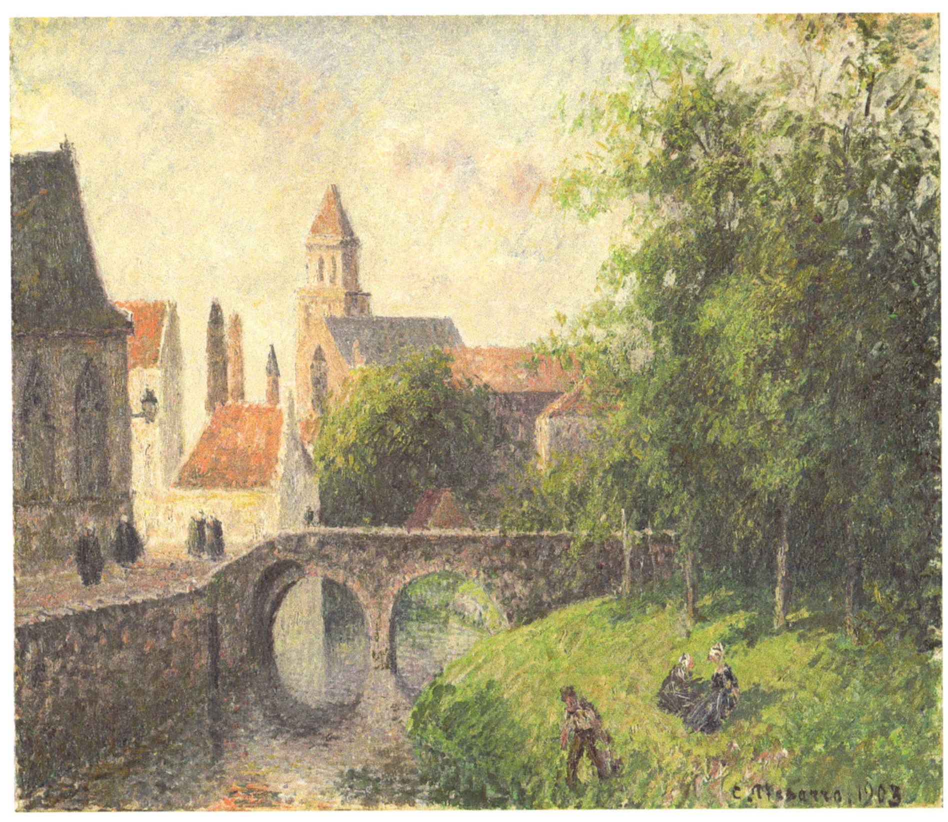

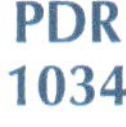

Pont de la Clef in Bruges, Belgium

1894, 1903

City Art Galleries, Manchester, UK

PDR 1034

This painting of an ancient bridge in Bruges was probably made from an upstairs window. The top of the arched bridge forms a horizontal line that intersects with the perpendicular church steeple, identifying the focal point of the painting.

The right side of the canvas is dominated by the luminous green trees that stretch to the top and leave no room for the cloudy blue sky. The sun bathes the grass below and casts short shadows under the trees.

The rest of the painting is dominated by warm colors of light red, pink, and mauve, complementing the green. The graceful arches of the bridge are reflected in the still surface of the river, creating a sense of tranquility.

On the left is a tall chapel with Gothic windows, distinguished by a large lantern and dark figures hurrying along the shadowy road. Their dark robes and white caps suggest that they may be Benedictine nuns, who are still frequently seen on the streets of Bruges.

in Gisors (a larger town near Éragny) and the region." Pissarro had been careful not to share his political opinions with his neighbors.

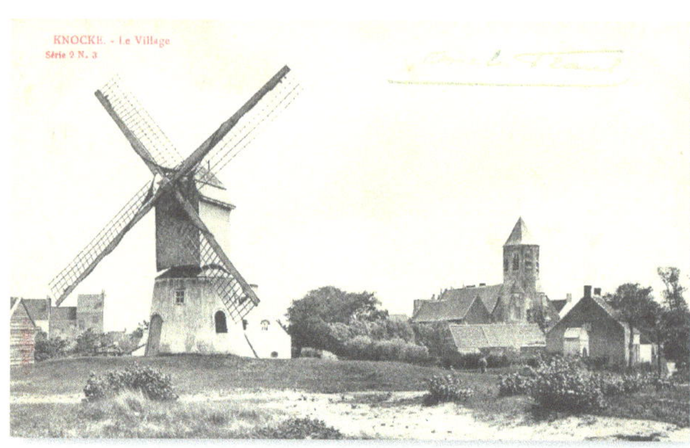

This postcard shows the old mill and church just as Pissarro painted them. The old mill is now in another location and is being preserved.

For many years, Pissarro had suspected that he was under surveillance. As early as 1883, Pissarro wrote Lucien that his most recent letter was a long time in delivery. *"Unquestionably it was opened by the postal authorities, for the envelope is smudged. One has only to read such or such a newspaper to be suspected and put on the index. I would not be surprised if something like that were responsible for the lateness of your letter."*

In the midst of the tumultuous events that followed the president's assassination, Pissarro was fearful of returning to France. Because he was born in the Danish colony of St. Thomas, Pissarro was never a French citizen. He may have feared that if authorities believed he was connected to the anarchists, that he might be expelled from France. And he distrusted certain people in Éragny who held grudges against his family.

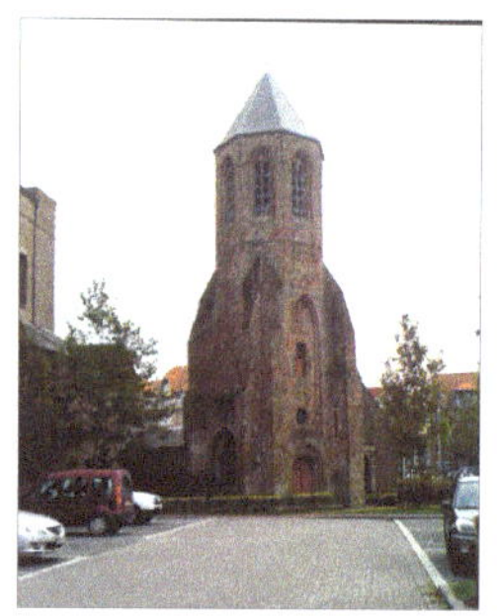
The small tower from the old church, which is seen in Pissarro's painting, has been preserved.

He wrote to Lucien, *"I rather fear I shall have to remain abroad for awhile."* Julie went back to Éragny, but Pissarro stayed in Belgium until October.

Knokke by the Sea

Most of Pissarro's time in Belgium was spent in the seaside resort of Knokke-sur-Mer on the North Sea. Today, Knokke is a luxurious resort that closely resembles Fort Lauderdale (Florida), with high-rise condominiums lining its wide beach. It is interesting to note that one of Pissarro's Knokke paintings, *Le Jardin du Presbytere a Knokke*, is in the collection of the Norton Museum of Art at West Palm Beach, Florida, just north of Fort Lauderdale. It pictures a garden, however, not the sand dunes along the ocean.

When Pissarro was there, Knokke was a small town surrounded by sand dunes and farm land. Wealthy people from Brussels and other parts of Europe went there on holiday. Pissarro's friend, van Rysselberghe, had a vacation home there. This made Knokke a friendly

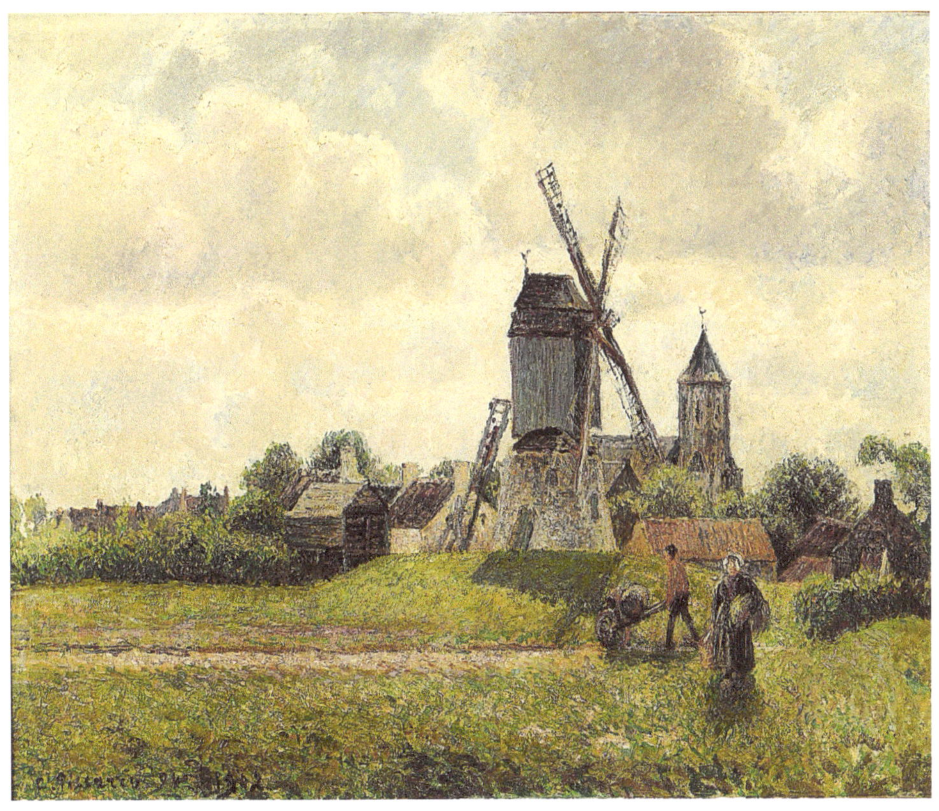

PDR 1038

The Vieux-Moulin, Knokke

1894, 1902
Tel Aviv Museum of Art, Tel Aviv, Israel
PDR 1038

Pissarro made thirteen paintings at Knokke. This painting, *The Vieux-Moulin in Knokke,* depicts what was at that time the heart of the seaside town. Although a cluster of houses stand near the church, the large gardens and farmland confirm the rural nature of the setting.

The old mill is indisputably the focal point of the painting, its four sails making a huge X, as the ancient tower of Marguerite Church stands sentinel in the background. The summer vegetation is green on the sandy soil and clouds thicken over the blue sky as local people go about their daily tasks.

This painting, like the one made in Bruges, also carries two dates: 1894, when it was originally painted, and 1903, when it was reworked in Pissarro's studio.

setting for Pissarro and his son Félix. They stayed in a new hotel recently built to accommodate the growing tourist business. The anarchist Élisée Reclus lived in Knokke, and Pissarro spent time discussing philosophical ideals with him and van Rysselberghe.

One of the paintings he made in Knokke depicts a very old windmill, the Vieux-Moulin, in the center of town right beside the church. A cluster of houses surround the church, but gardens and fields dominate Pissarro's canvas [See PDR 1038].

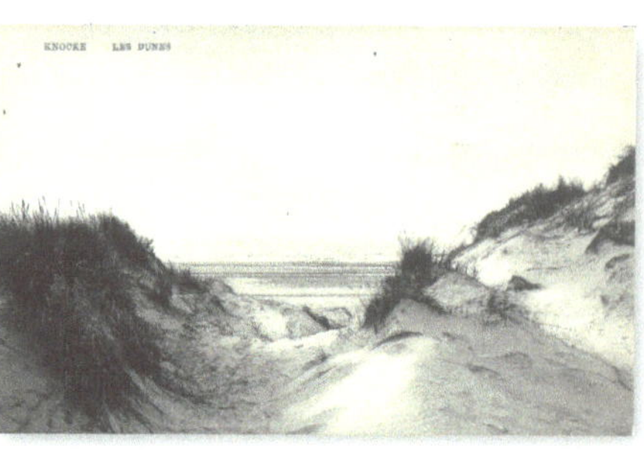

Pissarro made several paintings of the sand dunes.

Arriving at the train station at Knokke, we see the site of that painting across the intersection. The church tower, reportedly constructed in the fourteenth century, is still there, but the small chapel has been replaced by an enormous church with a very tall belfry. The old mill was removed in 1932 to a nearby location where it is still being preserved.

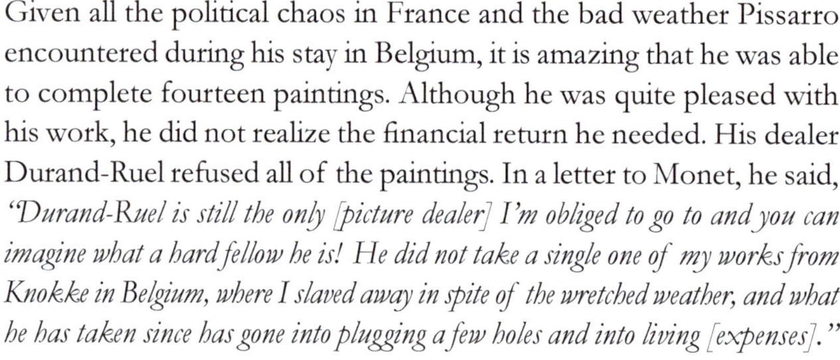

Given all the political chaos in France and the bad weather Pissarro encountered during his stay in Belgium, it is amazing that he was able to complete fourteen paintings. Although he was quite pleased with his work, he did not realize the financial return he needed. His dealer Durand-Ruel refused all of the paintings. In a letter to Monet, he said, *"Durand-Ruel is still the only [picture dealer] I'm obliged to go to and you can imagine what a hard fellow he is! He did not take a single one of my works from Knokke in Belgium, where I slaved away in spite of the wretched weather, and what he has taken since has gone into plugging a few holes and into living [expenses]."*

Though Pissarro determinedly shielded his paintings from any overt political implications, the reactionary environment in France continued to have a profound impact on his personal life and his philosophical beliefs.

Dieppe

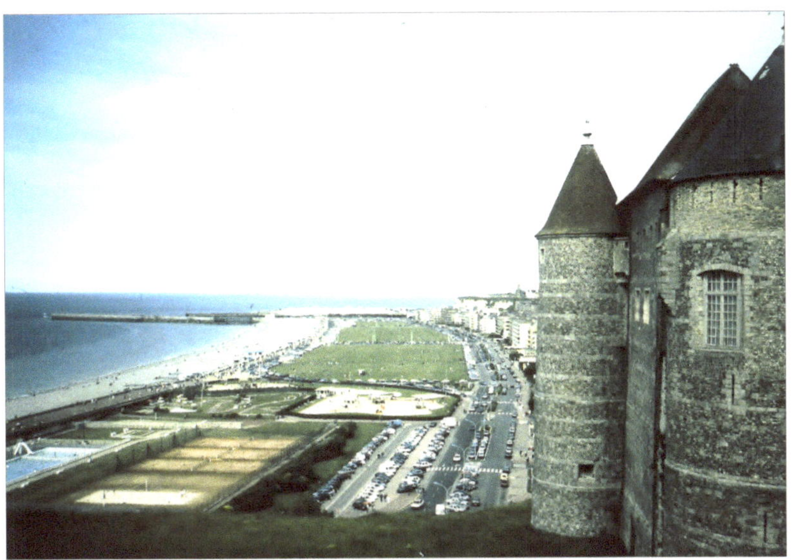

The Château de Dieppe, destroyed in the 12th century and rebuilt in the 14th century, sits atop massive white cliffs that face the ocean.

Dieppe by the Sea

The Dieppe cityscape is dominated by a wide beach, bookended by towering white cliffs and crowned by a medieval castle. But Pissarro painted neither the beach nor the castle. Perhaps he was reluctant to deal with the wind and sand of the beach because of the continuous problem of inflammation in his eye.

Any generalizations about Pissarro's œuvre, however, are dangerous because they are often disproved by fact. During a weekend visit with Monet's brother Léon in November 1883, he painted the ocean and cliffs at Les Petites-Dalles, a seaside resort west of Dieppe, despite the driving rain.

Dieppe – First Visit 1901

In the summer of 1901, Pissarro traveled to Dieppe for his first painting excursion. He stayed at the Hôtel du Commerce on the Place Duquesne (now the Place Nationale). From one of the higher floors, Pissarro looked down on the rue de la Boucherie and the Place Duquesne where the town fair was underway. At one point, he complained that the fair's carousel and street organs *"playing Gounod at top speed"* were keeping him awake at night.

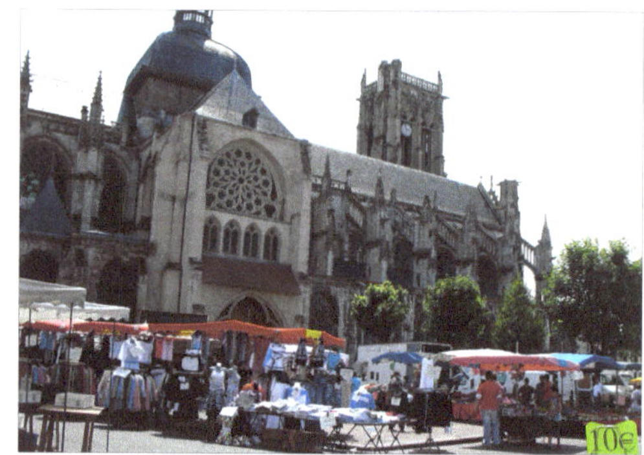

The Church of Saint-Jacques, originally built in 1168, burned and was rebuilt in the 1400s in Renaissance style. The lively Saturday market fills the streets around the church.

All the noise and bustle did not keep him from capturing the sun, shadows, and bright colors of the complex cityscape. In fact, despite the festive distractions, Pissarro managed to paint nine canvases during this time, and his art dealer Durand-Ruel bought three of them.

Dieppe – Past and Present

As it was during Pissarro's visits, the ancient Church of Saint-Jacques is still the center of community activity in Dieppe. Every Saturday, brightly colored stalls fill the church square, where merchants sell everything from lace curtains to dolls to jeans to candy. Flower stalls turn the market into a colorful garden. Butchers carve large chunks of meat while bakers lay out freshly baked loaves and friends and customers visit. Even though the market is held every week, there is an air of holiday.

Located on the English Channel just across from Newhaven (UK), Dieppe was first settled in 907 AD by the Vikings, who gave it the name "djupa" (deep) because of the natural harbors at the mouth of the Arques River. In 1195, Dieppe, then part of feudal Normandy, was attacked and destroyed by the King of France, Philippe Auguste. Walls were constructed around the city in the fourteenth century; the town gate, "Les Tourelles," made of sandstone and flint, is all that remains of the fortifications. The city was burned to the ground in 1694 by an Anglo-Dutch fleet, and only a few of the ancient half-timbered buildings were left standing. The church of Saint-Jacques, with its flying buttresses and gargoyles, constructed between the twelfth and sixteenth centuries, survived the onslaught and still marks the city's center today.

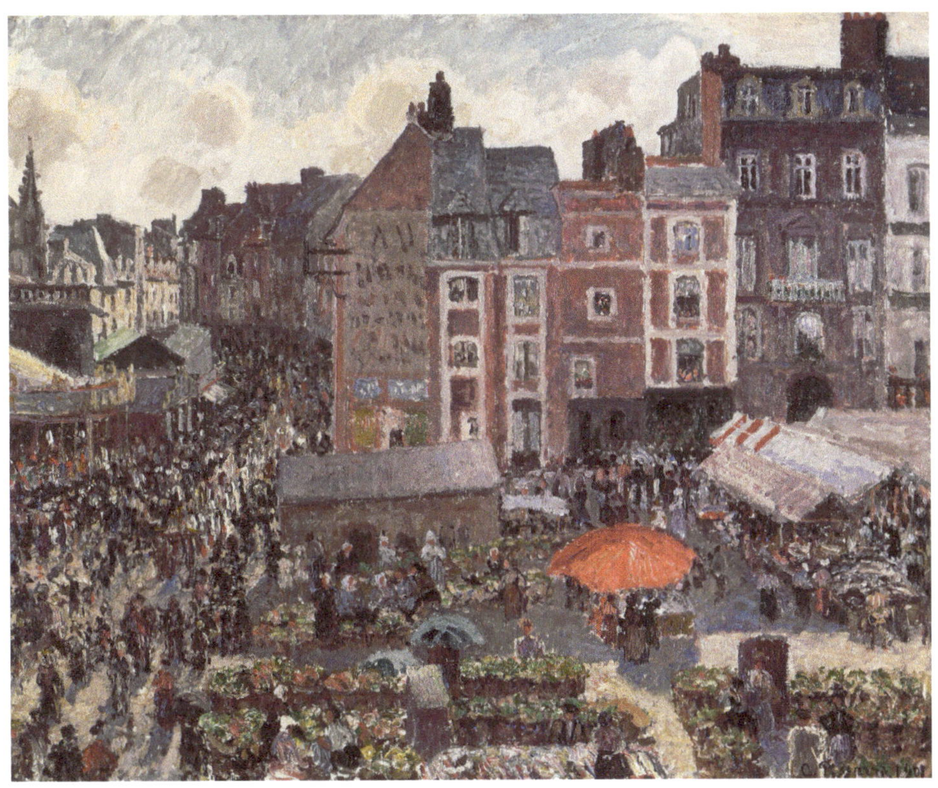

The Town Fair by the Church of Saint-Jacques, Dieppe, Effect of Sunlight, Afternoon

1901

Philadelphia Museum of Art, Philadelphia, PA

PDR 1388

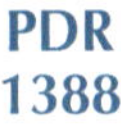

This scene of Dieppe is packed full of people and activity, leaving very little room for the blue sky and puffy clouds. The painting is a juxtaposition of curves and angles. On the left, we see the street reaching into the middle distance before it is ultimately blocked by tall buildings. Its curve mirrors the circular shape of the carousel, which conceals the sharp corner of the Church of Saint-Jacques. Behind the stream of people are towering buildings, their chimney pots touching the canvas edge.

Shades of red fill the picture—brick red on nearby buildings, darker red of distant buildings, and small patches of red on the produce tables. In the right foreground, Pissarro places a bright red umbrella, which punctuates the jumble of images and mimics the circular forms on the left. Although other reds in the painting are muted, the red on the umbrella is clear and bright. The umbrella is set halfway in the sun and halfway in the shadow, depicted by a slightly darker red edging the top of the umbrella's curve. Pissarro uses it to emphasize the contrast between the bright sunlight in the foreground with the gray-blue shadow from the surrounding buildings in the middle ground.

Dieppe's reputation as a holiday destination began in 1824. The Duchesse de Berry, then in her 20s, went to Dieppe with her court to bathe in the ocean for "therapeutic purposes." By the 1880s, Dieppe's pebble-covered beach was covered with tourists in nineteenth century striped swimsuits.

More recently, Dieppe was the site of heroic World War II battles as Canadian forces stormed the beaches hoping to liberate France from German occupation during World War II. The unsuccessful attempt cost hundreds of Canadian lives, and even today the people of Dieppe remember the courage of those valiant soldiers.

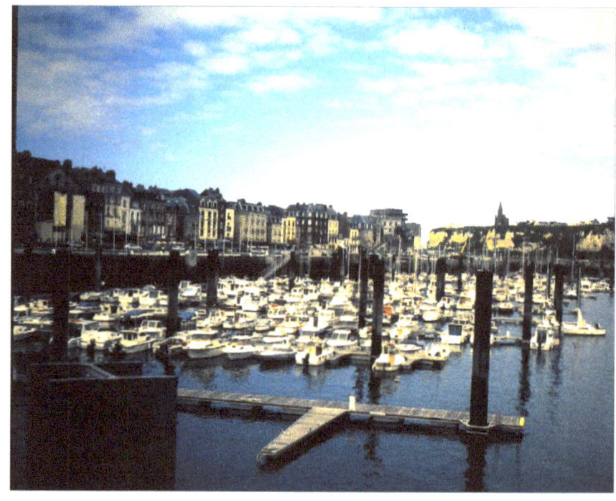

The outer harbor, once the dock for international shipping, is now the home of Dieppe's pleasure craft.

Dieppe – Second Visit 1902

In a letter he wrote to a collector the next year, Pissarro explained, *"Dieppe is a wonderful place for a painter who enjoys life, movement, color. I have some friends there and I know the motifs I would like to do. In spite of the dense crowds, I have decided to go back there again this year."*

Even though he stayed at the Hôtel du Commerce by the church of Saint-Jacques, Pissarro rented a separate room on the quay Duquesne to use as a studio. From his upper-story window, he had an excellent view of fish markets and outer ports to the left and the basin Duquesne to the right. In the early morning, Pissarro could watch the activity at the fish market when restaurant owners and housewives came to examine the fresh catch.

During this sojourn, Pissarro painted several views of the outer harbor, its blue water bordered by the sparkling white cliffs. The view has changed little since then. Pissarro presented one of these paintings to the mayor of Dieppe to be placed in the town's museum, where it can be seen today. [See PDR 1448]

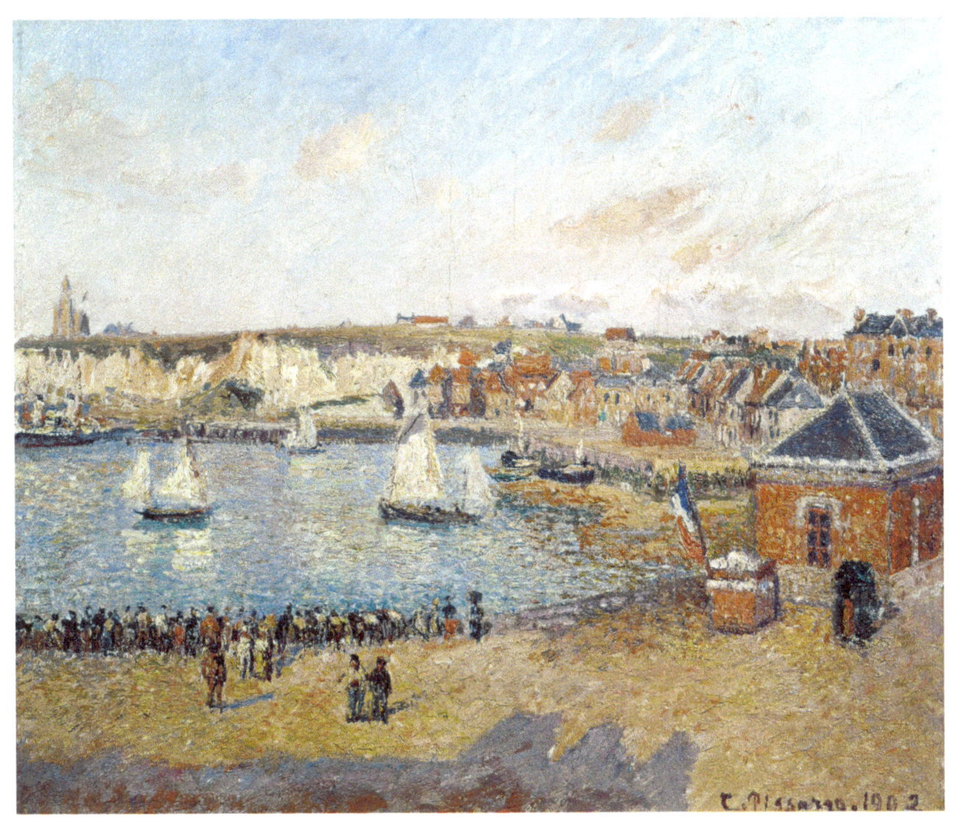

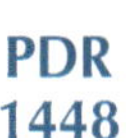

The Outer Harbour at Dieppe, Afternoon, Sunlight

1902

Château-Musée de Dieppe, Dieppe, France

PDR 1448

From his window on the quay Duquesne, Pissarro saw the outer harbor lined with people and filled with various types of boats. In the bright sunshine, the water is deep blue and reflections play on its rippling surface. The sailboats in the middle are taking advantage of the summer breezes.

Across the harbor is a modern steamship with two large smokestacks. Beside the fishermen's village of Le Pollet, the massive white cliffs continue their march to the sea. Atop the cliffs on the left is the tiny Chapelle Notre-Dame de Bonsecours marking the entrance to the harbor. The view is anchored at the lower edge by deep purple shadows in the foreground, which signify the sinking sun.

Near the small red brick building on the right we see a large French flag, blowing in the wind, an unusual touch for Pissarro, who gave this painting to the local museum.

When Pissarro's son Georges came to Dieppe for a visit, he noted, "As for Papa, he's been working hard and has done wonders: the port with the hustle and bustle of the crowd and the boats departing and arriving, the trails of smoke, and so forth and so on. It's tremendous, better than last year's churches." In all, Pissarro made 21 paintings during his second sojourn in Dieppe.

Pissarro was not alone in his admiration of Dieppe. Between 1815 and 1939, the city attracted a wide range of artists. In their own times, Dieppe and its environs hosted Turner, Corot, Delacroix, Renoir, Monet, Whistler, Sickert, Isabey, and Braque, who is buried at nearby Varangéville. But it may have been Pissarro who best captured the community spirit of Dieppe with its busy docks and joyful markets.

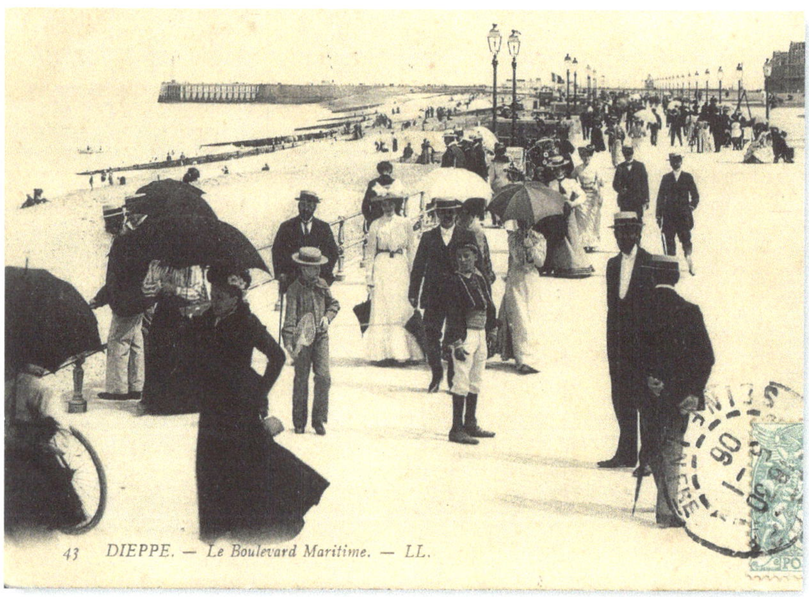

The boardwalk along the beach in the early 1900s

Le Havre

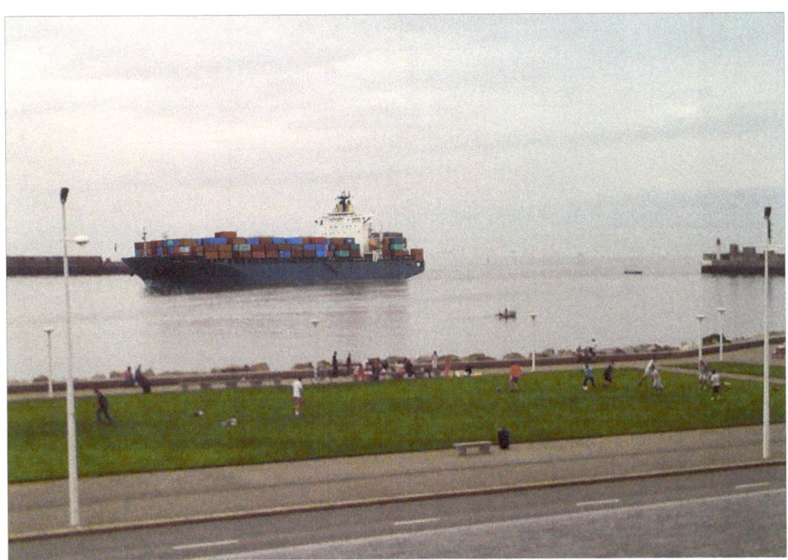

A ship piled high with containers enters the port of Le Havre.

Gateway to the Ocean

The Le Havre that Pissarro visited in 1903 was a bustling seaport accommodating both international commerce and pleasure boating. Perhaps it is appropriate that all of Pissarro's Le Havre paintings feature the docks because "the harbor" (translation of "Le Havre") is literally the town's name, the essence of its history, and its fate even into current times.

Before choosing to paint at Le Havre, Pissarro visited other places he thought worthy of consideration. This reconnaissance trip was an adventure in itself. Pissarro and Julie were transported via automobile by Pieter Van de Velde, one of

Pissarro's wealthy collectors. How modern this must have seemed to Pissarro who, for years, had traveled by train or simply walked from his home to nearby sites, carrying his easel on his back.

The search party explored the picturesque fishing port of Honfleur, which was the home of the artist Eugène Boudin. To this day, the town looks exactly as it did in the early nineteenth century when women climbed to the roofs of their narrow six-floor houses to watch for the fishing boats' return. But its charm did not win Pissarro's favor.

They also visited the Hôtel Saint-Simeon at Honfleur, where Boudin, Corot, Daubigny, and Monet had previously found painting motifs. However, the local sites no longer had the rustic look Pissarro sought: "*...nothing remains of this glorious past...,*" he wrote. "*It is hideously well-groomed and polished....*"

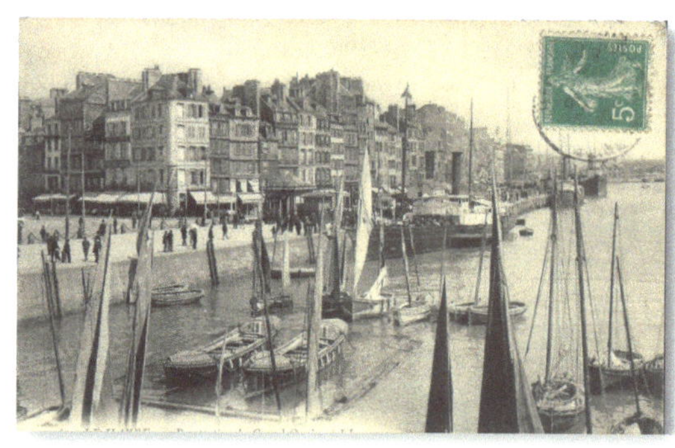

Large steam boats line the quai, surrounded by fishing boats.

As a young man, Monet had painted the beach at Sainte-Adresse, a suburb of Le Havre. But any location like this was out of the question for Pissarro because the wind and sand would cause inflammation in his damaged eye.

Finally, he made his choice: "*Searching for a place suitable for my work has caused me endless toing and froing. It was only yesterday that I decided to put down roots in Le Havre: I'm staying at the Hotel Continental, across from the Le Havre jetty, the spot where all the ships go by....*"

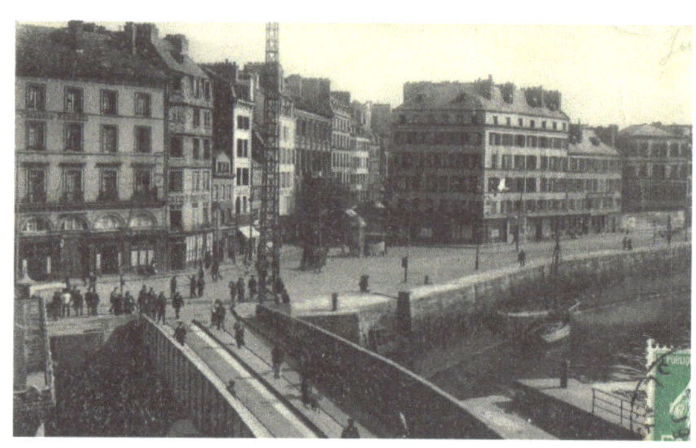

The Quai Notre-Dame near the hotel where Pissarro stayed and painted his Le Havre series

Painting the Action on the Docks

It was the busy ports at Le Havre's city center that attracted Pissarro's interest. At Rouen, he had painted the tidal Seine and the boats from Le Havre coming up river to the inland port. Now he would paint Le Havre itself, the port of entry for many products, such as coffee, cotton, spices, and exotic woods. Even more interesting, it opened directly onto the ocean, accommodating modern steamships from faraway Atlantic ports.

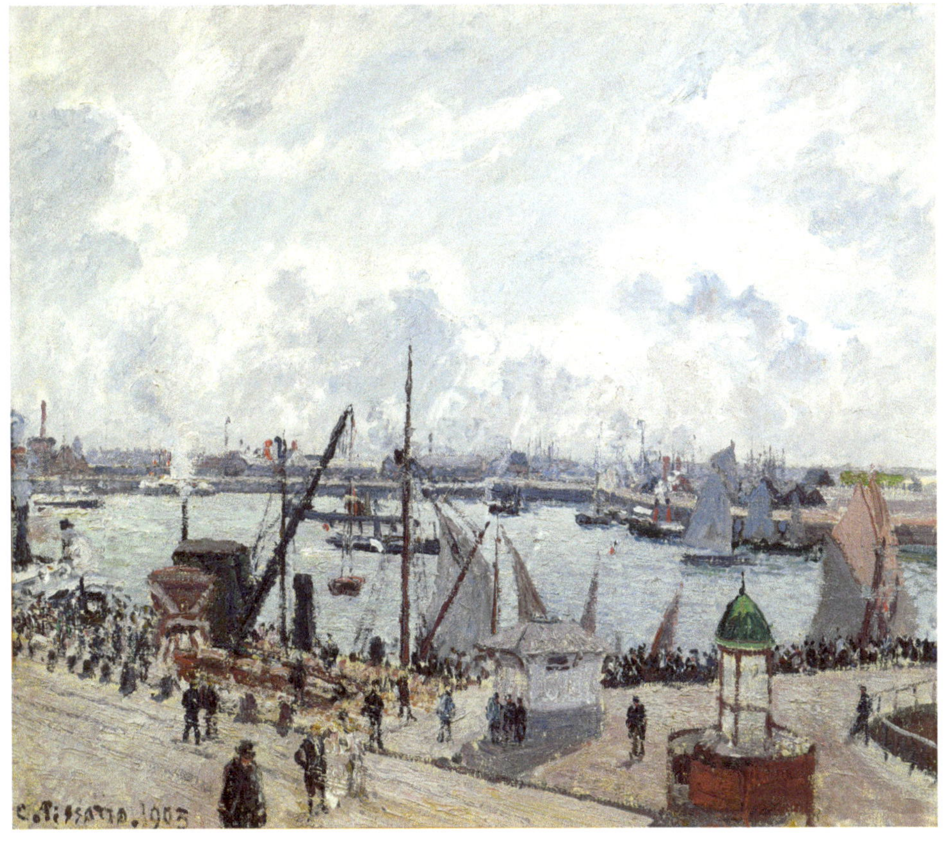

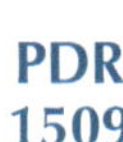

PDR 1509

The Anse des Pilotes, Le Havre, Morning, Sunshine, Tide Rising

1903
Musée Malraux, Le Havre, France
PDR 1509

This is one of the paintings purchased from Pissarro by the Le Havre museum. The complex scene documents the heavy traffic in Le Havre's port. The harbor is packed with boats, and commercial facilities line the water's edge. The left side of the canvas reveals a red brick factory with a tall smokestack, and billowy clouds fill the top half of the canvas.

Pissarro focused on a steamship in the left foreground, which is barely visible behind the huge steam crane discharging puffs of white smoke. A heavy consignment hovers in midair above the dock. The dark boom of the crane draws a heavy diagonal line, which, if extended, meets the top of the ship's tallest mast. This joined at the bottom with the ship's deck forms a large triangle that is repeated in the triangular shape of nearby sails. The boom also makes a distinct X with the ship's lower mast and forms a perfect parallel with a small boom on the ship. This highly geometric construction anchors the painting and provides a stable fulcrum around which the other elements can revolve.

Interestingly, the lower mast of the docked ship is flying the French flag. This may have been a local ship, carrying merchandise from the Le Havre docks inland to Rouen or Paris. Just to the right, another small ship in the middle of the harbor is also flying the Tricolor. To the left of the first flag, on the distant side of the harbor is a flurry of flags of red, white, and blue. The inclusion of French flags is unusual for Pissarro. We wonder why the anarchist painter included French flags in this particular painting, but it is almost always a mistake to second-guess him. He may have simply painted what he saw that day.

He settled in and began to capture the busy scene on the docks below him. Several basins lined the side of the Seine's broad estuary. Some were used to ship merchandise and goods; others accommodated a large fleet of pleasure boats. One was the boarding point for passengers sailing on gigantic oceangoing vessels.

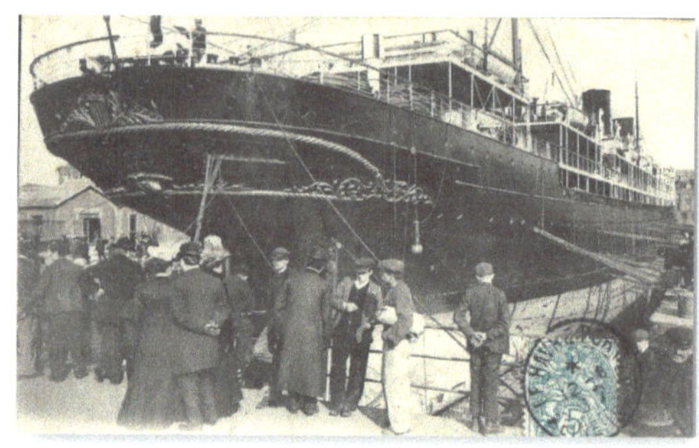

Passengers waiting to board Le Provence, an ocean liner owned by the French Compagnie Générale Transatlantique. The ship was used to transport troops during World War I and was sunk in the Mediterranean in 1916.

Pissarro was aware that the scenes he was painting would not be there much longer. It was common knowledge that the city of Le Havre had plans to enlarge the docks the following year to accommodate increasing ocean traffic. During his stay of about ten weeks, he completed 24 paintings that became reminders of the city and its docks in 1903, and a graphic illustration of how the city had outgrown its current docks.

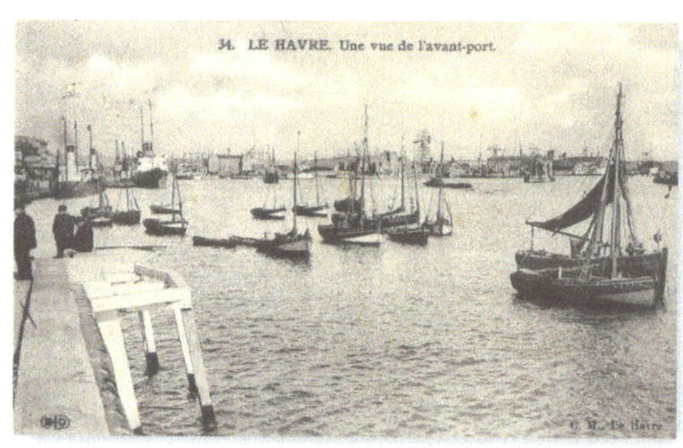

Fishing boats in the forward port at Le Havre

Looking out his window to the left, Pissarro had an exceptional view of Le Havre's lively cargo trade. He painted the frenetic activity of steamboats with sailboats darting between them. He included the modern tram that whisked passengers and dock hands from the jetty to the city center. He also seemed fascinated by the huge steam-driven cranes with their tall booms that moved heavy cargo between ship and shore [See PDR 1509].

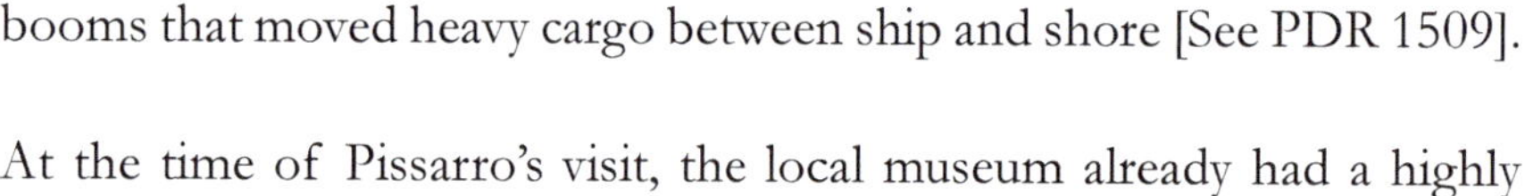

At the time of Pissarro's visit, the local museum already had a highly regarded collection of French paintings. Pissarro approached the museum about buying some of his work. He was aware of their significance to the city: *"I'm told [the pictures are] very important from the historical and documentary viewpoint! The harbor is being demolished to make room for a bigger one, and once it has been demolished I'm told [they] will be unique!!"*

The curator, who was himself a painter in the academic style, disapproved of Pissarro's work. However, Van der Velde, Pissarro's friend, and other local supporters urged the museum's acquisition committee to approve the purchase of two paintings. It was the first museum in France to purchase paintings by Pissarro. Musée Malraux in Le Havre, the museum built to replace the one destroyed by World War II bombing, now has six Pissarro paintings, including those two purchased during Pissarro's visit.

Le Havre – The Eternal Phoenix

Although the sites Pissarro chose were characterized by modernity, they were steeped in history. Located on the English Channel at the mouth of the Seine, Le Havre was just a small fishing village in 1517 when François I, king of France, built a fort there to defend the Seine estuary. In 1534, Jacques Cartier sailed from Le Havre with two ships and 61 sailors to find a route to Asia. Instead they found Canada and established New France. In the seventeenth century, Le Havre became a gateway for trade and exploration and a barrier to repeated attacks from the British.

The first ships from the United States entered the port of Le Havre in 1783, just seven years after that young country's independence. Scheduled service to New York was initiated shortly afterward. By 1847, the ships sailing to New York were steamboats.

Le Havre grew steadily into the twentieth century, making it a strategic target for German forces during World War II. Its liberation in 1944 came at a high cost, with almost total destruction of the town center and harbor. Immediate rebuilding of the docks paved the way for the phoenix-like reconstruction of the urban areas. However, very little remains of the city that was there during Pissarro's painting campaign.

Turning to Other Motifs

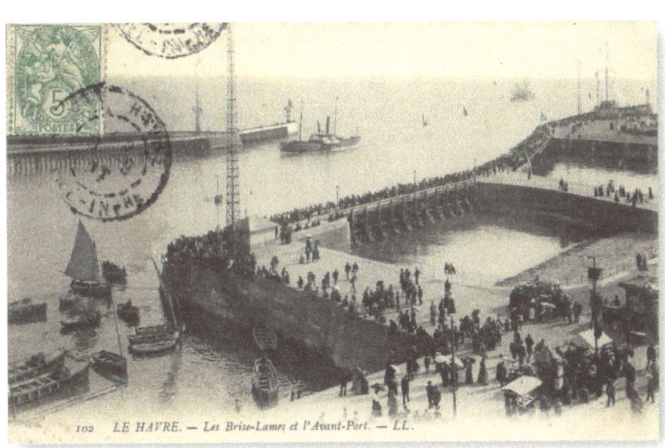

The forward port at Le Havre as shown by Pissarro in his painting

Directly in front of Pissarro's hotel window, the harbor was often filled with sailboats. Although Monet and other Impressionists had often painted pleasure boats, this was not a customary theme for Pissarro. More often, the vessels he painted were working boats on the Seine or Oise—barges, steamboats, even an occasional raft. In Le Havre, however, he seemed to delight in the billowing sails that gave him another bright surface on which to reflect light and color.

When Pissarro looked out his hotel window to the right, he saw the north jetty with its semaphore, and beyond, a direct view out to sea. He considered this a superb motif and captured the scene in both calm and rough seas. As he described it, "...*the Havre jetty happens to be in a part of [town] that is the pride of the citizens of Le Havre, and it does in fact have a grand character*".

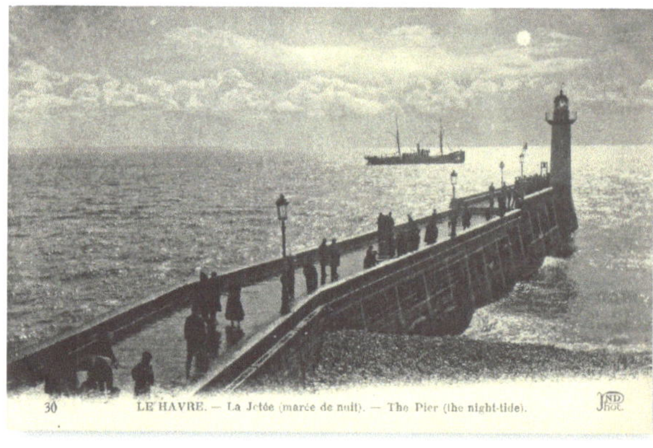

The people of Le Havre were very proud of the jetty, according to Pissarro.

Pissarro had a perfect view of the massive ocean liners and watched as they departed for foreign ports. He wrote his son Georges: *"All day long I see great transatlantic steamers passing by in front of my windows, and other [ships] from morning till evening, with the wharves, the traffic, it's grand, I think I'm onto a new series, which will be interesting."*

One of his paintings from this time depicts the *Lorraine*, France's largest passenger ship at that time, slipping away from the dock. Built in 1899, the Lorraine was made of steel and had two smoke stacks. It was a massive vessel, 563 feet long and 60 feet wide.

As he celebrated his 73rd birthday in Le Havre on July 10, Pissarro wrote letters to his children, *"I'll do my best to go quietly on with the life that has been allotted to me by doing as much work as I can, for the thread that holds me to this earth has nearly run out."*

The paintings from this trip to Le Havre would comprise Pissarro's last series. Not too long after leaving Le Havre, Pissarro became gravely ill and died in Paris.

Some historians believe that in his Le Havre series, Pissarro painted the small boats heading out to sea to foreshadow his own death. Despite what he prophetically wrote in his letter, this seems uncharacteristic. Pissarro did not approve of symbolism, religious or otherwise, in paintings. However, this may be a revealing exception. Pissarro was a man whose life was full of dichotomy and change. In fact, the only thing predictable about Pissarro was his capacity to surprise.

Paris

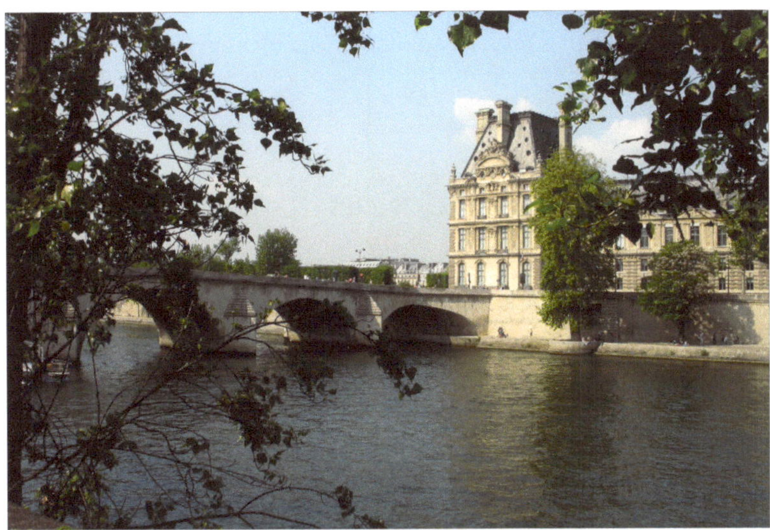

The Pavillon de Flore, built in 1595 by Henri-IV to link the Grande Galerie with the Tuileries Palace, was painted by Pissarro in 1903 from the balcony of a Left Bank hotel.

The Place of Paris in Pissarro's Life

Paris was the center of Pissarro's world in many respects. In the city, he had connections with family members, friendly exchanges with other artists and journalists, and contacts with business associates. He also enjoyed the cultural stimulus of the museums, theaters, and concerts.

As a child, Pissarro came to Paris for school and it was there that he learned to draw. As a young man determined to make his name as an artist in Paris, he fought the battles of the Paris Salon and spearheaded efforts to create the Impressionist movement. As an adult artist, he painted some of his most memorable cityscapes in Paris, and it is where he died at the age of 73.

Although he kept a studio when he could afford it, Paris was rarely a permanent residence for Pissarro as an adult. On the other hand, he was not a visitor in Paris as he was in Rouen, Dieppe, and Le Havre, where he made painting expeditions. For professional and personal reasons, Paris was his base, his touchstone.

Pissarro's paintings of Paris are the transcendental definition of the city for many people. They are seen illustrating everything from book covers to product packaging. These paintings are universally recognized as the image of Paris, whether or not people recognize the artist. Among the most familiar are the paintings Pissarro made of the Boulevard Montmartre [See PDR 1168].

The Paris of Pissarro's Childhood

In 1830, the year Pissarro was born in St. Thomas, the last monarch of France, Louis-Philippe, began his reign. Undoubtedly, the news of Paris was discussed in Pissarro's home in Charlotte Amalie. His French grandparents lived in Passy, then a small village west of Paris and now an elite neighborhood near the Trocadero. The young Pissarro's first political leanings may have been influenced by French politics as well as his own experiences with political unrest in St. Thomas.

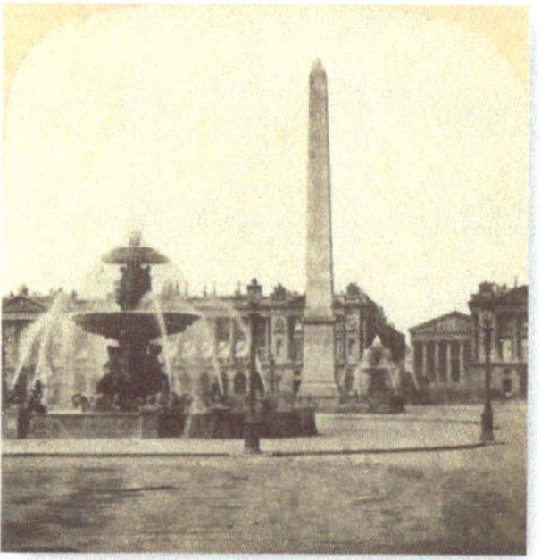

Place de la Concorde in 1865 when Pissarro was 35 years old

When Pissarro was 12, his parents sent him to France to get a proper education. He spent six years at the Pension Savary, an elite boarding school in Passy, where his fondness for drawing surpassed his interest in other subjects.

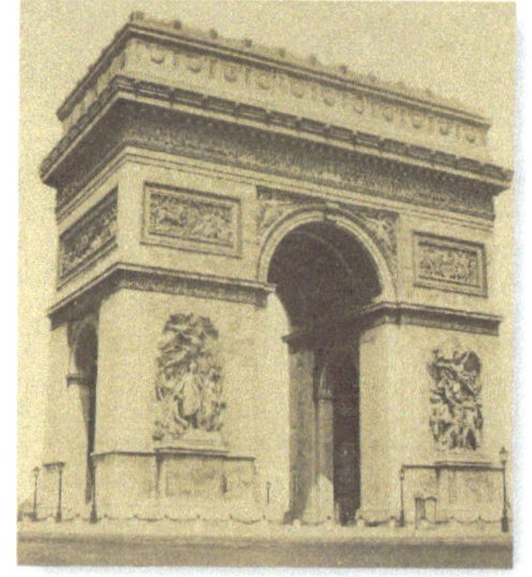

The Arc de Triomphe in 1867 when Pissarro was 37 years old

The Paris Pissarro knew as a schoolboy in 1842 had only 12 arrondissements and was enclosed by a wall, constructed to ensure collection of taxes on goods brought into Paris. Because Passy was located outside this wall, Pissarro had to go through one of the 52 toll gates to enter the city. A much larger circle of military fortifications built by Louis-Philippe in 1840 also surrounded Paris and its environs, including Passy.

At this time, the center of Paris was still a medieval city with tiny winding streets and alleys. Its two- and three-story buildings were overcrowded with vast numbers of people who had moved into the city from the countryside. Poverty was pervasive, sanitation was poor, and crime was rampant. The Île de la Cité was still the center of Paris, and the city stretched no farther west than the Place de la Concorde, which was muddy in winter and sandy in summer.

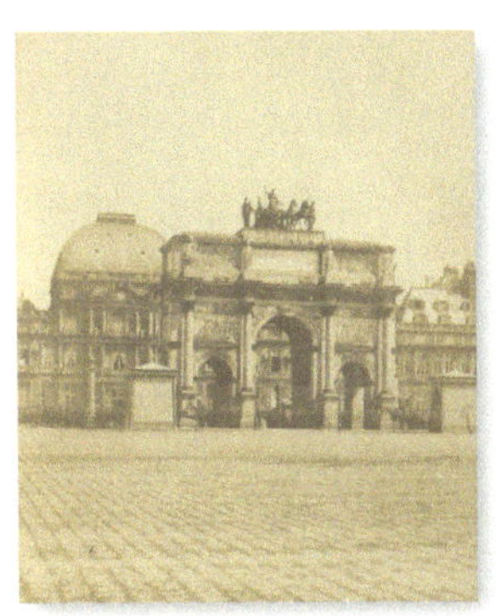

The Tuileries Palace behind the Arc de Triomphe du Carrousel, as Pissarro would have seen it when he visited the Louvre before 1871.

As a young student coming to the Louvre to look at paintings, Pissarro made his way through surrounding slums. At that time, the Louvre did not have the configuration of the museum we know today. Beyond the Carrousel Arch was the ancient Tuileries Palace built by Catherine de Medici in the sixteenth century. This grand castle, a blatant symbol of the monarchy, would have been a familiar sight to the young Camille. Some twenty years later in 1871, the palace was burned to the ground during the Commune uprising following the Franco-Prussian War. Pissarro was in exile in London at the time, but he would have seen the wreckage, which was not cleared away for several years.

Many of the Paris landmarks we know today were already in place when Pissarro came to Paris as a boy. The Arc de Triomphe, begun by Napoléon Bonaparte, was finished in 1836. It was standing alone in a grove of trees not far from Pissarro's school, its view in line with the tallest dome of the Tuileries Palace.

To the east where the Bastille had stood, Louis-Phillipe had erected the July Column after he took power in the Revolution of 1830. The Luxor Obelisk, erected in Concorde in 1836, was between the Tuileries Palace and the Arc de Triomphe.

The Effect of Napoléon III

Shortly after Pissarro finished his schooling in Passy and returned to St. Thomas, the Revolution of 1848 erupted in Paris. Louis-Napoléon, nephew of Napoléon Bonaparte, won the election that followed with 74 percent of the vote. At the end of his presidential term, Louis-Napoléon took over the country in a coup d'état and established himself as Emperor Napoléon III. He was in power when Pissarro returned to Paris at the age of 25.

These events had a major impact on Pissarro's life. It was Napoléon III, who in 1853 authorized Baron Haussmann to obliterate much of medieval Paris and construct the broad boulevards that Pissarro would immortalize in his paintings. In 1860, the city was enlarged and divided into twenty arrondissements.

It was Napoléon III who authorized the Salon des Refusés in May 1863, where hundreds of paintings rejected by the Salon were shown, including three by Pissarro. He also instigated the Franco-Prussian War in 1870, which caused Pissarro to spend an extended time in London.

Pissarro's Return to France

When Camille Pissarro came to Paris in 1855, he was already an accomplished artist. According to Richard Brettell, noted Pissarro specialist, he had "a large portfolio of highly competent drawings and paintings made before academic instruction."

The 25-year-old Pissarro arrived in Paris in September 1855 just in time to visit the Exposition Universelle, where he saw paintings by Delacroix, Ingres, Corot, and Courbet. He also visited Courbet's separate pavilion, built to protest the official exhibition. Thus, Pissarro learned firsthand about the passionate conflicts that were already shaking the Paris art world.

Rachel, Pissarro's mother, had previously moved to Paris from St. Thomas. When Pissarro arrived, he was able to live with his family in an exclusive neighborhood, now in the sixteenth arrondissement. At the urging of his father, Pissarro attended the École des Beaux-Arts for a short time, and then studied in private classes. In 1857, he enrolled in the Académie Suisse, where he could draw from live models, instead of copying plaster casts. There he met Armand Guillaumin, Claude Monet, and Paul Cézanne. Monet introduced him to Frédéric Bazille, Alfred Sisley, and Auguste Renoir. By 1863, many of the artists who would later be known as the Impressionists were friends and colleagues.

In 1860, Pissarro met Julie Vellay, a young woman from Burgundy who had come to Paris to find work. She was employed as a kitchen maid by Pissarro's mother. The alliance he forged with Julie was to last a lifetime, despite the adamant disapproval of his parents. Together, they had eight children, and with her industry and frugality, Julie gave Pissarro her support through good times and bad.

Working as an Artist in Paris

Camille and Julie made a home together in Paris, and it was there that their first child, Lucien, was born in the winter of 1863. They had no financial resources and depended on the allowance that Pissarro received from his father. To save money and find new motifs, the young family moved to a village on the banks of the Marne River. It was there that

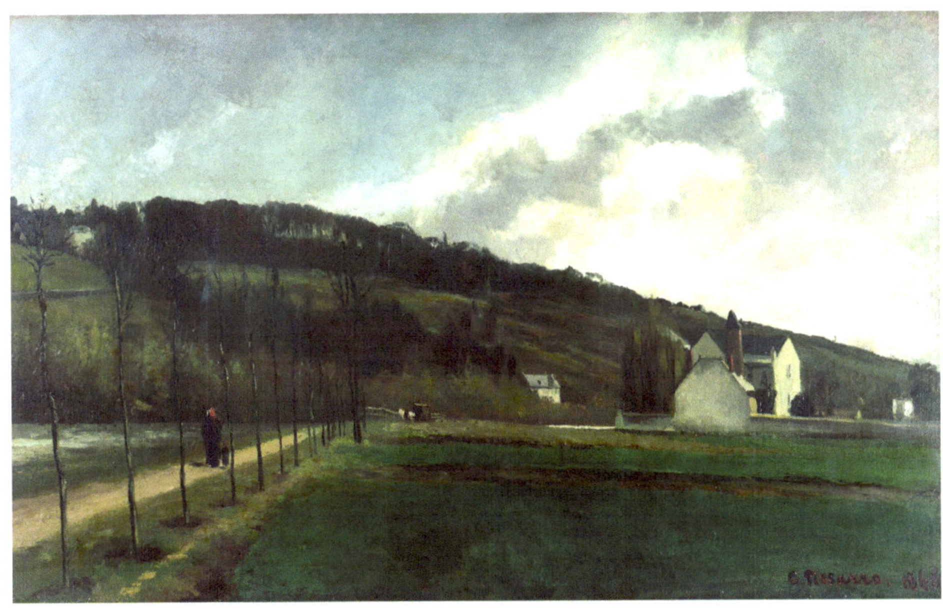

Banks of the Marne in Winter

1866
Art Institute of Chicago, Chicago, IL
PDR 107

PDR 107

The Banks of the Marne depicts a landscape in the dead of winter. Pissarro views the scene through the eyes of a minimalist. There is no vegetation to soften the view, and geometry dominates the landscape. Except for the row of trees leading our eyes back into the hills, the foreground is devoid of subject matter.

The hill and sky in the background fill two-thirds of the canvas. The rocky slope, dotted with evergreens, forms a diagonal line that separates the area into almost equal portions of land and gray-clouded sky. The bleakness forces us to look at the geometric shapes formed by the hill, the road, and the sky. Pissarro, the most innovative of all the Impressionists, may have been foreshadowing the concept of Minimalism. Certainly, that term was not invented until the twentieth century. But his eye was, even at this early point in his career, capturing and focusing on the simple elements of the landscape, a feature that would continue to be apparent in his paintings.

their first daughter, Jeanne-Rachel Pissarro, was born May 18, 1865. One of the paintings Pissarro made in that area, *Banks of the Marne in Winter,* was subsequently shown at the Salon of 1866. Émile Zola, a journalist and art critic, published his appreciation of Pissarro's work: "Thank you, Monsieur; your landscape refreshed me for a good half hour during my journey through the great wilderness of the Salon. I know you were admitted only with the greatest difficulty, and I sincerely congratulate you on this. Besides, you must know that you please no one, and that your painting is found to be too bare, too black. So why the devil are you so singularly clumsy as to paint solidly and make a frank study of nature! … An austere, grave style of painting, an extreme concern for truth and accuracy, a rugged and strong will. You are a great blunderer, sir—you are an artist whom I like" [See PDR 107].

Although Pissarro continued to have a studio in Paris from time to time, it was too expensive to support his growing family there. The young couple rented houses in nearby towns in the summer and stayed in Paris in winter. It was there on November 21, 1878, that Ludovic-Rodo, the couple's fourth son was born. In Paris Pissarro could sell his paintings, meet with other artists, and participate in the growing market for Impressionist art.

Gare Saint-Lazare

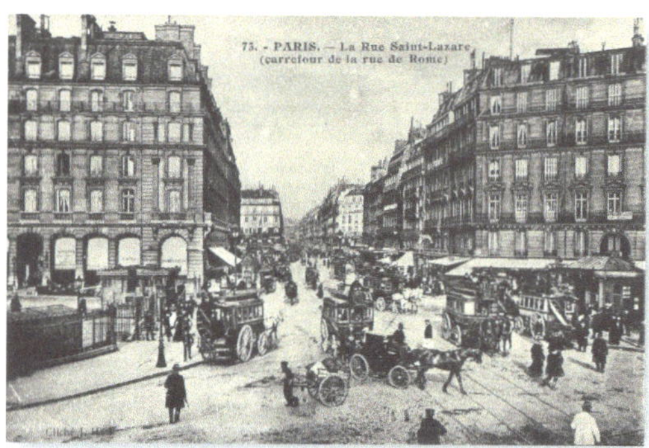

Place de Havre at the turn of the century

It was later in life, at the age of 63, that Pissarro began painting Paris streets and boulevards in earnest. Although he painted a few canvases around Montmartre in his early 30s, he generally did not make paintings during his frequent Paris visits. Later in life, problems with his vision caused Pissarro to view Paris differently.

In 1893, the abscess in one of Pissarro's eyes worsened, requiring daily treatment that kept him in Paris for nearly three months. He could not set up his easel on the street because the wind and dust would damage his eye. Instead, Pissarro painted four canvases from the window of his hotel room near the Gare Saint-Lazare, the railway station where he arrived on his frequent trips from Éragny to Paris.

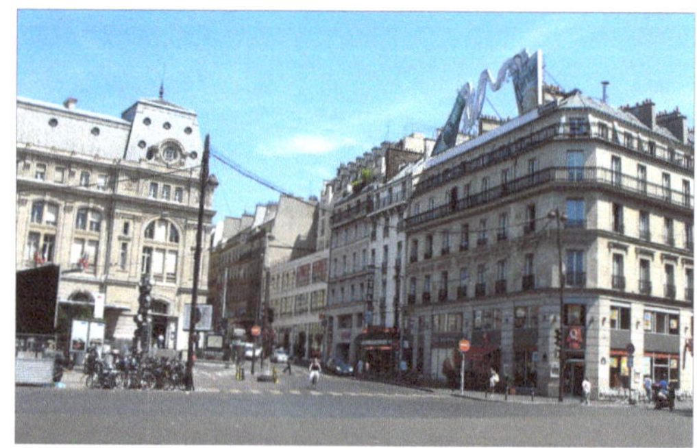
A current photo of the site looks virtually the same as Pissarro's painting

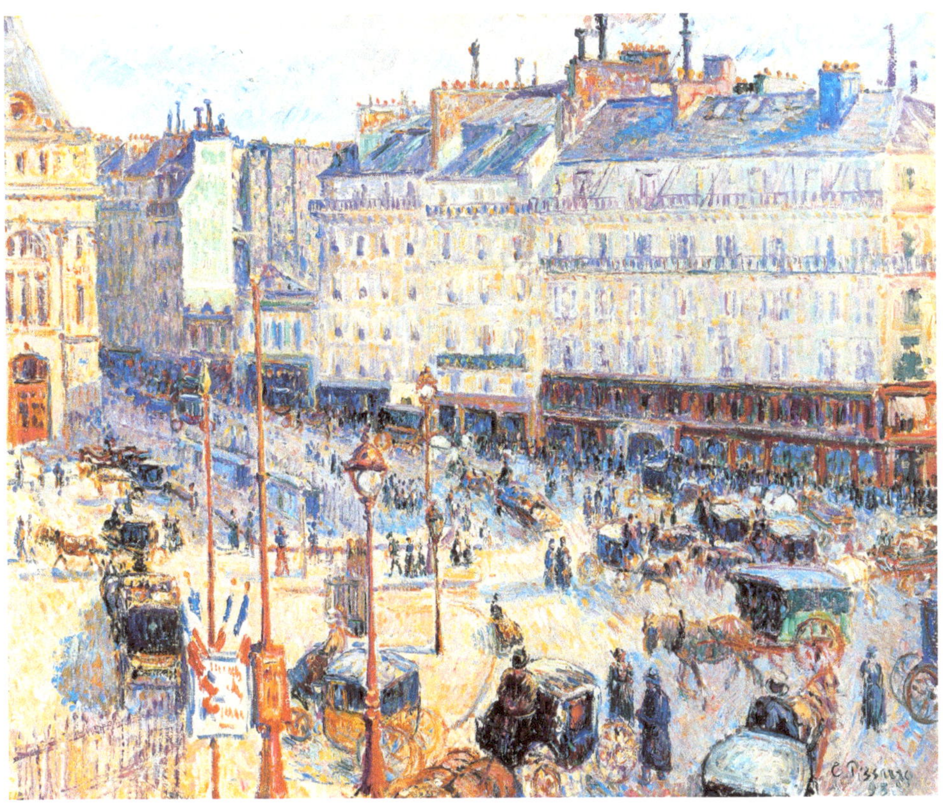

PDR
986

Place du Havre and Rue d'Amsterdam, Morning, Sunlight

1893

Art Institute of Chicago, Chicago, IL

PDR 986

This painting is a tour de force of Impressionist color. The scene is awash with bright sunlight that bathes the cobblestones in a yellow glow and creates deep blue and purple shadows in contrast. The Place du Havre with its circular traffic dominates the foreground and extends at an angle back into the rue d'Amsterdam. The background is filled with a block of tall buildings whose chimney pots touch the top edge of the canvas. Their solidity balances the fluidity of the moving traffic pattern below.

This scene is virtually the same today as when Pissarro painted it. Only a small sliver of the Gare Saint-Lazare is shown on the left. To the right, a light green geometric shape appears on an exposed side wall of a building deep in the shadows. Its purpose is unclear, but there may have been a colorful advertising message in the high-traffic area.

Standing close to the painting, we see only a multitude of tiny brushstrokes in rainbow colors. Farther back, the image of sunlight and shadows is quite clear. This painting is a sophisticated play of contrasting colors in a delicate balance that unites the composition.

One of his most luminous paintings of Paris resulted from this enforced sojourn [See PDR 986]. Today, the streets around the Gare Saint-Lazare are filled with automobiles, but the train station and the surrounding buildings are the same ones that Pissarro painted.

Pissarro visited this site again in January of 1897 and made more paintings of the streets around the train station. He wrote Lucien, *"During my stay here I was able to do six small canvases which will cover my expenses for the month, effects of snow in the rues Saint-Lazare and Amsterdam."*

His agent Durand-Ruel bought all six of these new Gare Saint-Lazare paintings. He suggested that Pissarro plan a series of paintings on larger canvases depicting Paris' new wide boulevards.

Boulevard Montmartre

In February 1897, Pissarro installed himself in a room at the Hôtel de Russie, where he had a good view of the Boulevard Montmartre. His son Lucien was enthusiastic about Pissarro's plan for a complete series of boulevard paintings: "What a good idea you had to install yourself in Paris, this will make you more successful in the eyes of the Parisians who love only their city, when all's said and done, not to mention the enjoyment you'll get from this thoroughly new series."

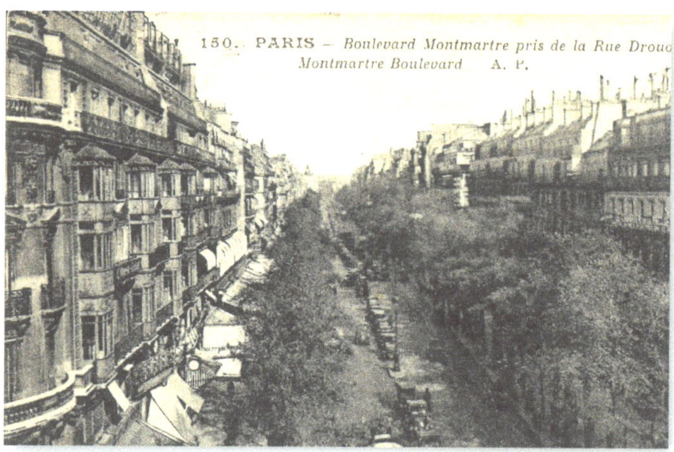

A view of Boulevard Montmarte similar to that painted by Pissarro

Pissarro stayed there until late April and completed 16 paintings; 14 of boulevard Montmartre and two of the boulevard des Italiens. Durand-Ruel bought twelve paintings from that series [See PDR 1168].

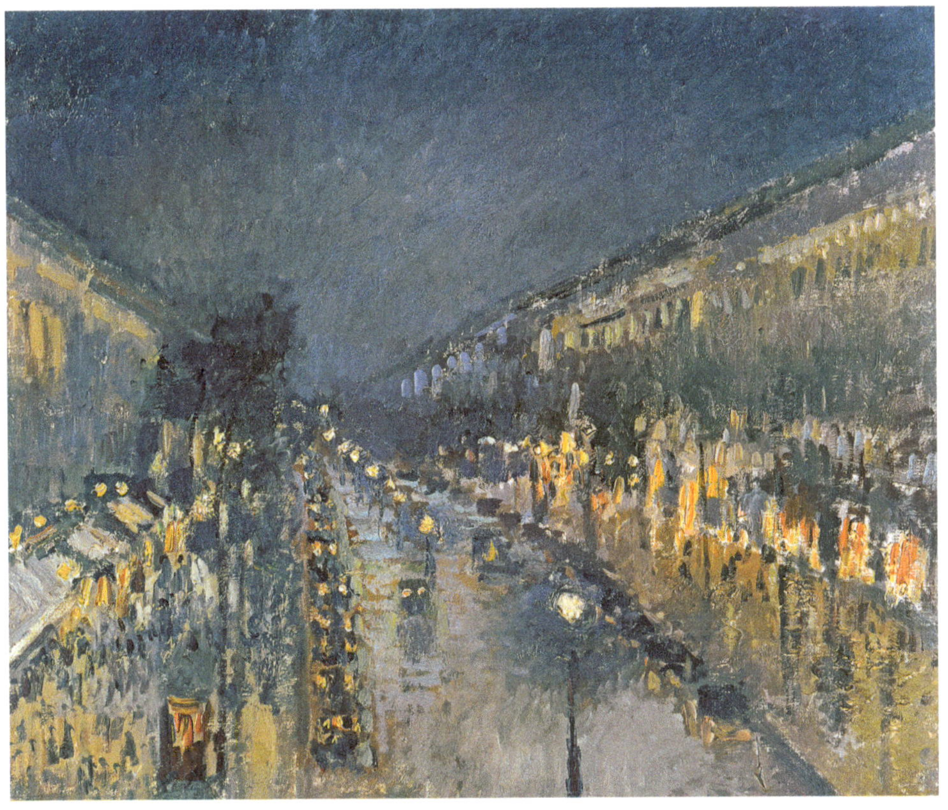

PDR 1168

Boulevard Montmartre, Night Effect
1897
National Gallery, London, UK
PDR 1168

Because this masterpiece is so familiar, we may not really see its distinctiveness. On this rainy night with lights reflecting on shiny streets, Pissarro allows the colors to mix and blur. The loose brushstrokes make no attempt at realism and only suggest forms. The elements in this painting are so indistinct that they would be unrecognizable if the context were not known.

In fact, looking at the images only as patches of color, we discover amazing views. If we turn the painting upside down, the dark areas support the bright shiny portions above and constitute a predictable arrangement. Turned on either side, it presents interesting asymmetrical configurations.

For all practical purposes, this is an abstract painting. This painting clearly establishes the fact that Pissarro's work was foreshadowing the art of the future.

Place du Théâtre-Français

When Pissarro came back to Paris on December 15, 1897, for another painting excursion, he was dealing with many problems. He was worried about his son Lucien, who had suffered a stroke-like paralysis that year, and saddened by the death of his 23-year-old son Félix from tuberculosis. As he had done in times of sorrow earlier in his life, he immersed himself in work.

He searched several locations and finally settled on a site overlooking the Place du Théâtre-Français (now called the Place André-Malraux). From his windows, he had a stunning view of the Avenue de l'Opéra and the sumptuous new Opéra Garnier.

Pissarro seemed pleased with the view and wrote Lucien, who was recuperating in London, *"I forgot to mention that I found a room in the Grand Hôtel du Louvre with a superb view of the Avenue de l'Opéra and the corner of the Place du Palais Royal! It is very beautiful to paint? Perhaps it is not aesthetic, but I am delighted to be able to paint these Paris streets that people have come to call ugly but which are so silvery, so luminous and vital. They are so different from the boulevards. This is completely modern!"*

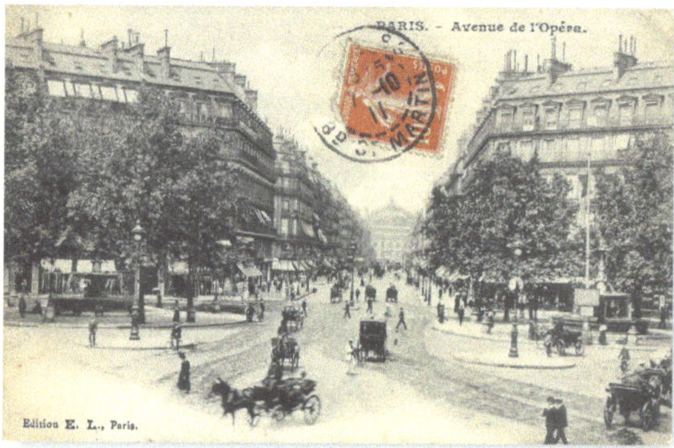

Place du Théâtre-Français about the time Pissarro painted his series of this site

Most of his paintings depict the large intersection in front of the hotel leading into the avenue de l'Opéra. He made only three paintings of the street to the left, rue Saint-Honoré, which must have been tricky to paint because of its oblique angle from his window [See PDR 1202].

Pissarro's paintings frequently include subtle details that provide great delight to the viewer observant enough to spot them. In eight of the ten paintings of the Place du Théâtre-Français, he pictures a pair of windows with muted red draperies, unique because most of the other windows are neutral in color. The red draperies are located on the upper balcony of the building on the right corner.

Interestingly, the red draperies are in exactly the same location in each painting, suggesting that this was not a fortuitous choice, but that the red draperies were actually there. We may wonder if Pissarro was being very meticulous in painting exactly what he saw, or if he happened to know who lived behind those red draperies. That mystery remains to be solved.

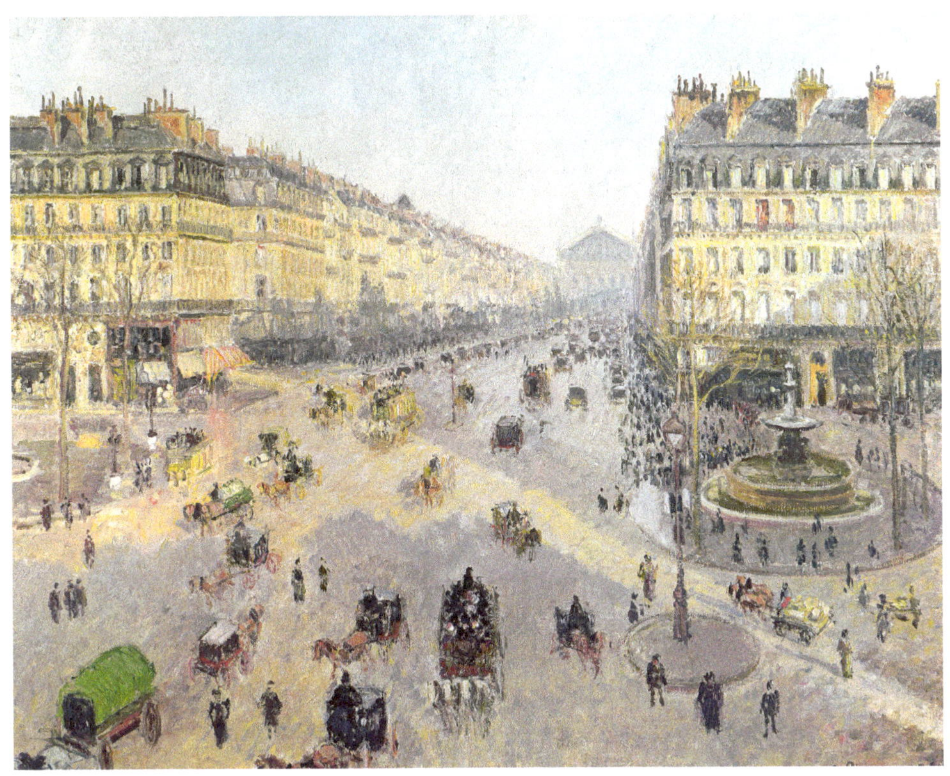

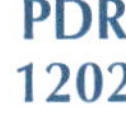
PDR 1202

Place du Théâtre-Français and the Avenue de l'Opéra,

Sunlight, Winter Morning
1898
Musée des Beaux-Arts, Rheims, France
PDR 1202

From his window in the Grand Hôtel du Louvre, Pissarro painted a cloudless Paris sky. The pale winter sunlight glows pink on the elegant façades and ironwork balconies. Even though the lavish opera house at the end of the avenue was already an important landmark, it is insignificant in this painting and appears almost in caricature, with no details apparent.

The variety of vehicles crowding the busy intersection is amazing. The top level of a large omnibus, pulled by three white horses, is packed with people. Private carriages and cargo wagons jostle for space with horse-drawn taxicabs. Fearless pedestrians cross the huge expanse, striding bravely through the stream of heavy traffic.

The shapes of the distinct shadows give this 1898 painting a Cubist characteristic as they distort the symmetry of the buildings and avenue. From the right, the silhouette of the Théâtre-Français, not seen in this view, shadows the circular fountain. In the foreground, the presence of the hotel is betrayed by its shadow. The sunlight that pours through the open spaces forms a vivid geometric pattern on the street, setting the traffic in motion. We can see the delicate differences in the color of the carriages as they move between sun and shadow.

The Dreyfus Affair

During this same painting expedition, Pissarro experienced firsthand the turmoil of the Dreyfus Affair. Four years earlier, Alfred Dreyfus, a French-Jewish army officer, had been accused of treason and sentenced to life imprisonment on Devil's Island, near French Guiana.

In subsequent years, it became apparent that the case had been false, and a huge governmental cover-up had prevented Dreyfus from receiving a fair trial. His case captured the attention of many notable individuals who believed in justice, including that of novelist Émile Zola. Zola penned a powerful editorial, "J'accuse!" to expose the miscarriage of justice to the general public. His statement brought international attention to the case and caused deep divisions among the French who vehemently took sides either for or against Dreyfus. The blatant anti-Semitism in France, supported by the Catholic Church, became all the more obvious as it gave great voice to Dreyfus's opponents.

The Dreyfus Affair triggered endless debates, protests, riots, and duels, even creating grave rifts between family members. The turmoil was boiling over into the streets during Pissarro's sojourn. Pissarro wrote in a letter, *'Don't worry too much about my safety here; for the moment there's only a few Catholic brawlers from the Latin quarter, encouraged by the government .They shout: 'Down with the Jews,' but nothing more.... Yesterday, while I was making my way along the boulevards to Durand's at five o'clock, I found myself in the midst of a band of little scamps followed by ruffians shouting: 'Death to the Jews! Down with Zola!' I passed calmly through them to the rue Laffite, they didn't even take me for a Jew!"*

The conflict also divided the artists of Impressionism, who before now had scarcely paid any attention to religious affiliation. Pissarro, a friend of Zola's, supported his initiative for the sake of justice. However, Renoir, Degas, and Cézanne took the opposite view, shunning Pissarro because he was Jewish, and creating breaches that were never repaired.

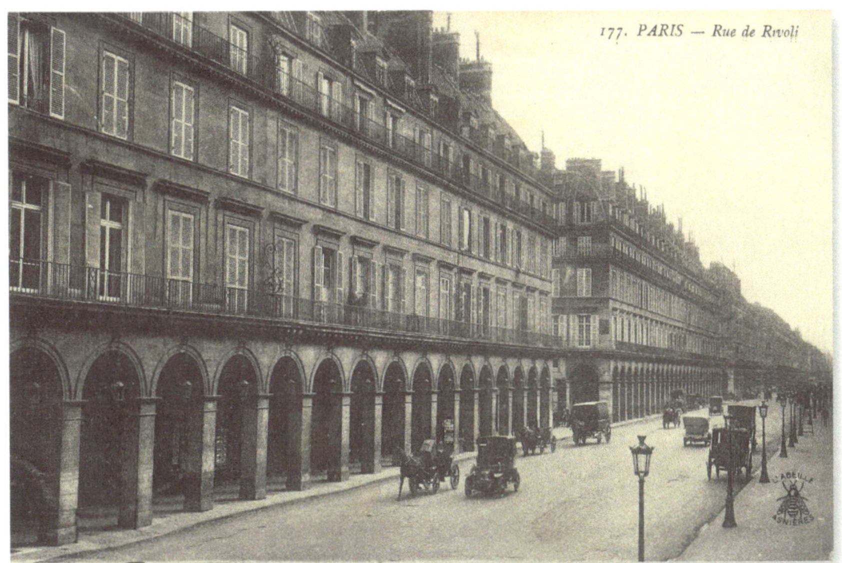

Rue Rivoli as it would have looked
when Pissarro lived there

Tuileries Gardens

The following January in 1899, Pissarro took his wife Julie and two youngest children, Cocotte and Paulémile with him to spend the winter and early spring in an apartment on rue Rivoli, near the Louvre.

Pissarro enthusiastically described his new motif, "*...opposite the Tuileries, with a superb view of the gardens, the Louvre to the left, in the background the houses on the quays behind the trees [and] to the right the dome of the Invalides, and the steeples of Ste. Clotilde behind clumps of chestnut trees. It's very beautiful.*"

By the middle of June of that year, Pissarro had painted 14 views of the Tuileries Gardens. Durand-Ruel purchased 11 of those paintings.

After painting at Éragny and Rouen during the summer, Pissarro brought his family back to the rue Rivoli apartment in November 1899, where they stayed until May 1900. Durand-Ruel bought seven of the 14 additional paintings he made that winter. At last, Pissarro and his family could enjoy some financial security.

Pissarro returned to that apartment once more during the month of June 1900 to have treatments for his inflamed eye. He made three last paintings from that perspective. This time, he was there in the summer, and his paintings contain a multitude of greens portraying the grass, shrubs, and a variety of trees.

Place Dauphine

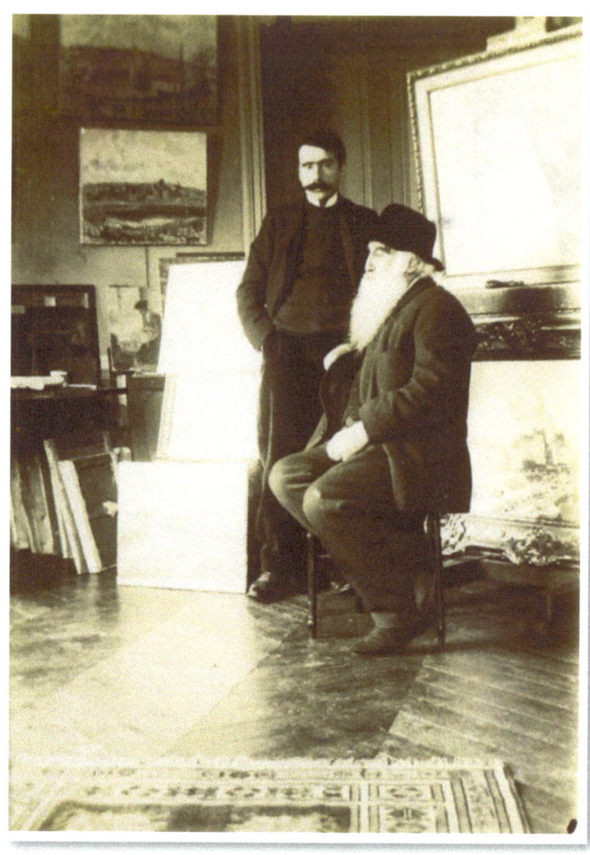

Camille Pissarro and his son Georges in the flat at 28 Place Dauphine with Pissarro's paintings in the background c. 1902
Lionel and Sandrine Pissarro Archives

Pissarro was ready to change locations, and in November 1900 he moved his family to an apartment on the Île de la Cité, the island in the middle of the Seine. From that place, he could see both the Left Bank and Right Bank. Across the Seine on his left, the Hôtel de la Monnaie and the dome of the Institut de France lined the quay; across the Seine to his right, was the Samaritaine department store, flags flying from its rooftops. The Pont Neuf, the oldest bridge in Paris, connected the two riverbanks and passed in front of his window. He had a panorama that included the river, barges and boats, traffic on the bridge, pedestrians, and interesting buildings on both quays. The places that he painted then look virtually the same today.

Between November 1900 and the end of April 1901, he completed 21 paintings. In one little-known painting, he captured the wreck of a barge against one of the piers of the Pont Neuf.

In October 1901, Pissarro and his family returned to the Place Dauphine and stayed until mid-May 1902. During that sojourn, he completed 26 oil paintings, capturing the familiar views in sunlight and under overcast sky, under frost and blankets of snow, and with fog and mist. He painted early in the morning and throughout the day, and he captured beautiful sunsets as night fell.

Directly in front of Pissarro's window was a large statue of Henri-IV, who was king of France from 1589 to 1610. Born a Protestant, Henri had converted to Catholicism in order to become king of France. However, he retained a deep concern for people of other faiths, and in 1598 he issued the Edict of Nantes declaring tolerance for all religions.

The following year from November to May of 1903, Pissarro repeated these scenes and added the Hôtel de la Monnaie on the

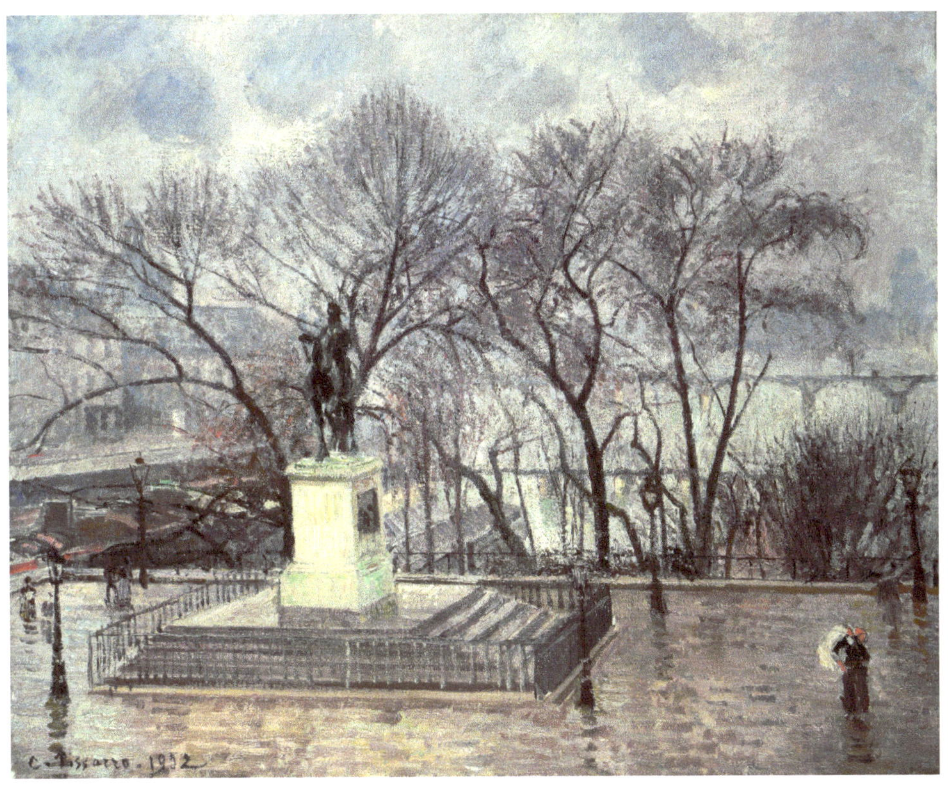

PDR 1421

The Statue of Henri-IV, Morning, Rain

1902

Arkansas Arts Center, Little Rock, AR

PDR 1421

Although he painted a wide variety of motifs, Pissarro did not usually paint landmarks or familiar sites. However, he made twelve paintings that include the statue of Henri-IV. It is likely that Pissarro, an avid reader of history, would have been aware of the beliefs of Henri IV, who championed religious tolerance. However, we cannot tell if he was subtly paying homage to the old king or if he was simply painting what he saw from his window.

On this rainy day, there are few pedestrians walking around the statue, and the view of the Louvre on the right is lost in the blue fog and mist. On the left, the dome of the Institut de France defines the Left Bank. Behind the screen of leafless trees, the Seine reflects the cloudy sky.

Most of the painting behind the statue is given over to the sky, the river, and the buildings, with blues, grays, and white predominating. Their coolness is contrasted by the warm golden color of the paving blocks in the foreground. The dark trunks of the tree connect the terrace with the sky and provide a soft frame for the statue.

Left Bank. Tiring of these views, he rented a room at a hotel on quay Voltaire to use as a studio during April and May. He finished this series of paintings by dividing his time between Place Dauphine, where he completed 13 paintings, and quay Voltaire, where he painted 14 canvases.

The paintings made on quay Voltaire included alluring views of the Pont Royal and the Pont du Carrousel, two of the bridges crossing the Seine, and the quay Malaquais with the dome of the Institut de France in the distance.

In September of that year, Pissarro and his family returned to Place Dauphine for a few weeks until their new apartment on Boulevard Morland in the fourth arrondissement was ready. He was eagerly planning the new series he would do from those windows when he became sick and died following a brief illness.

Just before the move, while he and his family were still at Place Dauphine, Pissarro painted a self-portrait showing himself at 73 years of age. Through the window behind him are the buildings of the Samaritaine. In this, his last self-portrait, Pissarro clearly locates himself in Paris, certainly one of his favorite places [See PDR 1528].

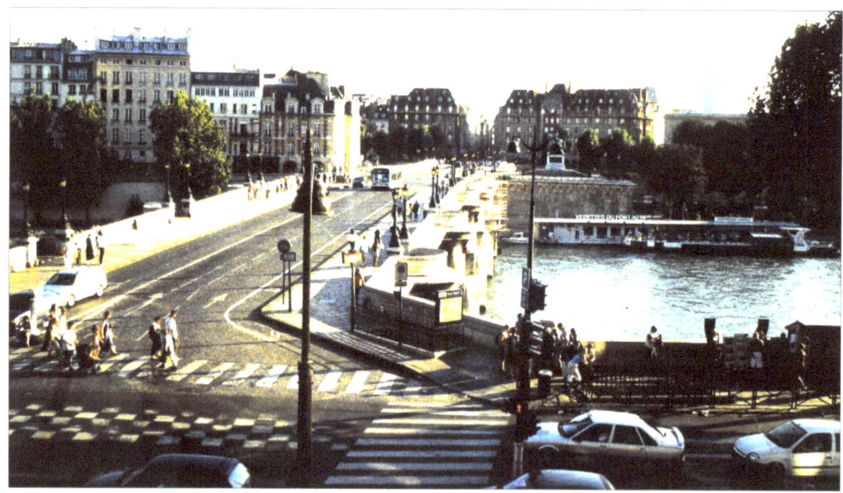

A view of Pont Neuf from the old Samaritaine department store. On the left of the bridge is the building at Place Dauphine facing the Henri-IV statue where Pissarro painted his self-portrait.

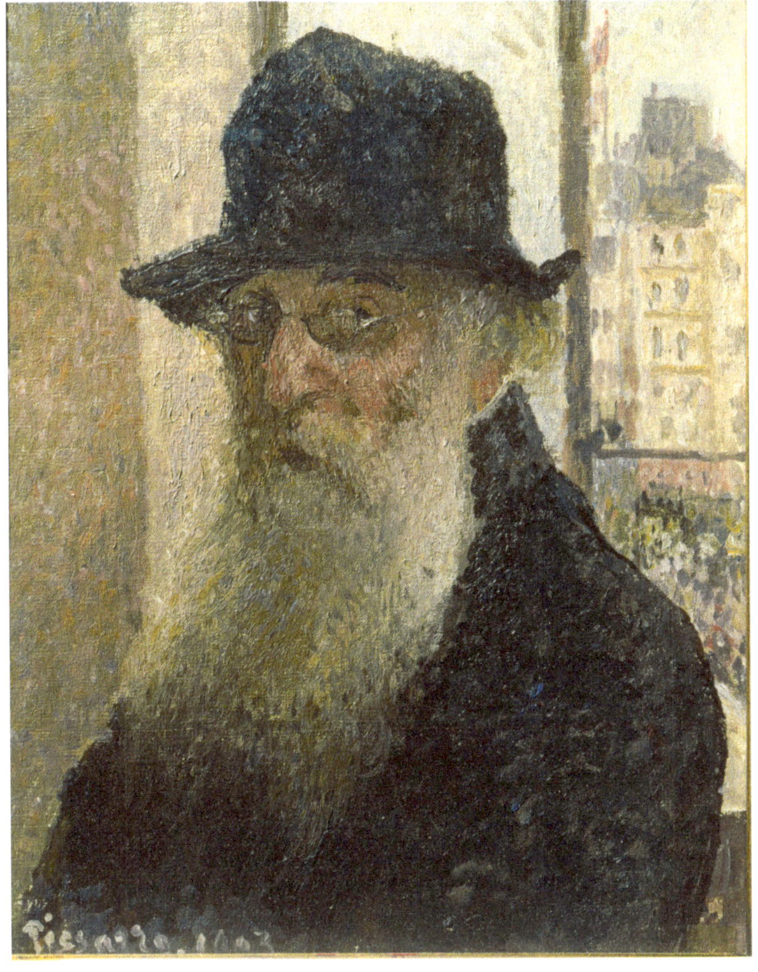

PDR 1528

Self-Portrait With Hat

1903

Tate Gallery, London, UK

PDR 1528

Pissarro made this self-portrait when he returned to Paris after completing his series at Le Havre. He painted himself standing in front of a window that reveals the familiar contours of the Samaritaine building he painted so many times before. He is 73 years old in this painting, and although his beard had been gray for many decades, his face and posture seem to reflect the passage of time.

Pissarro made four self-portraits in oils. When he made the first one, he was 43 years old and living in Pontoise. Already he had lost most of his hair and his beard was turning gray, but in that painting his face and stance conveyed his vigor and enthusiasm. After his second painting expedition in Rouen in 1896, Pissarro made a pair of self-portraits, depicting himself in a dark artist's smock, beret, and spectacles.

We see in this self-portrait of Pissarro a person who did what he loved and above all, remained true to himself.

Brief Chronology of the Life of Camille Pissarro

*[For a comprehensive chronology of Pissarro's life, see Volume I of **Pissarro: Critical Catalogue** by Joachim Pissarro and Claire Durand-Ruel Snollaerts, 2005]*

1830 On July 10, Camille Pissarro is born in Charlotte Amalie, St. Thomas, Virgin Islands.
1834 Young Camille begins school at the Moravian Protestant school with children of slaves.
1842 He studies at the "Pension Savary," located in Passy, a suburb of Paris. He learns to draw, and visits the Louvre.
1848 Back in St. Thomas, Pissarro works with his father in the family business.
1850 Pissarro becomes friends with the Danish painter Fritz Melbye.
1852 Pissarro goes to Venezuela for two years with Melbye, and they teach painting in Caracas.
1855 Pissarro moves to France. He studies at the École des Beaux-Arts for a short while.
1857 Pissarro enrolls at the Académie Suisse. He meets Camille Corot.
1860 Julie Vellay begins work in the Pissarro household, and she and Camille begin a relationship. Pissarro meets artists Ludovic Piette and Claude Monet.
1861 Pissarro meets Cézanne at Académie Suisse. He registers as a copyist at the Louvre.
1863 Monet introduces Pissarro to Frédéric Bazille, Alfred Sisley and Auguste Renoir. Lucien, first child of Camille and Julie, is born on February 20. Three of Pissarro's paintings are exhibited in the Salon des Refusés.
1864 Pissarro and his family visit the Piette family at Montfoucault for the first time.
1865 Two paintings by Pissarro are accepted for the Salon. Pissarro's second child, Jeanne-Rachel (Minette), is born on May 18.
1866 Pissarro moves his family to Pontoise. One of Pissarro's paintings is chosen for the Salon.
1868 Two Pissarro paintings are shown in the Salon.
1869 The Pissarro family moves to Louveciennes in the spring. One Pissarro painting is shown in the Salon.
1870 Two Pissarro paintings are accepted for the Salon. In July, the Franco-Prussian war begins. In September, Pissarro and his family flee to Montfoucault. Another daughter Adèle-Emma is born and dies after three weeks. That December, the Pissarro family flees the war again, taking refuge in London.
1871 Pissarro meets art dealer Paul Durand-Ruel in London. Camille and Julie are married on June 14 before they return to Louveciennes. Their son Georges is born on November 22.
1872 The Pissarro family moves back to Pontoise.
1874 The First Impressionist Exhibition opens in Paris on April 15. Minette dies on April 6 at the age of eight in Pontoise. Félix is born on July 24 in Pontoise. The Pissarro family spends the winter months at Montfoucault.
1875 Pissarro and his family spend the next fall and winter at Montfoucault.
1876 The Second Impressionist Exhibition runs from March 30 to April 30. The Pissarro family spends autumn at Montfoucault.
1877 The Third Impressionist Exhibition is held April 4—30.
1878 Pissarro's dear friend Ludovic Piette dies April 14 at Montfoucault. Ludovic-Rodo is born in Paris on November 21.
1879 The Fourth Impressionist Exhibition opens on April 10 for a month.
1880 The Fifth Impressionist Exhibition is held April 1—30.
1881 The Sixth Impressionist Exhibition runs from April 2 to May 1. On August 27, Jeanne-Marguerite (Cocotte) is born in Pontoise.
1882 The Seventh Impressionist Exhibition is held during March.
1883 Durand-Ruel presents a solo exhibition of 70 works by Pissarro. In October and November, Pissarro makes his first painting expedition to Rouen.
1884 The Pissarro family moves to Éragny-sur-Epte in April. On August 22, Paulémile is born.
1885 Pissarro meets Paul Signac and Georges Seurat and begins painting in the Pointillist manner.

1886 The Eighth Impressionist Exhibition (final one) opens in Paris on May 15, and Pissarro's works are shown with the Neo-Impressionists.

1888 An eye infection, which began in 1880, interferes with Pissarro's painting.

1890 Pissarro abandons Pontillism. The Boussod & Valadon Gallery in Paris mounts a show of Pissarro's work. In May and June, Pissarro and Lucien visit Georges in London. Lucien moves to London permanently in November.

1892 Durand-Ruel presents a retrospective of Pissarro's work. Pissarro travels to London to assist with Lucien's marriage. Julie borrows money from Monet to buy their house in Éragny.

1893 Confined to his hotel room in Paris with his eye infection, Pissarro paints a series of the Place du Havre. Durand-Ruel presents another solo exhibition of Pissarro's work. Pissarro converts his barn to a studio.

1894 Durand-Ruel holds another exhibition of Pissarro's paintings. In June, Pissarro, Julie, and Félix go to Brussels, where Pissarro remains until October.

1896 Pissarro spends January 20-March 30 in Rouen painting the quays and bridges.
In April and May, Durand-Ruel presents Pissarro's recent works at his gallery.
In September, Pissarro returns to Rouen for another two-month painting campaign.

1897 In January, Pissarro returns to Paris to make more paintings of the Place du Havre. He spends February to April in Paris painting a series of the Boulevard Montmarte. Durand-Ruel holds an exhibition of Pissarro's work in New York City. In May, Pissarro rushes to Lucian who is seriously ill and paints a new London series. Félix dies of tuberculosis on November 25 in London. In December, Pissarro begins a new series of the Place du Théâtre-Français in Paris.

1898 Pissarro spends January to April painting in Paris. Publication on January 13 of Emile Zola's letter "J'accuse!" ignites the Dreyfus Affair. In July, Pissarro begins a three-month painting expedition in Rouen.

1899 Pissarro moves his family to rue de Rivoli in Paris for the winter and spring, where he paints a series of the Tuileries Gardens. The Pissarro family goes back to Éragny for the summer, but returns to Paris in November.

1900 The following November, Pissarro moves his family to a flat on the corner of the Pont-Neuf to begin a new series of paintings.

1901 Pissarro makes a painting expedition to Dieppe in the summer. In October, he returns to Pont-Neuf for the winter.

1902 Pissarro paints in Dieppe from July to September. In November, the family returns to Pont-Neuf.
Seeking variety, Pissarro rents a hotel room to use as a studio on the Quai Voltaire.

1903 From July to September, Pissarro paints in Le Havre. Soon after, the family moves to a new apartment in Paris.
Pissarro becomes ill and dies on November 13 surrounded by his wife and children.
He is buried on November 15 at Pére-Lachaise.

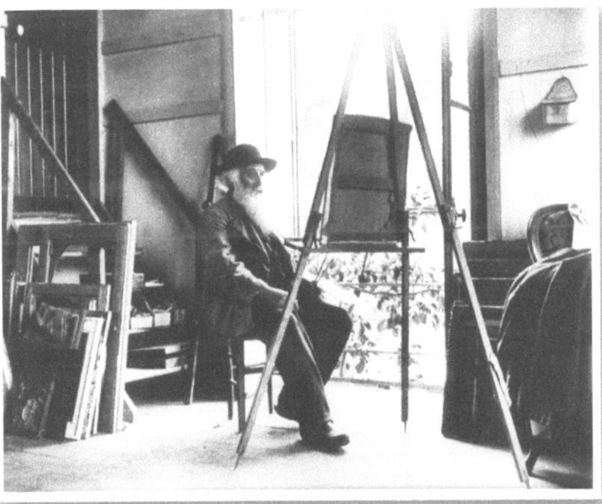

Camille Pissarro in his studio at Éragny-sur-Epte
Musée Camille Pissarro, Pontoise

INDEX

Bibliography

Adler, Kathleen. *Camille Pissarro: a biography.* New York: St. Martin's Press, 1977.

Adler, Kathleen. *A Time and a Place: Near Sydenham Hill.* Fort Worth, TX: Kimbell Art Museum, 2011.

Anderson, James Maxwell, and M. Sheridan Lea. *France:1001 Sights; An Archaeological and Historical Guide.* Calgary: University of Calgary Press, 2002.

Assouline, Pierre. *Discovering Impressionism: The Life and Times of Paul Durand-Ruel.* New York: Vendome Press, 2004.

Becker, Christoph. *Camille Pissarro.* Ostfildern-Ruit: Hatje Cantz, 1999.

Bredin, Jean. *The Affair: The Case of Alfred Dreyfus.* New York: G. Braziller, 1986.

Brettell, Richard, and Christopher Lloyd. *A Catalogue of the Drawings by Camille Pissarro in the Ashmolean Museum, Oxford.* Oxford: Clarendon Press, 1980.

Brettell, Richard, and Scott Schaefer. *A Day in the Country: Impressionism and the French Landscape.* Los Angeles: Los Angeles County Museum of Art, 1984.

Brettell, Richard R. *Pissarro and Pontoise: The Painter in a Landscape.* New Haven: Yale University Press, 1990.

Brettell, Richard R., and Joachim Pissarro. *The Impressionist and the City: Pissarro's Series Paintings.* New Haven: Yale University Press, 1992.

Brettell, Richard R., and Karen Zukowski. *Camille Pissarro in the Caribbean, 1850-1855: Drawings From the Collection at Olana.* St. Thomas, USVI: Hebrew Congregation of St. Thomas, 1996.

Brettell, Richard R. *Pissarro's People.* San Francisco: Fine Arts Museums of San Francisco, 2011.

Brown, Frederick. *For the Soul of France: Culture Wars in the Age of Dreyfus.* New York: Alfred A. Knopf, 2010.

Cahm, Eric. *The Dreyfus Affair in French Society and Politics.* London: Longman, 1996.

Carnevali, Gloria. *Pissarro in Venezuela: Works in Venezuelan Collections of Camille Pissarro's Venezuelan Oeuvre (1852-1854).* London: Vestey Group, 1997.

Celestin, Roger, and Eliane DalMolin. *France From 1851 to the Present: Universalism in Crisis.* New York: Palgrave Macmillan, 2007.

Cohen, Judah M. *Through the Sands of Time: A History of the Jewish Community of St. Thomas, U.S. Virgin Islands.* Hanover: Brandeis University Press, 2004.

Cook, Theodore Andrea. *The Story of Rouen.* Whitefish, MT: Kessinger Pub., 2008.

Dookhan, Isaac. *A History of the Virgin Islands of the United States.* Kingston, Jamaica: Canoe Press, 1994.

Duvivier, Christophe. *Camille Pissarro et Les Peintres de la Vallee de l'Oise.* Paris: Somogy, Eds. d'Art, 2003.

Giard, Michel. *Rouen.* Saint-Cyr-sur-Loire: A. Sutton, 1996.

Goubert, Pierre. *The Course of French History.* London: Routledge, 1991.

Gressier, James. *Pontoise: 2000 Ans d'Histoire.* Pontoise: Impr. Paris, 1973.

Hertzberg, Arthur. *The French Enlightenment and the Jews.* New York: Columbia University Press, 1968.

Jordan, David P. *Transforming Paris: The Life and Labors of Baron Haussmann.* New York: Free Press, 1995.

Lay, Jacques, and Monique Lay. *Louveciennes Mon Village.* 2nd ed. Louveciennes: Jacques Lay, 1989.

Lecanu, Gerald. *Le Havre.* 1st ed. Rennes: A. Sutton, 1995.

Lloyd, Christopher. *Pissarro.* Oxford: Phaidon, 1979.

Lloyd, Christopher. *Studies on Camille Pissarro.* London: Routledge and Kegan Paul, 1986.

Lurie, Patty. *A Guide to the Impressionist Landscape.* Boston: Little, Brown, 1990.

Lurie, Patty. *Guide to Impressionist Paris.* Manchester, N.H.: Robson Press, 1996.

Maloon, Terence. *Camille Pissarro.* Sydney, Australia: Art Gallery of New South Wales, 2005.

Markale, Jean. *The Templar Treasure at Gisors.* Rochester, VT.: Inner Traditions, 2003.

Marsland, William David, and Amy Louise Marsland. *Venezuela Through Its History.* New York: Crowell, 1954.

Pissarro, Camille. *Turpitudes Sociales.* Paris: PUF Editions, 2009.

Pissarro, Joachim. *Camille Pissarro.* New York: H.N. Abrams, 1993.

Pissarro, Joachim, and Stephanie Rachum. *Camille Pissarro: Impressionist Innovator.* Jerusalem: Israel Museum, 1994.

Pissarro, Joachim. *Pioneering Modern Painting: Cezanne & Pissarro, 1865-1885.* New York: Museum of Modern Art, 2005.

Pissarro, Joachim, and Claire Durand-Ruel Snollaerts. *Pissarro, Critical Catalogue of Paintings.* Milano: Skira, 2005.

Pissarro, Joachim. *Cezanne/Pissarro, Johns/Rauschenberg: Comparative Studies on Intersubjectivity in Modern Art.* Cambridge: Cambridge University Press, 2006.

Preston, Harley. *London and the Thames: Paintings of Three Centuries.* London: National Maritime Museum, 1977.

Rewald, John, and Lucien Pissarro. *Camille Pissarro: Letters to his Son Lucien.*1st Da Capo Press edition 1995. New York: Pantheon Books Inc., 1943.

Rewald, John. *Camille Pissarro.* 1st ed. New York: H. N. Abrams, 1963.

Rewald, John. *The History of Impressionism.* 4th rev. ed. New York: Museum of Modern Art, 1973.

Rewald, John, Richard Brettell, and Francoise Cachin. *Pissarro: Camille Pissarro, 1830-1903.* London: Arts Council of Great Britain, 1980.

Rothkopf, Katherine. *Pissarro: Creating the Impressionist Landscape.* Baltimore: Baltimore Museum of Art, 2006.

Russell, John. *Pissarro in England.* London: Marlborough, 1968.

Salome, Laurent, and Marie-Claude Coudert. *Musée des Beaux-Arts de Rouen: the Impressionists.* Paris: Reunion des Musées nationaux, 2003.

Salome, Laurent. *A City for Impressionism: Monet, Pissarro and Gauguin in Rouen.* Milan: Skira, 2010.

Schapiro, Meyer. *Impressionism: Reflections and Perceptions.* New York: George Braziller, 1997.

Shanes, Eric. *Impressionist London.* New York: Abbeville Press, 1994.

Shapiro, Barbara Stern. *Camille Pissarro; The Impressionist Printmaker.* Boston: Museum of Fine Arts, 1973.

Shikes, Ralph E., and Paula Harper. *Pissarro, His Life and Work.* New York: Horizon Press, 1980.

Stern, David, and Talma Zakai-Kanner. *Camille Pissarro and His Descendants: Impressionism to the Present.* Fort Lauderdale, FL: Museum of Art, 2000.

Thomson, Richard. *Camille Pissarro: Impressionism, Landscape and Rural Labour.* London: The Herbert Press Limited, 1990.

Thorold, Anne. *Artists, Writers, Politics: Camille Pissarro and His Friends.* Oxford: The Ashmolean Museum, 1980.

Thorold, Anne, and Kristen Erickson. *Camille Pissarro and His Family: The Pissarro Collection in the Ashmolean Museum.* Oxford: The Museum, 1993.

Weber, Eugen. *Peasants into Frenchmen: The Modernization of Rural France, 1870-1914.* Palo Alto, Calif.: Stanford University Press, 1976.

Willett, John, Anna Gruetzner Robins, and Sophie Bowness. *The Dieppe Connection: The Town and Its Artists from Turner to Braque.* London: Herbert Press, Brighton, 1992.

Credits

Front cover and p. 119: Musee des Beaux-Arts, Reims, France / Giraudon / The Bridgeman Art Library; p. xi: National Gallery of Art, Washington, DC. Collection of Mr. and Mrs. Paul Mellon; p. 4: Kimbell Art Museum, Fort Worth, Texas, USA / The Bridgeman Art Library; p. 5: National Gallery, London, UK / The Bridgeman Art Library; p. 11: Sterling & Francine Clark Art Institute, Williamstown, USA / The Bridgeman Art Library; p. 13: National Gallery, London, UK / The Bridgeman Art Library; p. 17: Musee d'Orsay, Paris, France / Giraudon / The Bridgeman Art Library; p. 21: Camille Pissarro, *The Hermitage at Pontoise* (*Les côteaux de l'Hermitage, Pontoise*), ca. 1867, Oil on canvas, 59 5/8 x 79 inches (151.4 x 200.6 cm), Solomon R. Guggenheim Museum, New York, Thannhauser Collection, Gift, Justin K. Thannhauser, 78.2514.67; p. 23: Musee d'Orsay, Paris, France / Giraudon / The Bridgeman Art Library; p. 25: Museum of Fine Arts, Boston, Massachusetts, USA / The Bridgeman Art Library; p. 27: Brooklyn Museum of Art, New York, USA / Purchased with funds given by Dikran G. Kelekian / The Bridgeman Art Library; p. 29: Sterling & Francine Clark Art Institute, Williamstown, USA / The Bridgeman Art Library; p. 37: Sterling & Francine Clark Art Institute, Williamstown, USA / The Bridgeman Art Library; p. 39: Musee d'Orsay, Paris, France / Giraudon / The Bridgeman Art Library; p. 43: The Art Institute of Chicago, IL, USA / The Bridgeman Art Library; p. 47: National Gallery of Art, Washington, DC. Collection of Mr. and Mrs. Paul Mellon; p. 49: Private Collection / The Bridgeman Art Library; p. 57: National Gallery of Art, Washington, DC. Collection of Mr. and Mrs. Paul Mellon; p. 61: National Gallery of Art, Washington, DC. Collection of Mr. and Mrs. Paul Mellon; p. 69: Dallas Museum of Art, Texas, USA / The Bridgeman Art Library; p. 73: National Gallery of Art, Washington, DC. Ailsa Mellon Bruce Collection; p. 77: © Samuel Courtauld Trust, The Courtauld Gallery, London, UK / The Bridgeman Art Library; p. 81: Philadelphia Museum of Art, Pennsylvania, PA, USA / John G. Johnson Collection, 1917 / The Bridgeman Art Library; p. 85: De Agostini Picture Library / J.E. Bulloz / The Bridgeman Art Library; p. 87: Image copyright © The Metropolitan Museum of Art, Image source: Art Resource, NY; p. 93: Manchester Art Gallery, UK / The Bridgeman Art Library; p. 95: Tel Aviv Museum of Art, Israel / Simon and Marie Jaglom Collection / The Bridgeman Art Library; p. 99: Philadelphia Museum of Art, Pennsylvania, PA, USA / Bequest of Lisa Norris Elkins, 1950 / The Bridgeman Art Library; p. 101: Musee des Beaux-Arts, Dieppe, France / Giraudon / The Bridgeman Art Library; p. 105: Musee des Beaux-Arts Andre Malraux, Le Havre, France / Giraudon / The Bridgeman Art Library; P. 113: The Art Institute of Chicago, IL, USA / The Bridgeman Art Library; p. 115: De Agostini Picture Library / The Bridgeman Art Library; p. 117: National Gallery, London, UK / The Bridgeman Art Library; p. 123: Private Collection / The Bridgeman Art Library; p. 125: ©Tate, London 2013. Presented by Lucien Pissarro, the artistÕs son 1931.

All current photographs with no credits are the work of the author; historic photographs on pp 110 -111 are the property of the author.

Pissaro's Places In France

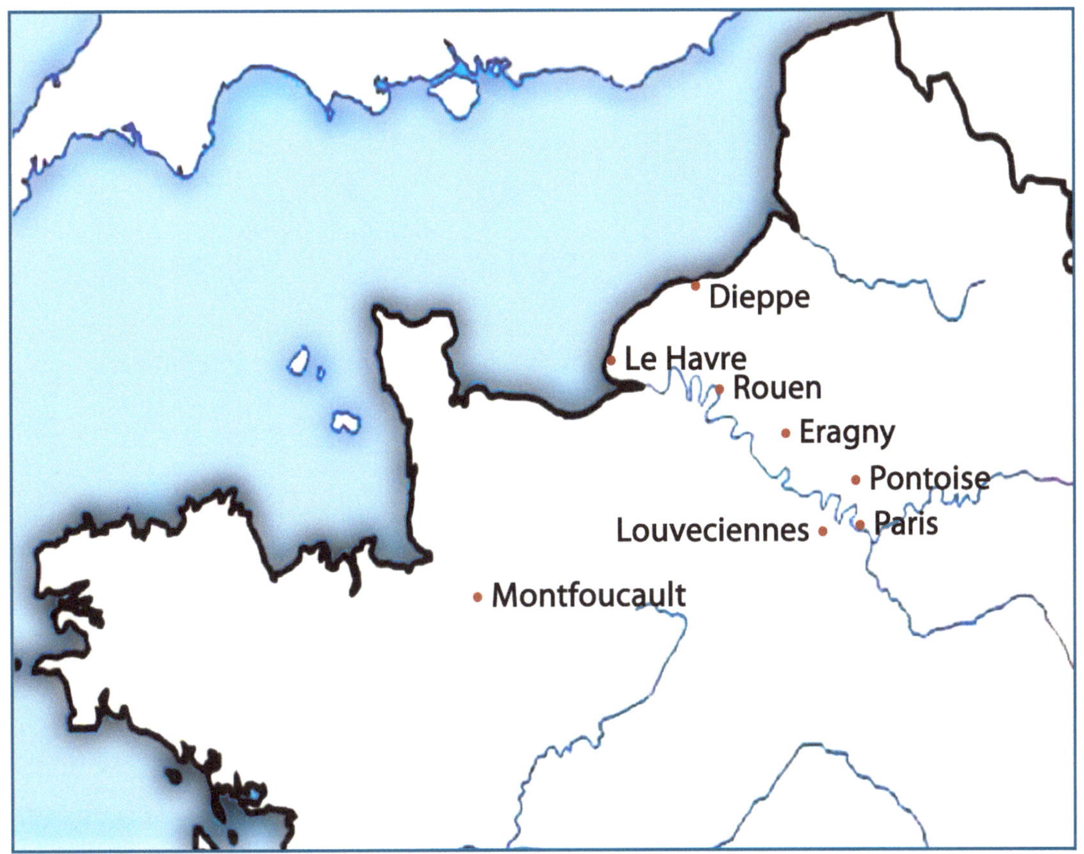

www.ingramcontent.com/pod-product-compliance
Lightning Source LLC
LaVergne TN
LVHW070124110826
845147LV00002B/180

9780988568501